I0530103

Words and Phrases Native English Speakers Prefer To Use

英語母語者常用詞和短語

鮮海濱 著

Canada International Press
加拿大國際出版社

Title: Words and Phrases Native English Writers prefer to use
書名：英語母語者常用詞和短語

Author: Robert Xian
作者：鮮海濱

Published by: Canada International Press
出版：加拿大國際出版社

First Edition in Canada: May. 2025
2025 年 5 月 加拿大第一版

First Printing: May. 2025
2025 年 5 月 第一次印刷

ISBN: 978-1-998479-48-1

ISBN 978-1-998479-48-1

9 781998 479481

Preface

Whenever time allows, particularly on weekends, I find great pleasure in leisurely wandering through local bookstores, hoping to stumble upon new reference books for English learning.

My persistent quest has been to find a book brimming with words and phrases frequently employed by native English speakers, meticulously extracted from the dazzling pages ofdictionaries. Alas, for the past two decades, my search has been in vain.

During my journey, I have encountered countless Chinese English learners who share a common grievance—their struggle with selecting the right words and phrases when expressing themselves in writing. They bemoan the overwhelming thickness of dictionaries, which often makes it arduous to discern the appropriate usage of words and ponder the specific vocabulary favored by native English speakers.

Regrettably, my quest for a satisfying book that meets my expectations remains unfulfilled. After much contemplation, I made a resolute decision to fill this void in English language learning market by writing a book of my own.

Today, after years of unwavering dedication and tireless effort, I am delighted to announce the successful publication of this long-awaited book. It has been meticulously curated with a unique design, tailored specifically for Chinese English learners aspiring to excel in their English writing skills. Within its pages, you will find a collection of words and phrases extensively used by native English speakers, offering an invaluable resource for all Chinese English learners. To facilitate quick and effortless access, the book incorporates the use of Chinese pinyin, enabling learners to pinpoint accurate words and phrases with ease by searching a word in the order of pinyin.

Allow me to clarify that this book is not a dictionary; it is a comprehensive handbook. It has been thoughtfully crafted to cater to a diverse readers, including secretaries, salespeople, marketers working in joint ventures and foreign enterprises, as well as students in colleges and universities who are preparing for various English language tests such as TOEFL, GRE, GMAT, IELTS, and those planning to embark on further studies abroad. Naturally, it is equally suitable for self-study English learners. By employing the words and phrases provided in this book in a random yet intelligent manner, you will be able to refine your writing skills and enhance the readability of your work, giving it the polish and sophistication of a native English speakers touch. One distinctive aspect of this book lies in its fusion of Chinese thinking patterns. It seamlessly bridges the gap between Chinese and English by offering equivalent English words and phrases for various Chinese expressions. For example, when you seek to convey the concept of lengkuwuqing; you can easily locate the English word callousness; under the corresponding pinyin section C. Similarly, the phrase yaowuyangwei; finds its English counterpart, saber-rattling; within the pinyin section dedicated to the letter Y; In my personal experience, regardless of the length of our English language studies, our mother tongue consistently infiltrates our attempts to express ourselves in English. I cannot wholeheartedly endorse the notion that proficient English learners can rival native English writers, particularly in terms of word choices and phrase selections. Whenever we speak or write, there is an inevitable tendency to unintentionally think in Chinese while conveying our thoughts in English. The ability to seamlessly switch between languages is a skill possessed by some, but remains a formidable challenge for others. As adult English learners, eradicating our mother tongue from our minds entirely proves to be an arduous task. Our mother tongue is akin to a pre-installed "hard drive" that has been embedded within us since we were born.

Furthermore, the market is saturated with a plethora of English-English dictionaries, English-Chinese dictionaries, and even Chinese-English dictionaries. While these resources provide a vast array of words and phrases, it is often challenging for learners to accurately identify and harness the exact vocabulary preferred by native English speakers, while retaining the same nuances as their Chinese counterparts. This is where a book that highlights nearly all conceivable idiomatic words and phrases repeatedly used by native English speakers becomes an invaluable asset for Chinese English learners. I sincerely hope that this book serves as the solution you have long been seeking — a remarkable and unparalleled resource that surpasses your expectations.

The crowning feature of this book lies in its ability to recalibrate your approach to word selection, guiding you away from Chinglish expressions and towards idiomatic English words and phrases in your writing. I am fully aware that due to the constraints of page limitations, I have only been able to include a fraction of the words and phrases that could be provided. My intention is to impart guidance and inspire you to select the most fitting idiomatic English words and phrases to enrich your writing. By presenting a small sample, I encourage you to explore and expand upon these words and phrases in real-world writing scenarios. Dedicate yourself to the diligent study and embrace the opportunity to utilize them boldly, regardless of the context. This steadfast commitment will undoubtedly propel your English learning journey forward.

Recognizing the limitations of my own proficiency in English, I acknowledge that errors must exist in this book. I wholeheartedly appreciate any assistance you may offer in identifying and rectifying these errors.

Robert Xian

前言

每當時間允許，尤其是在週末，我總是喜歡悠閒地逛逛本地書店，希望能偶然發現一些適合英語學習的新參考書。我一直在不懈地尋找一本書，它能夠收錄英語母語者常用的單詞和短語，並且是從琳琅滿目的詞典中精心提煉出來的。然而，過去二十年來，我的搜尋始終未能如願。

在這個過程中，我遇到了無數中國英語學習者，他們都有一個共同的困擾——在寫作時很難準確選擇合適的單詞和短語。他們常常抱怨詞典的厚重，讓他們難以辨別單詞的正確用法，同時也難以揣摩英語母語者偏愛的詞彙。

遺憾的是，至今我仍未能找到一本完全符合我期望的書。經過深思熟慮，我毅然決定填補這一英語學習市場上的空白，親自編寫一本書。

今天，經過多年的不懈努力和辛勤付出，我欣喜地宣佈，這本期待已久的書終於正式出版了。它經過精心策劃，採用獨特的設計，專為希望提升英語寫作能力的中國英語學習者量身打造。

本書收錄了英語母語者廣泛使用的單詞和短語，成為所有中國英語學習者不可多得的寶貴資源。
為了便於快速查找和使用，該書採用中文拼音排序，便於學習者通過拼音順序查找詞彙，精准而高效地定位所需的詞語和表達。

在此，我要特別說明，這本書並不是一本詞典，而是一本全面的英語寫作手冊。它旨在幫助不同群體的讀者，包括在合資企業和外資企業工作的秘書、銷售人員、市場行銷人員，以及正在備考 TOEFL、GRE、GMAT、IELTS 等各類英語考試的大學生，或是有意出國深造的學習者。

當然，它同樣適用于所有自學英語的愛好者。如果能巧妙地運用本書提供的單詞和短語，您的寫作將更具可讀性，甚至能達到英語母語者的表達水準，使文章更加流暢自然。

本書的一大特色是結合了中文的思維方式，在中英文之間架起了一座橋樑，為各種中文表達提供了相應的英語詞彙。例如，當你想表達"冷酷無情"時，可以在拼音索引 L 下找到其英文對應詞"callousness"；而"耀武揚威"在拼音索引 Y 下可以找到 "saber-rattling"。在我的個人學習經歷中，體會到無論我們學習英語多久，母語都會在潛意識中影響我們的英語表達。我無法完全認同"英語學得好的人能夠與英語母語者的寫作水準媲美"這一觀點，特別是在單詞和短語的選擇上。每當我們說或寫英文時，難免會在腦海中先以中文思維構思內容，然後再轉化成英文表達。雖然有些人可以做到流暢地切換這兩種語言，但對於大多數人而言，這仍然是一項極具挑戰的事情。對於成人學習者來說，徹底擺脫母語影響幾乎是不可能的。我們的母語就像一塊自出生起就被植入大腦的"硬碟"，深深紮根於我們的思維模式之中。

此外，市場上已經充斥著各種英英詞典、英漢詞典以及漢英詞典，雖然它們涵蓋了大量詞彙，但學習者往往難以精準地挑選出符合英語母語者習慣的表達詞和短語，並且能夠與漢語的表達方式相對應。因此，一本專門收錄英語母語者高頻使用的地道單詞和短語的書，必將成為中國英語學習者不可或缺的珍貴工具。我衷心希望這本書能夠成為你一直以來尋找的答案，為您的英語寫作之路提供幫助，並超越你的期待。

本書的核心價值在於幫助你重新調整單詞選擇的方式，避免"中式英語"（Chinglish），以引導你在寫作中使用地道的英語詞彙和短語。由於篇幅限制，本書只能收錄有限的內容，但我的初衷是為您提供方向，並激勵您進一步探索最恰當的英語表達方式。通過這本書所提供的詞彙和短語，您可以在不同的寫作場景中加以運用，並逐步掌握它們。堅持學習，並勇敢地在寫作中使用這些表達，你的英語水平定會穩步且快速提升。

當然，我深知自己的英語水準仍存在不足，因此本書難免會出現錯誤。如果您能幫我找出並改正這些錯誤，我將不勝感激。

鮮海濱

Foreword

I am delighted to endorse this book, which is designed to help Chinese English learners elevate their English writing to a native level. Whether you're a student or a working professional, this book offers practical tools and insights that go beyond traditional grammar and vocabulary reference books.

What sets this book apart is its focus on helping learners think and write like native speakers. Through engaging unique examples, authentic expressions, and culturally relevant usage, readers learn to express themselves more naturally, confidently, and fluently in English writing. From mastering commonly used words and phrases to understand how to use them in the right tone and context, this book guides learners toward a more sophisticated level of expression in writing

It also introduces advanced vocabulary in a way that is easy to seek, remember, and apply, making it ideal for anyone aiming to sound more professional or competent in their writing.

I highly recommend this book to all Chinese English learners who are serious about improving their written English and achieving native-like fluency.

Abiel Asefha

推薦本書

我非常樂意推薦這本書，它專為中國英語學習者打造，旨在幫助大家將英文寫作能力提升至母語者的水準。無論你是學生還是職場人士，這本書都提供了實用的寫作工具和深刻的語言見解，遠遠超越了傳統的語法和詞彙參考書。

本書的最大亮點在於，它著力幫助學習者真正做到"像母語者那樣思考和寫作"。通過富有吸引力的原創示例、地道自然的表達方式，以及貼近英語文化語境的用法，讀者能夠學會在英文寫作中更加自然、自信和流暢地表達自己。從掌握常用詞彙和表達，到理解如何在不同語氣和語境下恰當運用，它一步步引導學習者邁向更高級、更成熟的寫作風格。

書中還以簡明易查、便於記憶和實際應用的方式介紹了大量高級詞彙，非常適合希望在寫作中展現更強專業度或語言素養的學習者。

我衷心推薦這本書給每一位真正想提升英文寫作能力、並立志達到母語流利水準的中國學習者。

阿比爾·亞瑟法

Contents 目錄

A

1. querulous 愛抱怨的
例：His tendency to be querulous came from his parents, independent of his education. 他愛抱怨的性格是從父母那裡遺傳的，與他的教育無關。

2. pushy 愛出風頭的
例：Wherever and whenever you work, almost all people dislike pushy people.無論何時何地工作，幾乎所有人都不喜歡愛出風頭的人。

3. nosy 愛管閒事的
例：This guy loves being nosy, which annoys some of his buddies. 這傢伙喜歡愛管閒事，弄的一些朋友很不高興

4. fussy 愛挑剔的
例：How to provide a better service? from my point of view, we must be patient in dealing with fussy customers.如何提供更好的服務?在我看來，我們必須耐心地對待愛挑剔的客戶。

5. sedate 安靜的
例：Some experts say sedating kids that will be weak in innovation and creation in the future in comparison with the chirpy and proactive ones.一些專家說，與活潑、積極的孩子相比，安靜的孩子在未來的創新和創造能力會較弱。

6. to tee up 安排
例：She teed up the meeting for her boss. 她為她的老闆安排了這次會議。

通常，一說安排 ...人們往往第一時間想到的就是 arrange,如：to arrange a meeting. 似乎用 tee up 的並不常見，多見於以俚語的方式適用。不過，如果一篇文章中總是重複出現 arrange 會變得乏味，不妨穿插適用 tee up 會使文章讀起來更生動。 所以說，本書中的每個詞都有這種用途，在您的日常寫作中穿插選用，會有意想不到的效果。

7.solace 安慰之物
例：During a war or turbulent period, storing food and cash will be the best solace in making people feel calm and confident.在

戰爭或動盪時期，儲存食物和現金是會讓人們感到平靜和自信的最好安慰之物。

8. hubris 傲慢

例： I knew a person who boasted of saying "I am an adult with a degree" I disliked his hubris and, of course, retorted him immediately 我認識一個人，他突然自誇說:"我是一個有學位的成年人。"我不喜歡他的傲慢，當然馬上反駁他。

9. overbearing 傲慢的，盛氣凌人的

例：He looks like a humble person; however, he is actually quite overbearing.

他看起來像一個謙遜的人。然而，他實際上很傲慢.

再比如：She presents an overbearing attitude towards her employees, so all of them keep their distance from her.她對員工表現出傲慢的態度，因此他們都與她保持足夠的距離。

10. to strut 昂首闊步

例： After loading up the applause from the audience, she strutted wearing a purple jacket that looked elegant and noble. She was spotted by her fans instantly.在觀眾的掌聲中，她昂首闊步穿著一件看起來優雅高貴的紫色外套。 瞬間被她的粉絲們認出。

B

1. to liken sth. to sth. 把…同…相提並論、把 ...比作 ...

例：We liken the procedure to a solid channel that absorbs all kinds of knowledge.
我們把這個過程比作一條穩固的管道，能吸納各種知識。

再比如：Many men tend to avoid a second marriage

because many women have a habit of likening their current marriage to their previous one—something that annoys their partners tremendously. 許多男性傾向於回避再婚，因為許多女性習慣於把現在的婚姻拿來同之前的婚姻相提並論，而這讓她們的伴侶感到非常煩惱。

2. to be dubbed 被⋯稱為

例：The space shuttle to Mars has been dubbed "The Red Probe," and it is tasked with discovering whether life exists there. 前往火星的太空梭被稱為"紅色探測器"，其任務是探尋那裡是否存在生命。

3. to direct one's ire at 把⋯的憤怒轉向⋯

例：My manager was blamed by many employees, but since he couldn't identify who was specifically responsible, he directed his ire on me. 我的經理遭到了許多員工的指責，但由於他沒能查明具體是誰的責任，便把憤怒轉到我身上。

4. to bungle sth. 把⋯搞砸

例：You hired a bunch of people with no technical background, and they completely bungled our project. 你雇了一堆毫無技術背景的人，結果把我們的專案徹底搞砸了。

再比如：His boss bungled the implementation of the policy he himself had stipulated, which caused him to lose credibility among the employees. 他的老闆把自己制定的政策執行得一團糟，導致他在員工中失去了信譽。

5. to gum up 把⋯搞砸

例：Due to his lack of research, he gummed up the project. 由於他缺乏研究，他把專案搞砸了。

6. to pin the blame for 把⋯歸咎於

例：I'm afraid I have to disagree with the idea that we should pin the blame for the price surge on the Ukraine-Russia war. 恐怕我得不同意將價格上漲的責任歸咎於烏克蘭-俄羅斯戰爭。

7. the conflation of 把⋯混為一談

例：We must avoid the conflation of race and religion. 我們必須避免把種族和宗教混為一談.

例句中的 avoid 是個動詞，接下來的 conflation 表面上看是個名詞，可實際上有動詞的含義即"把 ...混為一談"，中文在一個句子中會出現幾個動詞連用，可英文一般來說要表達幾個連續動作時，句子中只出現一個動詞，接下去的動作就用名詞形式表達，或跟動名詞來表達連續的動作含義。用名詞來表達動詞含義在中譯英時非常普遍，大家要特別留意。

8. to cast ...as... 把…看作…

例：Some optimists cast a terrible human disaster as a reward from God, elbowing us to evolve to a higher level. 一些樂觀主義者將可怕的人類災難視為上帝的獎賞，認為這推動了人類向更高層次進化。

9. to align ...with ...把…同…聯繫起來

例：As parents, you must align your children's future with the hard work they are putting into their studies. 作為父母，你們必須把孩子的未來同他們在學習上付出的努力聯繫起來。

10.   to baffle 把…難住，讓…困惑

例：Your question baffled me, which made me feel quite awkward. 你的問題把我難住了，這讓我感到非常尷尬。

再比如：How you spent money baffled me; it was as if you were a billionaire, completely ignoring price tags and grabbing everything you liked. 你花錢的方式讓我困惑不解；就好像你是個億萬富翁，根本不在意標籤上的價格，喜歡什麼就拿什麼。

11. to botch sth... 把…搞砸了、把…弄得一團糟

例：He rudely botched the wedding party. 他粗魯地把婚禮宴會搞砸了。

12. to be no match for sb at 在某方面某人不是某人的對手

例：Jacob was no match for Levi when it came to basketball. 雅各在籃球上不是李維斯的對手。

13. to throw sth to the winds 把…拋到九霄雲外，拋到腦後

例：My leader went against the rules stipulated by our company; he threw principles to the wind, which put me in an awkward situation. 我的領導違反了公司的規定，他把原則拋到了

九霄天外，這讓我陷入了尷尬的境地。

14. to tuck into 把⋯塞到⋯
例：I felt embarrassed to accept her money; she tucked it into my hands and ran away. 我不好意思接受她的錢，她把錢塞到我手裡就跑了。

15. to sever .把⋯割裂開
例：They had always gotten along so well, and yet, without explanation, they severed the bond between faith and loyalty. 他們一直相處得很好，但不知為何，信任與忠誠之間的紐帶卻被割裂了。

16. to hollow sth. out 把⋯挖空
例：He hollowed out the tangerine, filled it with rock candy and honey, and then steamed it for 30 minutes. It is said to be one of the most effective remedies for a stubborn cough. 他把橘子挖空，放入冰糖和蜂蜜，然後蒸了 30 分鐘。據說這是一種治療頑固咳嗽的最有效方法。

17. to stake 把⋯押在⋯賭一把
例：His boss strongly supported her, staking his reputation and future on her promotion to team leader, even though she had made some mistakes. 他的老闆堅定地支持她，儘管她犯了一些錯誤，但還是將自己的聲譽和未來都押在了她升職為團隊領導上。

18. to butter up 巴結，討好
例：His wife was enraged by his behavior and demanded a divorce. Not wanting their relationship to worsen, he tried to butter her up in an attempt to salvage the deteriorating situation. 他的妻子被他的行為激怒，強烈要求離婚。為了避免他們的關係惡化，他試圖巴結她，挽救這場日益惡化的局面。

19. to fish sb. out of 把某人從⋯撈出來
例：This lawyer spent so much time trying to fish him out of jail. 這個律師花了大量時間試圖把他從監獄裡撈出來。

20. owe one's success to 把某人的成功歸為 ...
例：The award for my thesis owes my success to my

professor's effort and great support. 我的論文獲獎要歸功於教授的努力和大力支持。

21. to tether one's hope to 把某人的希望寄託在 ...

例: As seniors, we could once tether our hopes on our children to support and care for us in old age. Unfortunately, younger generations seem to have shifted their focus inward, prioritizing their own lives. Some even prefer the idea of their parents remaining independent rather than embracing the traditional role of caregivers. Consequently, parents must now learn to foster their own independence. 作為老年人，我們曾經可以把希望寄託在子女們身上，指望他們在我們年老時給予扶持與照料。可惜的是，如今的年輕一代似乎更關注自身的發展，重心也隨之發生了轉移。有些人甚至更傾向于讓父母保持獨立，而不是履行傳統上的贍養責任。因此，做父母的如今也必須學會培養自己的獨立性。

22. to tout something 把某事吹捧成

例：This company touts its latest chips as cutting-edge technology. 這家公司把其最新的晶片吹捧成是尖端技術。

23. to crank up 把聲音調大

例：Could you please crank up the radio? I love this melodious music 請你把收音機音量調大一點好嗎? 我喜歡這首旋律優美的音樂。

24. to bill oneself as 把自己標榜為

例：This enterprise billed itself as a champion of "green energy consumption," but unfortunately, it turned out to be the city's top polluter year after year and was ranked among the worst companies. 這家企業把自己標榜為"綠色能源消費"的典範，但不幸的是，它每年都是全市最大的污染源之一，並被列為最糟糕的公司之一。

25. a damp squib 白搭了，白費勁兒了

例：His attempts to persuade his brother to think it over turned out to be a damp squib. 他勸說他兄

弟三思而行的努力似乎白搭了。

26. to prostrate 拜倒在 ...
例：One principle everyone must follow is never to prostrate themselves before money. 每個人都必須遵守的一個原則就是絕不能拜倒在金錢面前。

27. dud 白費了，無用的，爛的
例：He made a dud effort, which led to absolutely no results. 他的努力完全白費了，毫無結果。

再比如：The editor deleted many dud words and expressions from an article written by a reporter. 編輯刪掉了記者寫的一篇文章中許多無用的詞句。

還有：That manufacturer produced a dud product with lots of issues — I'm not buying it. 那家製造商生產的產品很爛，存在很多問題。我絕不會買。

28. to besmirch 敗壞，玷污，誹謗
例：Since he intentionally spread rumors to besmirch my reputation, I decided to file a lawsuit and take him to court.
由於他故意造謠敗壞我的名譽，我決定起訴並將他告上法庭。

29. to disengage 掰了（多指關係上）
例：They used to be great friends, but now they've disengaged from each other after quarreling over how to divide some benefits. 他們過去是非常要好的朋友，但因為在分配利益時發生爭執，如今掰了。

30. to develop ...from scratch 白手起家
例：This entrepreneur became a billionaire, however, he developed himself from scratch. 這位企業家成了億萬富翁，然而，他是白手起家的。

31. rags-to-riches 白手起家
例：Nolan is one of the most famous entrepreneurs in our country, especially known for his rags-to-riches story. 諾蘭是我們國家最著名的企業家之一，特別以他的白手起家故事聞名。

32. to divest oneself of 擺脫
例：We must divest ourselves of conventional ideology in order to create a new, modern one. 我們必須擺脫傳統的思想觀念，以創造一種新的現代化理念。

33. to sow discord 搬弄是非
例：My bottom line is to distance myself from anyone who loves to sow discord. 我的底線是遠離任何愛搬弄是非的人。

34. to the strains of 伴隨著 ... 的旋律
例 ： While listening to the melodious song, Lili began to hum the tune to the strains of "I Love You, China."
在聆聽那首悅耳的歌曲時，莉莉開始哼起了《我愛你，中國》的旋律。

35. nifty 棒棒的，漂亮的
例：Sony used to produce a nifty portable CD player that was very slim and made of magnesium, making it extremely durable. Unfortunately, it has been discontinued. Frankly, it's a memory of my generation. 索尼曾經生產一款棒棒的可攜式CD播放機，非常薄，由鎂合金材料製成，很耐用。遺憾的是，它已經停產了。說實話，那是我們這一代人的記憶。

36. to enwrap 包，裹
例：The dumplings are made by enwrapping minced meat and vegetables, mixed with a touch of salt, soy sauce, and oil, in dumpling wrappers. 餃子是用加入少許鹽、醬油和油的肉末和蔬菜包在餃子皮裡做成的。

37. to keep mum 保持沉默，守口如瓶
例：I tried to keep mum about this case, which triggers a lot of debate among young people. 我儘量對這個在年輕人中引發大量爭議的案件保持沉默。

38. to maintain a laser-like focus on 保持高度關注
例：A lot of stuff was fervently stolen each month, which requires maintaining a laser-like focus on this issue. The upper management is seeking better solutions. 每個月都有大量物品被瘋狂盜竊，這要求我們對這個問題保持高度關注。

高層管理正在尋求更好的解決方案。

39. to keep one's toes 保持警惕

例：With the easing of the mandatory mask order, several waves of virus variants still keep people on their toes. 隨著強制戴口罩令的放鬆，幾波病毒變種仍然讓人們保持警惕。

40. to exercise restraint 保持克制

例：When someone insults you, you must exercise restraint, otherwise, the conflict will be unavoidable.當有人侮辱你時，你必須保持克制，否則，不可避免會發生衝突。

41. to keep somebody in good nick 保持某人身體健康

例： She often eats so-called healthy food to keep herself in good nick; however, from a long-term perspective, it won't be beneficial to her health. 她常常吃所謂的健康食品來保持身體健康；然而，從長遠來看，這對她的健康並沒有好處。

42. to plummet 暴跌

Due to the bad news, the stock market plummeted , which had buyers scared.由於利空消息，股市暴跌嚴重，令買家心驚肉跳。

43. to tumble 暴跌（指股市）

例：The stock market is tumbling due to the bad news released today.由於今天發佈的壞消息，股市正在暴跌。

44. to shear 剝奪

例：Shorn of his power by the emperor, he had no choice but to quit and return to his hometown. 皇上剝奪了他的權力，他只好告老還鄉。

45. upstart 暴發戶

例：This guy looks like an upstart, squandering a lot of money on purchasing luxury cars and jewelry. 這傢伙看起來像個暴發戶，在購買豪車和珠寶上揮霍了很多錢。

46. to plateau 飽和，達到平衡

例：After half a century, TV production and requirements

have plateaued.半個世紀後，電視製作和需求已經飽和。

47. to lay bare 暴露無遺、洩露

例：His ugly behavior has been laid bare, and he had no way to argue; the only choice for him is to claim guilty.他的醜惡行為已經暴露無遺，已無力辯解；　唯一的選擇就是認罪。

再比如：All the documents are the properties of the company, they shouldn't be laid bare to the outside world.所有的檔都是公司的財產，不應該把它們洩露給外界。

48. overarching 包羅萬象的

例: I am so interested in this discussion because it will cover overarching fields.
我對這個討論很感興趣，因為它將涵蓋的領域包羅萬象。

49. to keep sth under wraps 保密 （俚語）

例：Her acne skin suddenly became smooth and beautiful, A lot of people showed strong interest in how she quickly changed the texture of her skin, but she prefers to keep it under wraps. 她的痘痘皮膚突然變得光滑美麗，很多人對她如何快速改變皮膚的質感挺感興趣，但她卻保密。

50. underbelly 薄弱部分

例：Due to solid client complaints, the head office is trying to make up for its underbelly in the financial system.由於客戶的不滿，總公司正在努力彌補其在金融體系中的薄弱部分。

51. testy 暴跳如雷的

例：Some people are sensitive; any suggestions to them may get them testy.有些人明感；　對他們的任何建議都可能讓他們暴跳如雷。

52. goons 暴徒

例: During the turmoil, goons brazenly shouted, "Smash the police car!" It was evident that the situation was spiraling out of control, and the entire country was on the verge of descending into anarchy. 動亂期間，一群暴徒肆無忌憚地喊著："砸警車！"顯然，局勢已經徹底失控，整個國

家正瀕臨陷入無政府狀態的邊緣。

53. binging 暴飲暴食
例： To live a longer life, you must strive to avoid binging on all types of food. 如果你想長壽，必須儘量避免暴飲暴食各種食物。

54. to gripe about 抱怨
例：My mom is very diligent; she never griped about her hard work in her life.我媽媽很勤奮，她一生中從未抱怨過她的辛苦。

再比如：So many people gripe about the soaring price of gasoline. 許多人抱怨汽油價格飛漲。

還比如："Why I contributed more, but I got less?' he gripes"為什麼我貢獻的多，得到的少?" 他抱怨到。

55. to bemoan 抱怨，惋惜
例：The city council bemoaned the water shortage, so a new plan needs implementation.市議會抱怨 水資源短缺，因此需要實施一項新計畫。

56. to grumble about 抱怨，表示不滿
例：This guy always grumbles about his low salary paid by the company.這個傢伙總是抱怨公司給他的工資低。

再比如：With the deterioration of the currency devaluation, so many people grumbled about their poor quality of life. 隨著貨幣貶值的惡化，很多人抱怨他們糟糕的生活品質。

57. stroppy 暴躁的，難以控制的 （俚語，非正式的一種用法）
例： As a teenager, my son is too stroppy to communicate with me. 作為一個十幾歲的孩子，我的兒子太暴躁了，不願意和我交流。

58. tetchy 暴躁的，易怒的
例：He is too tetchy to control his mood correctly. But Overall he is a nice person. 他太暴躁了，無法適當地控制自己的情緒。除此之外，他是個好人。

59. irascible 暴躁的，易怒的
例：Anyone prone to be irascible may not have a bright future.

Sometimes, one's restraint and patience could bring him more chances.任何容易暴躁的人都可能沒有光明的前途。有時候，一個人的克制和耐心可以給他帶來更多的機會。

60. to get riled by 被 ...激怒
例：Claire is prone to get riled by any jokes, so be careful to try not to make any jokes with her.克雷爾很容易被任何笑話激怒，所以,儘量不要和她開玩笑。

61. to be dogged by 被 ...困擾
例：People living along the river are dogged by the flood.住在河邊的人們被洪水所困擾。

62. sleaze 卑鄙，不道德的人
例：This professor plagiarizes another person's essay to show it as his accomplishment, he was regarded as a sleaze.這個教授抄襲別人的論文來顯示自己的成就，認為是一個卑鄙無恥的人。

63. abject 卑鄙的
例：He won this game, but he is an abject winner.他贏了這場比賽，但他是一個卑鄙的贏家。

64. dastardly 卑鄙的
例：Indulging in dastardly gossip about someone behind their back is a reprehensible behavior, and we should never advocate for it. 在背後說別人的壞話是卑劣的行為，我們絕不應該提倡。

65. grubby 卑鄙的，骯髒的，髒兮兮的
例：She always gossips about some of her colleagues behind their backs, so almost all people will think her behavior as grubby. 她總是在背後說同事的閒話，所以幾乎所有人都會認為她的行為卑鄙無恥。

66. to get burned 被炒魷魚
例：Due to his miscalculation, all the figures have been messed up, so as a manager, the board decided to get him burned.由於他計算失誤，所有的數字都被弄亂了，所以作為一名經理，董事會決定炒他魷魚。

67. to saddle sb. with 背負
例：He splurged a significant amount of money on luxury items, which has saddled him with a heavy debt.

他在奢飾品上花了太多錢，這是他背負了沉重的債務。

68. to be saddled with 背負著 ...（債務）
例： I saw so many people saddled with a large number of mortgages, which laid heavy debt on their shoulders and plunged them into a hopeless future in their life. 我看到很多人背負著大量的抵押貸款，沉重的債務壓在他們的肩膀上，讓他們的生活陷入無望的未來。

69. to grovel for 卑躬屈膝
例：I dislike someone groveling for obtaining a promotion in a company by currying favor with top-level administrators. 我不喜歡有人為了在公司升職而卑躬屈膝去討好高層管理人員。

70. to carry the can 背黑鍋
例：Someone stole money in the office, but the manager couldn't find who did; I was alone in the office, which indicates I might carry the can for this case. 有人在辦公室偷了錢，但經理找不到是誰偷的，當時我一個人在辦公室，這表明我可能要為此事背黑鍋。

71. to be sacked. 被解雇了
例： Lots of female employees have been sacked due to their pregnancy. 很多女員工因為懷孕而被解雇。

還有另外一種表達方式就是 "you are fired" 比 you are sacked 程度上更重些。都是由於自己的過失造成的。最輕的是 you are laid off. 當然，更多的還是由於公司或廠方的原因導致你丟掉工作。另外， 英國人更偏向使用 you are sacked.

72. to be inflated by 被誇大
例：The functions of these AI gadgets are inflated by manufacturers. 這款人工智慧設備的功能被製造商誇大了。

73. to be boxed up 被困在
例：During the pandemic lockdown, he was boxed up in his house. 在疫情封鎖期間，他被困在家裡。

74. spellbound 被迷住的
例： The melodious song she sang leaves me spellbound 我被她唱的那首悠揚的歌給迷住了。

75. to be covetously eyed by someone 被某人貪婪地盯上

例：Never overexpose your talent and capability to avoid being covetously eyed by little shits.永遠不要過度展示你的才華和能力，以免被小人們貪婪地盯上。

76. to be binned 被扔進垃圾箱

（bin 本身是個名詞，在這裡卻用作動詞使用）

例：Elliana is crossed in love, so she binned all gifts and pictures related to her boyfriend thoroughly.艾蓮娜失戀了，所以她把所有與男友有關的禮物和照片都徹底扔掉了。

（美國英語中有很多名詞被用作動詞使用，尤其在口語中，這種現象尤為突出。可英國英語對此非常忌諱，認為這樣使用很粗俗，沒文化。）

77. to be riven with 被撕裂

例：She lost her husband and her son in a car accident. She was riven with pain when she recalled that story.她在一場車禍中失去了丈夫和兒子。當她回憶起那個故事時，有種被痛苦撕裂的感覺。

78. to be tipped 被推舉為 ...

例：As an ordinary employee, he was tipped as a member of the board in terms of his superior technical background and excellent personality.作為一名普通員工，他憑藉出眾的技術背景和優秀的人格被推舉為董事會成員。

79. perfidy 背信棄義

例：The severance of diplomacy among countries in the world resulted in perfidy of one another.世界各國之間外交關係的中斷是由彼此之間的背信棄義所導致的。

80. pent-up 被壓抑的

例：Research reckons pent-up sexual aspiration may lead to depression, especially among women.研究認為，被壓抑的性欲可能導致抑鬱，尤其是女性。

81. fallback 備用的，應急的

例：She is knowledgeable because she always prepares a fallback each time besides the essential plan.她很聰明，每次

都在關鍵計畫之外準備一個備用方案。

82. clunky 笨重的

例：The current technology didn't change the way of personal computers., which still look clunky even though manufacturers boasted that the design has become smaller and lighter. 目前的技術並沒有改變個人電腦的方式。儘管他們吹噓說設計變得更小更輕了，但看起來仍然很笨重。

83. to scamper 蹦蹦跳跳

例：I saw a group of kids scampering on the beach, which attracted a lot of people's eyeballs. 我看見一群孩子在海灘上蹦蹦跳跳，吸引了很多人的矚目。

84. to implode 崩潰

例：Deflation is just the beginning of the economy imploding. 通縮只是經濟崩潰的開始。

85. a shade better than 比…略好、比…稍好一點兒

例：This year's new generation iPhone design is a shade better than the year before. 今年新一代蘋果手機的設計比前一年略好。

86. wherewithal 必備的資金

例: I must prepare the wherewithal for enough tuition fees for the following semester. Otherwise, I have to drop out. 我必須為下學期學費準備足夠的錢。 否則，我必須退學。

87. to eschew 避免

例：He always tries to eschew any conflict with his wife to keep the whole family peaceful. I often wondered how long his tolerance could last. 他總是儘量避免與妻子發生任何衝突，以保持整個家庭的平靜。我經常想知道他的忍耐能持續多久。

88. to obviate 避免

例：The mechanics are trying to obviate the malfunction of the airplane to guarantee its safety. 該機械師試圖避免飛機的故障，以確保其安全性。

再比如：Automatic pilot technology can obviate errors occurring in human driving. 自動駕駛技術可以避免人為駕駛時發生的錯誤。

還有：To obviate errors during the exam, you must repeatedly check many times carefully.為了避免考試中出現錯誤，你必須反復仔細檢查很多次。

89. to push sb. 逼迫 ...
例：Please don't push me too much. I will almost become crazy. 別逼我太緊，我都快瘋了。

90. to corner someone 逼某人
例：Nolan was trapped in deep debt, which cornered him to work almost 24/7 to pay back the debt. 諾蘭陷入了沉重的債務中，這逼得他幾乎全天候工作來償還債務。

91. to sport 變（臉）
例：Normally, when someone drinks too much, their face turns red. However, one of my friends sported a pale complexion, which indicated that he could handle a much larger quantity of alcohol. 通常情況下，一個人喝得太多後，臉會變紅。然而，我的一個朋友的臉色卻呈現出蒼白，這顯示他可以喝更多。

92. to pervade 遍佈，遍及

例：iPhones are pervaded everywhere worldwide, they are still listed as No.1 in sales in the market. 蘋果手機遍佈世界各地，它仍然是市場上銷量第一的產品。

93. to be morphed into 變成
例：The current world has been morphed into a paperless digital one.當今世界已經變成了一個無紙化的數字世界。

再有：SARS 2.0 has been morphed into another lethal virus namely Delta plus Omicron. SARS 2.0 已經演變成另一種致命病毒，即德爾塔＋奧密克戎。

不同於 be changed into 只是形式上的轉變，而 morph into 卻有著本質的改變。

94. to get cold feet 變得冷淡
例：After marriage, their relationship was getting cold feet, which finally led them to divorce. 婚後，兩人的感情越來越冷淡，最終導致兩人離婚。

95. to blur 變得模糊，不清楚

例：The difference between men and women nowadays has become much more blurring because our concept is changing. 如今，男女之間的區別變得越來越模糊，因為我們的觀念正在改變。

96. to become so entrenched 變得如此根深蒂固的。

例： He is stubbornly sunk into his old ideology, I literally can't understand when and why he became so entrenched. 他固執地陷入他的舊意識形態中，我真不明白他是什麼時候以及為什麼變得如此根深蒂固的。同義詞有： deep-rooted, deep-seated

97. to downplay 貶低

例： As parents, you shouldn't downplay your kids' capability and proactiveness.作為父母，你不應該貶低孩子的能力和主動性。

98. to disparage 貶低

例：We must keep in mind to avoid disparaging others to lift ourselves. 我們必須牢記，不要貶低別人來抬高自己。

99. to spin a story 編故事 ...

spin 的意思太多了，比如：織紗，某物體快速旋轉，疾馳，某人急轉身，頭部感到眩暈，球旋轉，傾向性地報導，洗衣服後的甩幹，釣魚，播放電影，拋硬幣，乘車兜風等等 ...具體的用途大家可以參閱詞典。我們今天要重點說的是這個詞的另外一個用法表示編故事。

例：Stop spinning stories in front of me. 別在我面前編故事了.

100. to budge 變化、動搖

例：I didn't see him budging not only in his negative outlook but also in his spirit. He has been intoxicated into gaming and even forgetting to eat anything.我沒有看到他的負面態度和精神有任何變化。他一直沉迷於遊戲，甚至忘記了吃任何東西。

再比如: At this vital moment, no one will ever budge.
在這關鍵時刻，誰也不動搖。

101. inconstancy 變幻莫測

例：The inconstancy of the global economic situation may lead to a deepened gap between the rich and poor.全球經濟形勢變幻莫測，可能導致貧富差距進一步擴大。

102. pejorative 貶義的

例：She raised her tone while saying "thank you," implying a pejorative sense. 她提高了語氣說"謝謝"，表明帶有貶義的意思。

103. marginal 邊緣化了，微不足道了

例：Even many celebrities feel marginal after their retirement.即使是許多名人在退休後也感到被邊緣化。

再比如：The possibility leading to the third World War within a short time would be marginal. 在短時間內導致第三次世界大戰的可能性微乎其微。

104. to concoct 編造、捏造

例：He always concocted his feeling to deceive his girlfriend, and the consequence is that she recognized it finally and decided to depart from him。他總是編造感情來欺騙他的女朋友，結果她終於認清了他，決定和他分開。

再比如：The truth is that they concocted the facts and framed their colleague. It is unacceptable and intolerable.事實是他們捏造事實陷害同事。 這是不可接受和不能容忍的。

105. rancid 變質的，不新鮮的

例：Storing green leafy vegetables in the refrigerator for an extended period may cause them to become rancid, leading to an undesirable taste and potential degradation of nutritional quality, which is not conducive to good health. 將綠葉蔬菜長時間存放在冰箱中會變質，產生不良口感並導致營養品質的降低，這對健康不利。

106. doughty 彪悍的

例：Jordan is a doughty owner of this store and works almost 24/7, rarely sleeping and taking only one meal per day.喬丹是這家商店一位彪悍的老闆，幾乎

全天候工作，很少睡覺，每天只吃一頓飯。

再比如： During the strong earthquake, Audrey tried to save her 3 daughters. She looks pretty thin and weak, however, she actually is a very doughty woman. 在強烈的地震中，奧黛麗試圖拯救她的 3 個女兒。她看起來很瘦、很弱，但實際上她是一個很堅強的女人。

107. profess 表示
例： My partner professed his satisfaction with the distribution. 我的合夥人對分配表示滿意。

108. to fare 表現
例： The teacher praised his student, saying that he fared better than before.老師表揚了他的學生，說他比以前表現得更好了。

109. duff 蹩腳的，錯誤的
例： In the beginning, you may feel your oral English is duff, but with more practice, your spoken expression will become fluent.一開始，你可能會覺得自己的英語口頭表達有些蹩腳，但是通過更多的練習，你發現表達會變得順暢。

110. ulterior motives 別有用心
例： Strangers' sudden good care of you almost indicates ulterior motives, so you must be highly alert.陌生人對你的突然關心幾乎是別有用心的表現，所以你必須高度警惕。

111. on the cusp of 瀕臨，正處於
例： This company is on the cusp of bankruptcy; every employee feels rattled, panicked, distraught, and is trying to look for another job quickly. 這家公司瀕臨破產；每個員工都感到不安、恐慌、心煩意亂，並試圖迅速尋找另一份工作。

112. not...because...並不會因為⋯而⋯
例： He won't become rich because he tries to save money. 他不會因為努力存錢而變得富有。

113. to be lukewarm about 並不感興趣、並不熱衷

例： I am lukewarm about his explanation, no matter how rhetorical it was. 不管他的言辭多麼花言巧語，我對他的解釋都不感興。

114. to be not without 並非沒有

例：Reese put some money in the stock market and gained some profits; however, her investment was not without loss.瑞茜在股票市場投入了一些錢，並獲得了一些利潤，然而，她的投資並非沒有損失。

115. to ditch （非正式）摒棄

例：The custom for bride prices in China must be ditched. Given that more and more men can't afford it. Meanwhile, it will indirectly affect young people's vision on marriages and babies born from a long-term point of view. Strategically speaking, it won't be beneficial for the further development of the country.中國的彩禮習俗必須摒棄。鑒於越來越多的男人承擔不起。同時，從長遠來看，也會間接影響到年輕人的結婚生子觀念。從戰略角度上講，不利於國家的進一步發展。

116. to set aside 撥出

例:Each year, the company tried to set aside 3m dollars to enhance the welfare of senior retirement。公司每年都試圖撥出 300 萬美元來提高退休人員的福利。

117. to wow 博得 ...追捧

例："Niang Pao" effeminate nature wowed so many young people, which has twisted young kids' worldviews and brought them a lot of psychological issues.《娘炮》的娘娘腔博得那麼多年輕人追捧，扭曲了青少年的世界觀，給他們帶來了很多心理問題。

118. to strike a chord with sb. 撥動著某人的心弦

例：She sang a melodious song that strikes a chord with me。她唱了一首旋律優美的歌，撥動著我的心弦。

119. to earmark 撥款

例：The board earmarked 600bn dollars to develop the 2nm chips; the total investment will reach 1 trillion dollars.董事會撥

出 6000 億美元開發 2nm 晶片； 總投資將達到 1 萬億。

120. to earmark...for ... 撥款給

例：The government earmarked $87 billion dollars for supporting the civilians during the pandemic. 政府在疫情期間撥出 870 億美元用於支持平民。

121. to go ballistic 勃然大怒

例：My son broke a valuable antique; my wife went ballistic. 我兒子打碎了一件珍貴的古董，我妻子勃然大怒。

122. choppy 波濤洶湧的

例：The choppy ocean is reminiscent of my childhood when my grandma brought me to take a ship traveling to Europe in 1939. 波濤洶湧的大海讓我想起了我的童年，1939 年我奶奶帶我乘船去歐洲。

再比如：Our ship encounters a severe choppy ocean and it had almost sunk. 我們的船遇到了波濤洶湧的大海，差點沉沒。

其實，choppy 還有很多意思，比如：不穩定，大起大落等

等。大家有時間可以進一步查詢該詞的更多用法。

123. erudite 博學多才

例：He pretends to be erudite, but in reality, he knows nothing. 他裝作博學多才，實際上一無所知。

124. skittish 不安的、膽怯的

例：I am very concerned about children watching TV filled with violent content, which makes their parents skittish. 我非常擔心孩子們觀看充滿暴力內容的電視節目，這讓他們的父母感到不安。

再比如：As I was feeding some food to the skittish puppy, it cautiously tried to approach me, uncertain about my intentions. 當我給這只膽怯的小狗餵食時，它試圖小心翼翼地靠近我，對我的意圖感到不確定。

125. to be not inferior to 不比…差

例：Your performance is not inferior to others; you made an effort just not enough. 你的表現

不比別人差；你只是付出的努力不夠。

126. misfire 不發揮效力的

例:Santiago failed to motivate the misfiring team to be proactive , leading it to be disorganized. 聖地牙哥未能激勵這支不發揮效力的團隊主動作為，結果導致團隊變得混亂低效。

127. to be not much more than 不超過，僅僅

例 ： The total output of this special kind of material is not much more than a 1000 ton per year, that's why its prices can't come down. 這種特殊材料的總產量不超過每年 1000 噸，所以它的價格降不下來。

128. unviable 不成功的，行不通的（特質財政方面）

例：He lost nearly all his money in the stock market, and his investment turned out to be unviable. 他在股市中幾乎賠光了所有的錢，他的投資最終證明是不成功的。

129. to replenish 補充

例：Replenishing enough organic food into your body in the morning can enhance your energy for a whole day. 早上補充足夠的有機食物可以增強你一整天的能量。

再比如：I am swamped replenishing the stock of supplies because the goods were trendy and sold very quickly.我忙於補充庫存，因為這些商品很時髦而且賣得很快。

130. willy-nilly 不得不，不情願地

例:Unconditional acceptance of unequal treaties can only show their power and strength was not enough. There was no other choice, the rulers had, willy-nilly, agreed to sign it. What on earth was the reason behind it? 無條件接受不平等條約，只能說明他們的實力和實力還不夠。 別無選擇，統治者不得不同意在上面簽字。 背後到底發生了什麼？

131. neck and neck 不分上下，並駕齊驅

例： Both of the students in my class studied very well, and they are neck and neck. Eventually they were enrolled at Harvard University.我們班的兩個學生

學習都很好，他們不分上下，最後他們被哈佛大學錄取了。

132. Gone （be) 不復存在了，消失

例：Gone are her beauty and youth, her husband doesn't love her anymore. 她的美貌和青春不復存在了，她的丈夫也不再愛她了。

133. unyielding 不服輸的，不屈的

例：Due to his unyielding personality, he was appreciated by his boss and was promoted very quickly. 由於他不服輸的性格，他得到了上司的賞識，很快得晉升了。

134. to override 不顧

例：One of my friends overrode my feeling and decided to withdraw his investment. 我的一個朋友不顧我的感受，決定撤回他的投資。

135. to live up to 不辜負，名副其實

I definitely will live up to your expectation. 我一定不辜負你的期望。

還有，live up to one's reputation. 不負盛名。

136. regardless of 不分、不管、不顧

例：We reject any discrimination in this country, we advocate equality regardless of their race, and color. 在這個國家，我們拒絕接受任何歧視，提倡不分種族和膚色一律平等。

137. murky 不光彩的，不可告人的等

例：He played tricks in the bidding. He won, but I am shamed of his murky behavior. 他在投標中耍了花招。他贏了，但我為他不光彩的行為感到羞恥。

138. to be unabashed 不害臊，不知羞恥，不害羞，厚顏無恥

例：He was unabashed in his lying to the public. 他對公眾說謊而不感到害臊。

139. sheepishly 不好意思地，難為情地

例：He sheepishly glimpsed at the instructor while he was almost hitting a pedestrian.當他差點撞到一個行人時，他不好意思地瞥了教練一眼。

140. to be not up to snuff 不合格
例：Almost all the EVs are not up to snuff, and I don't want to buy them, because it means I am wasting money.幾乎電動汽車都不合格，我不想買，這意味著我在浪費錢。

141. ill-timed 不合時宜的
例：Any ill-timed behaviors will totally ruin the image of celebrities. 任何不合時宜的行為都會徹底破壞名人的形象。

142. dissonant 不和諧的
例：He looks pleased even though he sings a dissonant song in a low voice. 雖然他低聲唱著不和諧的歌，但他看起來很開心。

143. not be plain sailing 不會一帆風順
例：Starting your own business will not be plain sailing. You'd better do more marketing feasibility studies and surveys to make a realistic strategy to compete with your counterparts. 創業不會是一帆風順的，你最好多做市場可行性研究和市場調查，以便制定一個現實的策略與同行競爭。

144. fallow 不活躍的
例：After more than 300 years, this fallow volcano revived, and the local government is closely monitoring its activity. 300 多年後，這座不活躍的火山再次復活，當地政府正密切監視其活動。

145. to blurt out 不加思考脫口而出
例：Anyone randomly blurting out complaints without considering the consequences can potentially harm others and damage relationships. 不加思考隨意脫口而出的人不考慮後果可能會傷害他人且破壞彼此關係。

146. sputtering 不景氣的,氣急敗壞的，霹靂啪啦，
例: Facing the sputtering economy, each country took the most effective measures to turn it

on the right track.面對不景氣
的經濟，各國都採取了最有
效的措施使其走上正軌。

147. flaky 不靠譜的

例：This young man is too flaky
to guarantee it will be done well.
這個年輕人太不靠譜了，不
能保證這件事辦得好。

148. unviable 不可行的

例：During the presentation of
the project to his clients, some of
the points were deemed unviable,
which left the clients confused
and disappointed. 在向客戶介
紹專案的過程中，某些方面
被認為是不可行的，這讓客
戶感到困惑和失望。

149. implacable 不可調和的

例：After many years of
separation from her husband,
their relationship became
implacable, which at the bottom
line led to their divorce.與丈夫
分居多年後，他們的關係變
得不可調和，最終導致他們
離婚。

150. lukewarm 不冷不熱的，微溫的

例：I prefer the food lukewarm.
Overheating food probably burns
my mouth and esophagus，
which may cause cancers. 我更
喜歡不冷不熱的食物。 過熱
的食物可能會灼傷嘴和食
道，這可能會導致癌症。

151. take no heed 不理會，不重視

例：I sincerely gave him some
advice benefiting him for his future
studies, unfortunately, he takes no
heed.我真誠地給了他一些有
利於他未來學習的建議， 可
是他不理會。

152. to shamble about 步履蹣跚

例：He was drunk, and he
shambled about. He shouted. 他
喝醉了，步履蹣跚。他大聲
喊道。

153. to be littered with 佈滿，充滿

例：This region is littered with
so many traps to catch animals.
這個地區到處都佈滿了捕捉
動物的陷阱。

154. cobwebbed 佈滿蜘蛛網的

例：Jonah accidentally ran into an abandoned house and was surprised to see all the stuff was cobwebbed. He felt terrified.約拿不小心跑進了一座廢棄的房子，驚訝地發現所有的東西都被蜘蛛網覆蓋了， 他感到害怕。

155. can't feel willy-nilly to do sth. 不能任性做 ...
例： I can't feel willy-nilly to make a decision myself; I have to discuss it with them even though I am a supervisor. 我不能任性做出自己的決定； 即使我是主管，我也必須與他們討論。

156. stout 結實的，頑強的 、不屈不撓的，
例： I still prefer a pair of stout shoes rather than cheaper ones. 比起便宜的鞋，我還是更喜歡一雙結實的鞋。

157. unfashionable 不是新鮮事了，不時髦了
例： Injecting toxic reagents into the fish to keep them fresh has been unfashionable. 向魚體內注射有毒試劑以保持新鮮早已不是新鮮事了。

158. unencumbered 不受阻礙的、無拘無束的
例： If the rumors spread unencumbered, my fame will be spoiled and wreaked up unpredictably.如果謠言不受阻礙地傳播，我的名聲就會毀於一旦。

再比如：I love the unencumbered lifestyle instead of the 9-5 life cycle.我喜歡無拘無束的生活方式，而不是朝九晚五的生活週期。

159. incessant 不停的
例： Almost all the residents couldn't fall asleep because the noise made by the next door neighbor was incessant.幾乎所有的住戶都無法入睡，因為隔壁的噪音不停。

160. recalcitrant 不聽話的
例： She was annoyed by her recalcitrant son, who is at the age of 15 years old. Her son is experiencing adolescent rebellion. She felt bewildered.她對 15 歲不聽話的兒子感到惱火。 她的兒子正在經歷青春期的叛逆。 她感到不知所措。

161. patchy 不完整的

例：With its patchy financial information, this company is on the brink of bankruptcy.從不完整的資訊來看，這家公司的金融危機已經到了破產的邊緣。

162. precarious 不穩定的

例：In the Western world, jobs are usually precarious, and you often work more than one job on the same day to afford your higher expenditures.在西方世界，工作通常是不穩定的，你經常在同一天做不止一份工作來支付你更高的開銷。

163. to go out of one's way to 不惜一切代價

例：For true love, he went out of his way to woo her. Unfortunately, she didn't love him back. 為了真愛，他不惜一切代價去追求她。 可惜，她不愛他。

164. unremitting effort 不懈的努力

例：With all the colleague's unremitting efforts in the past 20 years, our company finally has been listed in the Nasdaq stock exchange.在全體同仁近 20 年來的不懈努力下，我公司終於在納斯達克上市。

165. jarring 不協調的

例：He looked jarring with improper clothes and colors.他穿著不得體的衣服且顏色看起來很不協調。

166. undying 不朽的

例：Teresa Teng left behind an undying melodious voice that captivated billions of Chinese fans.鄧麗君留下了她那不朽而婉轉的嗓音，令億萬中國歌迷為之傾倒。

167. to be never wonky about 不存僥倖

例：He was never wonky about his studies at university. While other students were content to scrape by with passing grades, he stayed committed to every assignment and his thesis. As a result, he was honored as the Best Student in the final term.他在大學時從不對學業存僥倖。別的學生只圖勉強及格，他卻認真完成每一項作

業和論文。最終，他被評為
該學期的最佳學生。

168. to be less susceptible to sth, 不易受 ...影響

例：Daniel is less susceptible to any poor judgment from other persons.丹尼爾不太容易受到其他人不良判斷的影響。

169. in spades 不遺餘力地

例:He dedicated himself to children's education in spades.他不遺餘力地致力於兒童教育。

170. to pay no heed 不用在意，不予理睬

例：Pay no heed to what others think of you go forward with confidence and do whatever you truly enjoy. 別在意他人的看法，帶著自信去做任何你真正喜歡的事。

171. to be reticent about 不願意，保持沉默

例：Everybody was reticent about the responsibility of failure for this project. 每個人都不願對這個項目的失敗承擔責任。

172. to be loath to 不願意 ...

例： Wyatt is loath to move too far from his hometown due to his deep sense of nostalgia. 懷亞特因思鄉情結濃重，不願搬離故鄉太遠。

173. wheeling and dealing 不擇手段，爾虞我詐

例：I'm quite annoyed by all the wheeling and dealing that goes on among colleagues in the company. 我對公司同事之間那些不擇手段，爾虞我詐感到非常煩。

174. unwittingly 不知不覺的

例： I was talking with one of my friends on the phone; however, I was so tired that I unwittingly fell asleep during the conversation. 我

和一個朋友在電話上聊天，但因為太累，我不知不覺地在通話中睡著了。

175. it is off the cards for 對…不可能

例： It is off the cards for all current vehicle manufacturers to change into EV production quickly because of the high investment cost. 由於投資成本高，目前所有汽車製造商都

不可能快速轉向電動汽車生產。

176. to throw off 戒掉，擺脫

例：So many young men can't throw off the addiction to drugs which will be lethal to their health. 許多年輕人都戒不掉毒品，這對他們的健康是致命的。

177. to wean sb off 擺脫對…放棄，迷惑

例：The reason I prefer a freelance job is to wean myself off the constraints of a 9-5 jobs. 我喜歡自由職業的原因是想讓自己擺脫朝九晚五的束縛。

再比如：Some scientists recently found that Chinese herbal medicines can quickly wean high blood pressure patients off blood pressure pills, which may cause serious side effects or even some cancers. 最近，一些科學家發現，中草藥可以很容易地讓高血壓患者放棄降壓藥，而降壓藥可能會導致嚴重的副作用，甚至致癌。

178. to maroon someone 被困在…

例：Loneliness marooned me in a strange place so I am often nostalgic of my hometown. 孤獨把我困在一個陌生的地方，所以我經常懷念我的家鄉。

179. to tout something 把某事吹捧成

例：This company touts its latest chips as a cutting edge technology.這家公司把其最新的晶片吹噓成尖端技術。

180. to cut euphemism 不要繞彎子

例：I hope you can directly expose your opinion instead of cutting euphemisms. 我希望你能直接表達你的觀點，不要繞彎子。

C

1. savvy 聰慧的，精明的(非正式用法表示)

例：Elon Musk is one of the savviest money makers in the

world.埃隆馬斯克是世界上最聰慧的賺錢者之一。

2. to trod on one's toe 踩了某人的腳

例：I am sorry that I accidentally trod on your toe; please forgive me.對不起，我不小心踩著你的腳；請原諒我。

3. deep-pocketed 財力雄厚的

例：The most deep-pocketed persons in the world are almost all in the US.世界上財力雄厚的人幾乎都在美國。

4. to adopt a stance of 採取了一種姿態

例：To avoid any depression being occurred, we must adopt a positive stance in facing any difficulties and challenges.為了避免任何抑鬱的發生，我們必須採取積極的態度面對任何困難和挑戰。

5. suck "菜"

例：You literally suck since you've already found your true love—why don't you have the guts to pursue her? 你是真的"菜"！都已經找到真愛了，咋不敢去追啊？

6. bonanza 財源滾滾，幸運

例：I sincerely hope your investment can bring a big bonanza for you. Good luck! Buddy.衷心希望您的投資能為您帶來財源滾滾。祝好運！哥們兒。

7. scintillating with wit 才思敏捷，妙語連珠

例：We have a new guy joining our team, and he brings a scintillating wit with him. 我們團隊來了一個新同事，他才思敏捷，妙語連珠。

8. spotty 參差不齊的，有好有壞的，

例：It is challenging for ordinary people to pick a watermelon that tastes sweet, given that its quality is spotty.普通老百姓很難挑到味道甜的西瓜，因為它的品質參差不齊。

9. dry 慘澹的，冷清的

例：When entering the supermarket, I found their business was dry.一進超市，我發現他們的生意很慘澹。

10.　thuggishly 殘忍地

例：To fight for the benefits from money left by their mom, three brothers thuggishly killed their sister. My question is, what was wrong with our human instinct? 為了爭奪媽媽留下的錢財，三兄弟殘忍殺害了妹妹。 我的問題是，我們人類的本能出了什麼問題？

11. poignant 慘痛的，悲傷的

例：My uncle told us about a poignant life experience in the early year of his stay overseas. 我叔叔給我們講了他早年在國外的慘痛經歷和生活。

12. to perpetrate 參與犯罪的

例：Anyone who perpetrated making poisonous food should be heavily penalized.任何製造有毒食品的人都應該受到重罰。

13. to scramble 倉促收尾

例：Due to the client's specified deadline, the design team is scrambling to wrap up. 由於客戶指定的截止日期，將至，設計團隊正在倉促收尾。

14. to rig 操控

例："The election has been rigged，" President Trump says."選舉已被操縱，" 特朗普總統說。
注：rig 的含義還有很多，大家可以參閱詞典查詢相關的其它用法。

15. sloppy 草率的

例：He provided the project plan, which looked pretty sloppy; his boss required him to design it in detail. 他提供了專案計畫，看起來很草率； 他的老闆要求他詳細設計。

16. clattery 嘈雜的，喧鬧的

例：The clattery sound gradually winds towards us; My curiosity spurs me to find out what is happening.嘈雜的聲音漸漸向我們走來，好奇心驅使我去弄清楚發生了什麼事。

17. to contrive 策劃，設計

例：He is busy contriving a specific marketing plan for this strategy so the sales team can follow it.他正忙著為這個策略設計一個具體的行銷計畫，以便銷售團隊能夠遵循它。

18. stratagem 策略
例：He crafted an effective marketing stratagem to face the challenge of the competitors.他制定了有效的行銷策略來應對競爭對手的挑戰。

19. tack 策略，方法
例：Persistence doesn't indicate you can stubbornly go into the dead end, you must change your tack to adapt to its dynamic transformation 堅持不代表你可以頑固地走進死胡同，你必須改變策略以適應它的動態變化。

20. strident 刺耳的，尖叫的
例：Don't talk to me with a strident voice, it is too impolite and rude.不要對我發出刺兒的大叫聲，太不禮貌且粗魯。

21. to goad 刺激
例：To avoid unnecessary wounds or death, don't goad the criminals; instead, try to figure out a better way to escape or call 911.為了避免不必要的傷亡，不要刺激罪犯，而是試圖找到一個更好的辦法逃跑或報警。

22. to sting sb 刺激某人、惹某人
例：This letter has stung him, he finally decided to leave this city
這封信刺激到了他，他終於決定離開這個城市.

再比如：Don't sting him in words and action, otherwise, he will commit suicide.別惹他，不然他會自殺的。

23. to come hurtling in 從 ...疾馳而來
例：The UFO came hurtling in from the outer space
不明飛行物從外太空疾馳而來。

再比如：Andrew saw a bullet train hurtling in from farther away
安德魯看見一列子彈頭火車從遠處疾馳而來。

24. to hustle to 匆忙，趕緊
例：No sooner had this guy remembered his friend's birthday than he hustled to buy a bottle of wine on the way to the visit. 這傢伙剛想起朋友的生日，便匆

忙趕去拜訪的路上順手買了一瓶酒。

25. to bustle 匆忙
例：In Beijing, so many young people bustled in and out every day. They walked very fast; I couldn't even catch up with them. 在北京，如此多的年輕人每天都很匆忙且走得很快。 我甚至無法趕上他們。

26. to ply 從事 ...
例：Even though the online ride sharing business just started, so many people worldwide are plying in that job. 儘管線上叫車業務剛剛興起，全世界就有很多人從事這項工作。

27. to flog 從中盈利,向某人賣東西
例：The manufacturers don't make anything that can't flog, because they want to earn good money. 生產廠家絕對不會製作任何不盈利的東西，因為他們想從中盈利。

再比如:After the senior students graduated, they started to flog their expensive textbooks to their junior classmates. 高年級學生畢業後，開始把他們昂貴的教材低價賣給低年級的同學。

28. to get by 湊合著過日子
例：A survey shows that many couples don't have true love, but considering their kids, they pretend to show their happiness to others; however, they will only just get by. 一項調查顯示，許多夫妻沒有真愛，但考慮到他們的孩子，他們假裝向別人展示他們的幸福，然而，實際上他們只能湊合著過。

再比如：Despite facing financial hardships, she managed to get by relying on her part-time job and frugal lifestyle. 儘管面臨經濟困難，她通過兼職工作和節儉的生活方式勉強湊合著過。

29. gruff 粗暴的
例：His statements and behavior are very gruff, a lot of his colleagues would rather keep a certain distance from him. 他的言行舉止很粗暴，他的許多同事都與他保持距離。

再比如：Two guys were fighting each other on the bus ,a lot of passengers ignored their gruff behavior.兩個男人在公共汽車上打架，不幸的是，許多乘客忽視他們粗暴的行為。

30. madcap 粗魯的，狂妄的

例：People with madcap behavior almost all lack a well-educated background.有這種粗魯行為的人幾乎都缺乏良好的教育背景。

31. cluster round 簇擁

例：Her grandpa passed away, and she went to bid him farewell. As she entered the funeral home, she saw the coffin placed in the center of the room, surrounded by clusters of roses. 她的爺爺去世了，她去向他告別。當她走進靈堂時，她看到棺材被擺放在房間的中央，四周簇擁著成群的玫瑰。

32. sketchy 粗略的

例：Aiden only provides some sketchy descriptions of his journey to the Antarctic.艾登只是粗略地描述了他的南極之旅。

33. to gee up 促使

例：The failure gees him up to refigure out a better way to face the challenge. 這次失敗促使他重新想出更好的方法來面對挑戰。

34. to tamper with 篡改，損害

例: Apparently, someone tampered with this document. We must look into it.顯然，有人篡改了這份文件。我們必須調查一下。

再比如：We must not be involved in other people's privacy. Otherwise, it will tamper with the good relationship with your colleagues.我們不能干涉別人的隱私。否則，會損害你和同事的關係。

35. to garble 篡改，歪曲，斷章取義

例：His counterpart garbled his original statement to mislead public opinion. 那個對手為了誤導輿論而歪曲了他原來的聲明。

再比如：You garbled my intended meaning, leading to a significant misunderstanding, and it was quite disappointing for both of us. 你曲解了我的本意，產生了很大誤解，這令彼此相當失望。

36. to lay waste to 摧毀

例：Russia's invasion of Ukraine laid waste to peace in that region. 俄羅斯入侵烏克蘭摧毀了該地區的和平。

37. to knock out 摧毀，弄壞

例：Switching the gear to reverse position while the car doesn't stop completely will totally knock out its transmission. 當汽車沒有完全停止時，將檔位切換到倒車位置將完全摧毀其變速器。

38. devastate 摧毀，蹂躪

例：Locusts could seriously devastate the crops in the southwestern part of China. 在中國西南地區，蝗災可能會嚴重摧毀整個地區的農作物。

39. to leach 萃取

例：This medicine pill is leached from organic herbs. 這種藥丸是從有機草藥中萃取的。

40. to be blindsided by 措手不及

例：She appears humble and nice, however, she covertly gossips about her colleagues. I was blindsided by her hypocrisy. 她看上去和藹可親，但卻在背後對同事說三道四。她的虛偽讓我措手不及。

41. blunder 錯誤（常指愚蠢的錯誤）

例：We advocate avoiding more blunders and becoming smarter. 我們提倡避免更多錯誤，變得更聰明。

42. convoluted 錯綜複雜的，曲折的

例：The convoluted plot in this novel attracted me. 這本小說錯綜複雜的情節吸引了我。

43. quiescent 沉默的，不動聲色的

例：During the negotiations, he keeps quiescent to observe the other party and figure out what he would do in the next step. 在談判過程中，他會保持沉默，觀察對方，並弄清楚他下一步要做什麼。

觀察對方，並弄清楚他下一
步要做什麼。

44. nigh on 差不多
例: I've already invested nigh on a million dollars in this stock, but unfortunately, it has been delisted. All my money is gone. 我已經投資差不多一百萬美元在這支股票上，不幸的是，它已經被摘牌。我的所有資金都沒有了。

45. lame 差勁的，蹩腳的
例：The design of this car is extremely lame, no one would like to buy it.這種汽車的設計太差勁了，沒有人願意買。

46. to slot 插入
例：Before exiting the toll parking lot, you are required to slot your valid credit card into the machine for payment. Once the payment is successfully processed, the barrier arm will be raised, allowing you to proceed with your vehicle. 在離開收費停車場之前，您需要將有效的信用卡插入機器進行支付。支付成功後，道閘才會升起，允許您駕駛通過。

47. to chip in 插嘴
例：Try to avoid chipping in while I am talking with my professor. 我和教授談話時，儘量不要插嘴。

48. to chime in 插話
例：It is impolite to chime in before the other person has finished speaking. 在對方沒有說完之前插話是不禮貌的。

49. to beget 產生
例：One person's persistence and perseverance can beget an outstanding achievement.一個人的堅持和毅力可以產生卓越的成就。

50. trills 顫音
例：I prefer trills embedded into the songs because they can fully express passions burried deeply in people's souls.我更喜歡將顫音嵌入歌曲中，因為它們可以充分表達人們靈魂深處的感情。

51. to drawn-out 長期的
例：We should try to avoid trying so-called new medications even though it ostensibly and effectively works well but they may churn out drawn-out side

effects. We have to focus on the observation of their prolonged usage in the public.我們應該儘量避免嘗試所謂的新藥，即使它表面上有效果，但這些新藥可能會產生長期的副作用。 我們必須專注於觀察它們在公眾中的長期使用效果。

52. oft-cited 常引用的

例： The rise of Walmart is a frequently oft-cited case in Master of Business Administration learning. 沃爾瑪的崛起是工商管理碩士學習中經常被引用的案例。

53. to overtake 超車，超越

例： I saw so many drivers crazily overtaking the others on the highway. It seemed to be dangerous behavior.我在高速公路上看到很多司機瘋狂超車，這似乎是非常危險的行為。

再比如： The speed of development in China's economy overtakes any other country in the world.中國經濟的發展速度超過世界上任何一個國家。

54. to go beyond 超出；勝過

例： Her performance goes beyond everyone's expectations. 她的表現超出了大家的預期。

55. overstretch 超出承受的能力

例：Nowadays, so many young people borrow money online; its high-interest rate overstretched the capability of paying back their debt.如今，很多年輕人在網上借錢；它的高利率超出了他們的償債能力。

56. sardonic 嘲諷的

例： She is not welcome because she always shows a sardonic smile to everybody. 她不受歡迎，因為她總是對每個人都露出嘲諷的微笑。

57. to outstrip 超過

例：Zoey outstripped all of her classmates by getting the highest scores for her final exam this year.佐伊在今年的期末考試中得了最高分，因此超過了她所有的同學。

再比如： To realize interstellar travel, we must invent an

outstripping speed of light shuttle. 要實現星際旅行，我們必須發明一種超越光速的太空梭。

58. rowdy 吵鬧的

例：I believe that only a minority of individuals would prefer a rowdy environment; instead, the majority would prefer a tranquil and tidy one.我相信只有少數人會喜歡喧鬧的環境，相反，大多數人喜歡寧靜整潔的環境。

59. a deluge of 潮水般湧來

例：The complaints from their clients, like avalanches, pump up a deluge of calls and letters from all over the country, so the company was forced to set up a special team to make an investigation.客戶投訴如雪崩，全國各地來電來信如潮水般湧來，公司被迫成立特別團隊進行調查。

60. to snicker 嘲笑

Snickering at someone's misfortune is immoral; we should offer them kindness and support instead.嘲笑別人的不幸是不道德的，我們應該提供給他們更多的善意和支持。

61. poke 嘲笑，奚落

例：He failed to win the tender so he got pokes from colleagues. 他投標失敗，因此受到同事們的嘲笑。

62. derisive 嘲笑的

例：His outlandish hairstyle was often derisive, which was very painful for him. He decided to cut his hair off, 他奇怪的髮型常常引來嘲笑，這讓他非常痛苦。後來，他決定把它們剪掉。

63. to leapfrog 超越

例：Brielle is classified as the second-best student in her class, however, it is very difficult for her to leapfrog the one in first place. 布瑞爾被評為班上第二優秀的學生，她很難超越第一名。

64. to blanch 焯菜

例：Some vegetables should be blanched before cooking; otherwise, they may produce toxic substances that could be harmful to people. These vegetables include green beans, spinach, kale, broccoli, Brussels sprouts, kidney beans, fiddlehead ferns, cauliflower, chrysanthemum greens, and some others. 一些蔬菜在烹飪前需要焯水，否則它們可能會產生對人體有害的有毒物質。這些蔬菜包括四季豆、菠菜、羽衣甘藍、西蘭花、孢子甘藍、四季豆、蕨菜、花椰菜、茼蒿等。

65. to bicker 吵嘴
例:The couple often bickers with each other over some trivial issues, which may affect their long-term relationship.這對夫妻經常因為一些瑣碎的問題而爭吵，這可能會影響他們的長期關係。

66. to hype up 炒作
例：Nowadays, a lot of media prefer to hype up something to attract people's eye balls.現在，很多媒體都喜歡炒作一些東西來吸引人們的眼球。

再比如：Some pharmaceutical manufacturers dedicated themselves to promoting this medication, which boasted the most effective cancer treatment. Unfortunately, the fact is that it is only marketing hype.

一些製藥企業致力於推廣這種號稱治療癌症最有效的藥物。不幸的是，事實是這只是一種行銷炒作。

67. downright 徹頭徹尾的
例：He always promised something to us but never cashed it, so someone told me he was a downright deceiver.他總是向我們承諾一些東西，但從來沒有兌現過，所以有人告訴我他是一個徹頭徹尾的騙子。

68. bromide 陳詞濫調
例：This movie, inflated with bromides, made readers feel disgust.這部電影充斥著陳詞濫調，讓讀者感到噁心。

再比如：This company threw out a bromide statement to hide their ugly behavior to be fraudulent by producing fake brands and earning illegal profits from it。這家公司發表了一份陳詞濫調的聲明，以掩蓋他們生產假冒白蘭地的醜惡行為，騙取非法利潤。

69. time-worn rhetoric 陳詞濫調

例：Nowadays, young people dislike the time-worn rhetoric; they have become very realistic. Some even prefer the "lying flat" lifestyle. 如今，年輕人厭倦了陳詞濫調，他們變得非常現實。甚至有些人更喜歡"躺平"的生活方式。

70. to swoop in 趁機，趁虛而入

例：Her company declared bankruptcy, so he swooped in to acquire it by paying less of a price.她的公司宣告破產，於是他趁機以更低的價格出手收購。

71. to be steeped in 沉浸

例：The story of the movie is very complex and attractive, I am almost steeped in it.這部電影的故事非常複雜且有吸引力，我幾乎沉浸其中。

72. to be immersed in 沉浸在

例：I guess everyone will be immersed in the happiness of the spring festival even though the pandemic is still haunting us.我想，雖然疫情還在肆虐，但每個人都會沉浸在春節的快樂中。

73. ropey 陳舊的，破舊的，劣質的

例：The US government plans to invest trillions of dollars in renovating its ropey facilities, involving public transportation, road, electricity, energy, etc.美國政府計畫投資數萬億美元翻新其陳舊的設施，涉及公共交通、道路、電力、能源等。

74. drab 沉悶的

例：The weather is drab, and I have no passion for doing anything, just sleeping at home. 天氣沉悶，我無心做任何事，只是在家睡覺。

75. to revel in 沉迷於

例：My son revels in gaming but abandons his studies unpredictably. I am very concerned about his future.我兒子沉迷于遊戲，出乎意料地放棄了學業。我很擔心他的未來.

再比如：I literally enjoy the holiday atmosphere, I'd love to revel in，especially during the spring festival，scrumptious food, magical colorful dazzling lights, and all varieties of folk stage performances with too many beautiful things.我很享受節日氣氛，尤其是在春節期間我很想陶醉美味的食物，神奇的五光十色的炫彩燈光，還有各式各樣的民俗舞臺表演，美不勝收。

76. to mediate 促成
例：The U.S. is trying to mediate a ceasefire between Ukraine and Russia.美國正試圖在烏克蘭和俄羅斯之間斡旋，促成停火。

77. ruminative 沉思默想的
例:The team made a very smart decision by collecting all ruminative suggestions from its members.該團隊通過從隊員收集沉思默想的建議，做出了一個非常明智的決定。

78. whiplash 沉重的打擊
例：His flunk on the university entrance exam gave him whiplash, even though he had prepared for it for a long time. 儘管他已經為此準備了很長時間，大學入學考試的失利給了他沉重的打擊。

79. to christen 稱…為
例：Now young people prefer to spend all their salary within a month, some people christened them a "moonlight clan" Yueguangzu" and some can even splurge to buy luxury stuff by borrowing high-interest loans. I literally can't read them. 現在年輕人喜歡在一個月內花光所有工資，有人稱他們為"月光族"，有的甚至可以借高息貸款大手大腳地買奢侈品。 我真的看不懂。

80. to clinch 成功獲得
例：She was so excited to tell me she clinched an offer from a famous enterprise.她很興奮地告訴我，她成功獲得了一家著名企業的錄用。

81. to concede 承認
例：Anyone can make a mistake, the point is we must concede it otherwise no one can respect you.任何人都可能犯錯，關鍵是我們必須承認，否則沒有人會尊重你。

82. to can ill afford to 承受不了

例：This world cup competition is so important that the whole team can ill afford to lose.這場世界盃比賽是如此重要，整個球隊都輸不起。

83. to underlie 成為…的基礎，是…的根源

例：All that you are studying today will underlie your future exploitation of your capability.你今天所學的一切都將成為你未來能力開發的基礎。

再比如：The poor understanding of culture underlies the lack of mutual communication.對文化的瞭解不足是缺乏相互交流的根源。

84. to become a stain on someone 成為某人的污點

例：Falling in love with his staff in the company runs against the rules and becomes a stain on Mr. Harry, so he, as a CEO, was eventually forced to step down. 在公司裡與員工談戀愛違背了公司規定，成為哈里森先生的污點，為此，作為首席執行官的他最終被迫下臺。

85. to bear weight 承受，負重

例：The bridge apparently is too old to bear weight. 這座橋顯然太舊了，承受不了重量。

86. to laud 稱讚

例：As parents, they must laud their children as "talented guys," "you did a pretty good job," etc., or " you are brave and strong" instead of blaming them as "stupid" or " timid". They must benefit them with more positive encouragement, less groaning and growling, which explores the potential to lay the foundation for their success. 作為父母，一定要稱讚自己的孩子"有才"、"你做得好"、"你勇敢堅強"，而不是指責孩子"愚蠢"、"膽小"，多一些積極的鼓勵，少一些抱怨和咆哮，發掘孩子的潛力，為孩子的成功奠定基礎。

87. stigma 恥辱、陰影

例：Our Chinese people endured a lot of stigma in history. Now we have stood up and will never tolerate any bullies at all.

我們中國人在歷史上遭受了很多恥辱，現在我們站起來，絕不容忍任何欺淩。

再比如：I wouldn't say I like the stigma of slandering without any evidence, which will overshadow my life. 我不喜歡沒有證據的誹謗汙名，這會使我的生活蒙上陰影。

88. "a fall into the pit can yield a gain in your wit". 吃一塹，長一智

例：The only way we learn lessons from our failure, namely:" a fall into the pit can yield a gain in your wit" we can tremendously move forward and achieve great success.只有我們從失敗中吸取教訓，即："吃一塹，長一智"，我們才能大踏步向前邁進，取得巨大成功。

89. to make a fetish of 崇拜

例：Chinese people must maintain their own traditional characteristics of living instead of making an aimless fetish of living styles in the western world.中國人必須保持自己的傳統生活特色，而不是盲目地崇拜西方世界的生活方式。

90. to be awash with 充斥著

例：The market is awash with a lot of fraudulent brand bags. 市場上充斥著許多假冒品牌的包。

91. to be inundated with 充斥著

例：Nowadays, almost all the websites are inundated with violent language and insulting comments ... 如今，幾乎所有的網站上都充斥著暴力語言和侮辱性的評論。

robert xian
2025-06-24 20:58:56
----

92. momentum 慣性

例：Experienced drivers typically leverage the vehicles' own momentum when driving downhill by easing off the accelerator pedal. 有經驗的司機在下坡行駛時，通常會鬆開油門來利用車輛自身的慣性。

93. to bristle with 充滿

例：He bristled with hatred toward the invaders after his son was killed. .因為兒子被侵略者殺害，他對他們充滿了仇恨，怒髮衝冠。

94. to be loaded with 充滿了 ...

例：Her kindness is loaded with full positive energy, which is very impressive.她的善良充滿了正能量，讓人印象深刻。

95. convulsion 抽搐

例：Covid-19 can trigger convulsions because the virus intelligently attacks people's brains. 冠狀病毒病會引發抽搐，因為該病毒會智慧地攻擊人的大腦。

96. grotesque 醜陋的，奇形怪狀的

例：The designs of vehicles nowadays are getting more grotesque.現在車輛的設計越來越醜。

97. to reek 臭氣熏天，散發著臭氣

例：This guy rarely took a shower, so he reeks, and nobody dares to be close to him. 這傢伙很少洗澡，臭氣熏天，沒人敢靠近他。

再比如：His father lived alone, his room was filled with garbage, and everything was messy due to his poor management of himself, which reeked of weird smells.他的父親一個人住，由於他自己管理不善，他的房間裡堆滿了垃圾，一切都很亂，散發著怪味。

98. to get around 抽時間做 ...

例：I am too busy to get around to deal with this matter.我太忙了，抽不出時間來處理這件事。

(當然，get around 的意思很多，比如：到處走走；逃避；說服；傳開來等）

99. at every turn 處處，到處

例：Recently, he encountered a lot of trouble at every turn.最近，他處處遇到麻煩。

100. among other things 除此之外

英語國家的人們非常喜歡用這個短語來表達此外這類的轉折含義。

例：Liliana works for the government as an administrator; Among other things, she is also a French tutor.莉蓮是政府的管理員;此外，她還是一名法語教員。

101. to sally out 出發，出擊

例：Camel trains sallied out in the early morning and launched their long journey through the Sahara Desert.駱駝隊一大早就出發了，開始了穿越撒拉沙漠的長途旅行。

102. notoriously 出了名地，臭名昭著地

例：The quality of the cars made by some countries is notoriously unreliable and inferior. Anyway, it sounds bizarre that there are so many people still going ahead to snap them up.一些國家生產的汽車品質是出了名的不可靠和劣質。 無論如何，讓人奇怪的是仍然有那麼多人去搶購。

103. to pepper with 充滿 ...

（pepper 除了有胡椒的意思外，它還可以作為動詞表示充滿）

例：The statement issued by this company is peppered with discrimination and bias. No employees can tolerate and accept it.該公司發表的聲明充滿歧視和偏見。 任何員工都不能容忍和接受。

再比如：In today's society, many young people have a tendency to pepper their expressions with an abundance of rhetoric, resembling the writing style of the official news. Unfortunately, this trend often results in the loss of their own unique personalities. 現如今，許多年輕人傾向于在表達中大量使用修辭手法，使其類似於官方新聞的寫作風格。不幸的是，這種趨勢往往導致他們個人獨特性的喪失。

104. to stick out 出色，顯眼

例：My classmate's academic achievements really stick out, leaving everyone on campus astonished.我的同學的學術成就非常出色，讓校園裡的每個人都感到驚訝。

105. brilliant 出色的

例：I often told my son that he needs brilliant communication skills to get along well with his colleagues or some other people he knows. 我常告訴我的兒子，他需要出色的溝通技巧才能與同事或其他認識的人相處得很好。（實際上，這個詞的中文解釋非常多，有

時候要根據上下文或不同場
景來判定和選用)

106. to be fraught with 充滿了 ...

例：This room is fraught with horror.這個房間充滿了恐怖。

107. to be on the back foot 處於劣勢

例：The final basketball competition is on; team A got 88 points vs. Team B 78 points, and team B is on the back foot.籃球決賽開始了，A 隊得了 88 分，B 隊得了 78 分，B 隊處於劣勢。

108. on the crust of 處在 ...的頂點，或風口浪尖

例：It's said that at 12 years of age, a girl's beauty is on the cusp of her whole life.據說，12 歲女孩的美麗正處於她一生的頂點。

109. to be in jeopardy 處在風險中，岌岌可危

例：Due to a shortage of funds, this project is now in jeopardy of being abandoned. 由於資金短缺，該項目現在正面臨被擱置的風險。

110. to emanate from 出自

例：Nobody can believe this ridiculous statement which emanates from a famous expert. 沒有人會相信這種荒謬的說法出自一位著名專家之口。

111. to be relayed back to 傳回

例：The pictures and data from Mars were relayed back to Earth. 相關圖片和資料從火星傳回地球。

112. to clad in 穿著

例：This lady, clad in a red cheongsam, anchored the program.這位身穿紅色旗袍的女士主持了節目。

113. dapper 穿著整潔的

例：Today is my graduation day, and as people crowded around, a dapper middle-aged man in a finely tailored suit walked onto the stage, instantly capturing everyone's attention. He turned out to be the president of our university, the youngest leader ever, which left us all in awe.今天是我的畢業典禮，人群擁擠在一起，突然，一個穿著精緻西裝，穿著整潔的中年男子走上舞臺，吸引

了所有人的目光。原來他是我們大學的校長，也是有史以來最年輕的領導。這讓我們都感到非常敬佩。

114. moribund 垂死的、停滯不前的
例：During the pandemic, all business became moribund.在大流行期間，所有業務都陷入垂死的狀態。

115. tantalizing 垂涎三尺，令人矚目的
例：He cooked beef so well, which was tantalizing.他把牛肉煮得很香，讓人垂涎三尺。

再比如：This diligent student's unwavering commitment to academic excellence has earned him a coveted spot at a prestigious university. The potential rewards of this achievement are both tantalizing and impressive.這位勤奮的學生通過刻苦努力獲得了頂尖大學的入學資格。這一成就所帶來的回報令人矚目且令人印象深刻。

116. to crow about 吹噓

例：Nathaniel always crows about his family's wealth and luxury; you will instead feel sick if you listen to it endlessly. 納旦尼爾總是吹噓他家的財富和奢華，你聽了沒完沒了反而會覺得噁心。

117. to brag of 吹噓做 ...
說到 brag 很多人都會立馬想到其後跟的介詞是 about,
比如：This company bragged about its product everywhere, which is inferior in its quality. 這家公司到處吹噓自己的產品，但品質很差。

而 brag of +動詞 ing 的表達方式不多。
例：This professor bragged of pouring so much of his energy and money in the essay guidance of his students.這位教授吹噓在指導學生寫論文上，他投入了很多精力和金錢。

當然，這個例句中 brag 後面應該使用 about,可當今的英語表達方式非常不拘一格，似乎帶有所謂創新。有時，按語法規則去衡量一些表達方式，會覺得怪怪的。但實際上語言就是交流的工具，

只要表達者能清晰地把意圖說明白，語法的局限就顯得非常蒼白了。當然，我這麼說並不是鼓勵大家撇開語法隨便亂講，只是想說語法固然重要，但只要能準確清晰把自己想表達的內容傳達出去，對方可以接受就基本達到預期目的了。如果一味地死扣語法來表達內容，在實際生活中就顯得古板生硬了。

118. folly 蠢事

例：It is folly to splurge money on stuff you rarely use daily. I see some girls buy a lot of skirts but never wear them.Years later, you can still find that some of them still have tags.把錢花在日常很少使用的東西上是愚蠢的，我看到一些女孩買了很多裙子，但從不穿，多年以後，你仍然可以看到其中一些還掛著標籤。

119. to debunk 戳穿

例：To get along with people, you must never forget that you ought not to debunk their natures even though you have seen through them.與人相處，切不可忘記，即使看透了人的本性，也不要戳穿。

120. to be conceived 懷上

例：When my brother was conceived 20 years ago, my mom got through her most difficult period.我媽媽 20 年前懷上我弟弟的時候，度過了她最艱難的時期。

121. lingering 持續的，延綿不斷的, 揮之不去的

例：The war between Russia and Ukraine will put a lingering influence on the global economy 俄烏戰爭將對全球經濟產生持續的影響。

122. to jump the queue 插隊、加塞兒

例：I saw a couple of young men jumping the queue among seniors who had been lining up there for almost a couple of hours. They didn't feel ashamed of their behavior.我看到幾個年輕人在排隊將近幾個小時的老年人中插隊。 他們不會為自己的行為感到羞恥。

123. to piggyback 傳播 （原意: 馱運）

例：This kind of virus can piggyback from one person to another. 這種病毒可以從一個人傳染給另一個人。

124. to get a square dinner 一頓豐盛的晚餐

例：After being busy for the whole week, I prefer to sit together with all my family members to get a square dinner. 忙碌了一周後，我更喜歡和所有的家人坐在一起吃一頓豐盛的晚餐。

125. to rehash 重複

例：Learning the lessons from history will help us avoid rehashing the obsolete, unrealistic, and discarded ideas; so we absorb its essentials and get rid of the rest. 從歷史中吸取教訓將幫助我們避免重複過時的、不切實際的和被拋棄的方式，我們吸收它的精華，拋棄它的垃圾。

126. to reflate 重新提升

例：To reflate the popularity of our tourism, we must enhance both the infrastructure and the services. This includes retraining our tour guide teams and elevating the quality of the services we provide. 要重新提升我們旅遊業的知名度，我們必須改進硬體和軟體設施。這包括對導遊團隊進行再培訓以及提高服務品質。

127. to perk up 重新振作起來

例：He lost his job and became depressed. The big challenge for him is how to perk himself up. 他失業了，變得很沮喪，對他來說最大的挑戰是如何重新振作起來。

128. to remain in one's infancy ...仍處於初級階段

例：The current research and study in robotics and AI remain in their infancy.
目前關於機器人和人工智慧的研究仍處於初級階段。

129. to seethe with 充滿

例：Tenants are sometimes seething with hostility towards landlords, and it is hard for me to understand why. 租戶有時對房東充滿敵意，我很難理解這種情緒。

130. to be the last straw 成為壓垮某人的最後一根稻草

例：Losing her pension savings was the last straw. 失去她的養

老金儲蓄成了壓垮她的最後
一根稻草。

D

1. a plethora of 大量的
表達更大數量上的變化。
例：Peter found a plethora of
job opportunities on the website
which listed millions of jobs.彼得
在網上找到大量的工作，而
這個網站每天上傳數以百萬
的工作機會。

我們常說所謂信息量很大，
一般意義上的 a lot of 所表達
的那種多不足以顯示量上的
巨大，故此，母語英語者常
用 a plethora of 來表達大量
的。

另外，表達信息量巨大也可
以說 a plethora of information,
表達大量出口 a plethora of
exports, 還有表達巨大的資料
量 a plethora of data 相當於
data mining 等等。希望大家
方便能深入查詢這個短語的
更多用法，以達到舉一反三
效果。

2. to noodle about 對⋯一竅
不通
例：I noodled about math but
my son became an expert in
math.我對數學一竅不通，我
兒子卻對數學很精通。

3. myriad 大批的
例：In terms of the struggling
economy, the property market
became saggy and myriad
builders went bust because of
slow consumer demand.
在經濟低迷的情況下，房地
產市場疲軟，消費者需求放
緩，導致大批建築商破產。

4. to splurge 大把花錢
例：He splurged much more on
education instead of food.他大
把錢花在教育上，而不是花
在食物上。

5. outflank 打敗
例：To outflank your
competitors, you need
exceptional talent and superb
skills.要打敗你的競爭對手，
你需要非凡的才能和高超的
技能。

6. to spiffy up 打扮

例：It is a big day for him because he is gonna date an unknown girl someone introduced to him days ago. In the morning, he got up early and started to spiffy him up to show his best to the girl.這對他來說是個大日子，因為他要和幾天前有人介紹給他的陌生女孩約會。早上，他起得很早，開始打扮自己，向女孩展示他最好的一面。

7. to spruce up 打扮的整齊漂亮

例：They picked up a lucky day to hold a wedding ceremony, so one day ahead, they tried to spruce up the whole room and dazzlingly decorated it.他們選了個舉行婚禮的吉日，所以提前一天，他們盡可能把整個房間打打扮的整齊漂亮。

8. skimp 對…不得不節省；捨不得給

例：Owing to the devaluation of the currency, the purchasing power of my income has shrunken, so I have to skimp on food expenditure. 由於貨幣貶值，購買力縮水了，所以我不得不節省食品開支。

9. to vaunt 大吹大擂

例：Sometimes the manufacturers vaunted the quality of their products. In fact, their quality is inferior. 有時製造商大吹大擂他們產品的品質。事實上，它們的品質是劣質的。

10. to apply a broad brush to 大刀闊斧地做 ...

例：The new board chairman applied a broad brush to cut off the expenditure and lay off many employees throughout the current difficulties. 為了渡過目前的難關，新任董事長採取了大刀闊斧削減開支和解雇許多員工的措施。

11. brawl 打鬥

例：Each year, road rage frequently occurs on the road, which leads to drivers' brawls, even on highways. 每年，道路上經常發生路怒，導致司機打鬥，甚至在高速公路上也是如此。

12. to wager 打賭

例：Do you dare wager to enter this dark room? Anyway, I felt scared. 你敢打賭進入這個黑暗的房間嗎？ 無論如何，我感到害怕。

13. a hiccup 打嗝

例： The better way to ease off your hiccup is that you can drink a small cup of water and keep it in your mouth without taking a breath for over seven seconds. After then, you can swallow it down. Your hiccup can stop immediately. Of course, you can repeat the same procedure if you don't think it works. 緩解打嗝的更好方法是，你可以喝一小杯水，含在嘴裡，屏住呼吸7秒鐘以上，最後，你可以把它吞下去。你的打嗝可以立即停止。當然，如果你認為它不起作用，你可以重複同樣的過程。

14. to wallop 顛覆

例：What if a future resource shortage happens on earth, does it wallop human life? Undoubtedly, the question arises: we must move to another planet like Mars or someplace in the deep cosmos. Nobody knows what we should do. 毫無疑問，未來地球上的資源短缺會顛覆我們人類生存？ 問題是我們是否要搬到另一個星球，比如火星，或者宇宙深處的一些地方。沒人知道我們能做什麼。

15. to clamp down on 打擊

例：With the increasing money laundry, the bank made a final decision to clamp down on this illegal behavior.
隨著洗錢行為的增多，銀行最終決定打擊這種非法行為。

16. to clobber 打擊（嚴厲）

例：I fully support our government clobbering the fabrication of poisonous food and child trafficking. 我完全支援政府打擊製造有毒食品和販賣兒童的行為。

再比如：His brother clobbered his wife with a cudgel, so everyone thought he was so stupid. 他哥哥用棍子打他老婆，為此大家都認為他很愚蠢。

17. to whip up

（這個片語的含義太多，原意是激起、激發等。但如果用在做飯方面比如打雞蛋，準備一頓豐盛的飯菜都可以用這個短語）

例：As a 12 -year old boy, he couldn't cook anything but only fried tomato with eggs, so he skillfully whipped up eggs and fried them with tomato, which smelt very tasty.12 歲的時候，他只會做雞蛋炒番茄，所以他熟練地把雞蛋打散，和番茄塊一起煎，味道很香。

再比如：The fraudulence by this company whipped up public rage.這家公司的欺詐行為激起了公憤。

還比如：He adepts to whipping up people' passions due to his personality and characteristics.由於他的個性和特點，他很善於激發人們的熱情。

18. alarmist 大驚小怪的，聳人聽聞的
例：Don't be such an alarmist, the worst scenario will be that I can resign.別弄得大驚小怪的，大不了也不過是我辭職而已。

19. the profusion of 大量的
例：The detector unraveled the case by meticulously studying the profusion of data, ultimately discovering the essential clues. 探測器通過詳細研究大量的資料，最終找到了關鍵的線索。

20. copious 大量的
例：Kentucky fried chicken requires copious amounts of processed chicken every month in order to maintain its sales supply 為了維持銷售供應，肯德基每個月都需要大量的加工雞肉。

再比如：Nowadays, kids are facing copious amounts of homework; I think they are overloaded 如今，孩子們面臨著大量的家庭作業，我認為他們是超負荷的。

21. a torrent of 大量的，如潮水般的
例：Layla felt very frustrated about a torrent of rumors spreading about the failure of her promotion. 蕾拉對大量謠言散

佈她晉升失敗的消息感到非常沮喪。

22. to spawn 大量繁殖，大量生產（這個詞的意思太多，在使用時，需要根據上下文來把握）

例：Crayfish and carp spawn very quickly in this region, which spoils the balance of the local environment. 小龍蝦和鯉魚在這個地區大量繁殖，它們破壞了當地環境的平衡。

23. to churn out 大量生產出

例：Apple iPhones occupy 2/3 of the mobile phone market in the world, so revenue is tremendously surmountable. The other manufacturers put their greedy eyes on it and churned out similar products. 蘋果手機佔據了全球 2/3 的手機市場，所以收益是非常可觀的。其他製造商眼紅，大量生產類似的產品。

再比如：To meet the requirement of people who are eager to wear masks in order to protect them from getting the infection of Covid, this factory readjusted its assembling line to churn out a tremendous amount of masks within a short time to ship them out worldwide. 為了滿足人們保護自己不感染新冠病毒而迫切戴口罩的需求，這家工廠重新調整了生產線，在短時間內大量生產口罩，並銷往世界各地。

24. to decimate 大批殺害，大量毀滅

例：Millions of chickens have been decimated due to a new virus called N5H1. 一種名為 N5H1 的新型病毒導致數百萬隻雞被大批屠殺。

25. to quip 打趣，譏諷，嘲弄

例：I knew a guy who bought a Mercedes car but just six months later, he sold it to one of his friends at half price; no one can imagine how rich he was, I quipped. 我認識一個人，他買了一輛賓士車，但僅僅 6 個月後，他就以半價賣給了他的一個朋友，沒人能想像他有多富有，我打趣道。

26. to slurp 大聲吃喝

例：I was sitting in a restaurant waiting for my bowl of noodles, but the person sitting opposite me was slurping his noodles so quickly that he finished them in an instant. I was completely astonished. 我坐在餐館裡等一碗面，然而，對面坐著的那個人大聲吃面且吃得非常快，幾乎在一瞬間就吃完了。我感到非常驚訝。

27. to bellow 大聲吼叫

例：He is a good-natured person. Unfortunately, he was enraged to bellow while facing unfair treatment and abuse.他是一個脾氣很好的人。 不幸的是，他在面對不公平的待遇和虐待時大聲吼叫。

28. hubbub 大聲喧嘩

例：In public areas, we must try to avoid hubbubs to bother others. Bothering others is impolite behavior. Unfortunately, many people ignore it. 在公共場所，我們要儘量避免大聲喧嘩打擾到他人。 打擾別人是不禮貌的行為。 不幸的是，為此，許多人忽略了。

29. to rant 大聲喧嘩，大吼大叫，誇誇其談，慷慨陳詞

例：At the airport, I saw a lot of people ranting at each other, which literally annoyed the people around them. 在機場，我看到很多人互相大聲喧嘩，這簡直惹惱了周圍的人們。

30. carnage 大屠殺

例：From my point of view, any wars, no matter big or small, indicate carnage for the local people.在我看來，任何戰爭，無論大小，對當地人民來說都是一場大屠殺。

31. to back down 打退堂鼓,

例：Apparently, you want to back down, but I won't. I am very disappointed with your attitude. 顯然，你想打退堂鼓，但我不會，我對你的態度非常失望。

32. incontinent 大小便失禁

例：Some seniors became incontinent. They need exceptional medical help to ease off their awkward situation.一些老年人變得大小便失禁。 他們需要特殊的醫療說明來緩解他們的尷尬處境。

再比如：When the court sentenced his death, he instantly became incontinent and fell over to the ground.當法庭判處他死刑時，他瞬間大小便失禁，倒地不起。

33. a mish-mash 大雜燴

例：This show is a mish-mash of all varieties of performances. It is impressive and attractive.這個節目是各種表演的大雜燴。這是令人印象深刻和有吸引力的。

34. to rake in , 大賺了一把，迅速大量取得

例：By investing in this project, Leah raked in a billion dollars in cash.通過投資這個專案，利亞賺了數十億美元。

35. to make a killing 大賺一把

例：After renovating this old house, Isaac sold it and made a killing. 翻修這幢老房子後，伊薩克把它賣了，大賺了一筆。

36. clockwork 帶發條的

例：I love the toys with the clockwork feature, which does not necessarily have to use batteries to power it.我喜歡有發條功能的玩具，它不一定要用電池供電。

37. to dribble 帶球，運球

例：As a famous soccer player, he runs very fast and has superior dribbling skills. Suddenly, unpredictably he drives a volley into the roof of the net, which impressed the audience. 作為一名足球名將，他跑動速度極快，帶球技術出眾，突然出其不意地凌空抽射入網，給觀眾留下了深刻印象。

38. vicarious 代替的

例：Recently, some colleges and universities caught some students illegally hiring vicarious examinees. The school board decided that the admission office would eliminate their scores no matter who they were. 最近，一些高校發現某些學生非法代考。學校董事會決定，無論他們是誰，招生辦公室都會刪除他們的分數。

39. bespectacled 戴眼鏡的

例：She is a bespectacled senior lady who is amiable, and kind-hearted.她是一位和藹可

親、心地善良、戴眼鏡的年長女士。

40. to tinged with 帶有…氣息、色彩

例：His newly published book cover was tinged with the thick country style and romantic air.他新出版的書帶有濃厚的鄉村和浪漫氣息。

41. flimsy 單薄的

例：He looked flimsier, so I fully nudged him to eat more and exercise to become stronger.他看起來太單薄了，所以我完全鼓勵他多吃點東西，多做運動，讓他變得更強壯。

42. to be passionate about 對 ...有熱情，有激情

例：Our parents should encourage their children to be more passionate about whatever they choose to do so they can excel. Without this passion, it is very difficult for them to be successful.我們的父母應該鼓勵孩子們對自己所做的事情充滿熱情，這樣他們才能做得更好，否則很難取得成功。

43. to get in the way 擋路，妨礙

例：A sculpture standing nearby the door seems to get in the way. It made so many visitors feel uncomfortable.
門附近的一座雕塑似乎擋路。它使許多遊客感到不方便。

再比如：He looks on the surface as pretty nice person, but in terms of his character, he often speaks ill of others. His behavior may get in the way of his success in the future.他表面上還不錯，但背地裡經常說別人壞話。 他的行為可能會妨礙他未來的成功。

44. defunct 倒閉的，失靈的

例：The turmoil of the economy left so many companies defunct. 許多公司因經濟動盪倒閉。

45. to feel aggrieved 感到倒楣，感到委屈

例： It took me almost 2 hrs. to queue, but unfortunately, I couldn't get the product. I felt aggrieved 排了差不多 2 個小時，可惜還是沒買到。 我感到很倒楣。

再比如：This company suddenly fired her, so she felt very aggrieved because she had no idea what was happening .這家公司突然解雇了她，讓她感到很委屈，因為她不知道發生了什麼。

46. to occasion 導致

例：You must never forget that it's better to talk less while working in the company, no matter what kind of situation, because an ignorant statement might occasion your removal.你必須時刻牢記，無論在何種情況下，你最好在公司保持沉默，因為你無心的說辭可能會導致你被炒魷魚。

47. to court 導致，招致

例：The wrong decision made by the board may court the bankruptcy of the company, and all employees will start to protest against it. 董事會做出的錯誤決定可能會導致公司破產，所有員工都會開始抗議。

48. to result in 導致 ...

例：Failure to control high blood pressure may suddenly result in cerebral hemorrhage. 如果高血壓得不到控制，可能會突然導致腦出血。

49. jauntily 得意地

例：He was so excited to shake his head jauntily, and suddenly he started to cry, which stunned every guest on the scene.他激動得得意地搖了搖頭，突然哭了起來，在場的每一個人都驚呆了。

50. heady 得意忘形的，濃郁醇厚的

例：I always kindly reminded my son not to be heady about his minor achievement. 我總是親切地提醒我的兒子不要為他的小成就而得意忘形。

再比如：This wine has been reserved for dozens of years, and its taste is heady. 這酒已經保留了幾十年，它的味道濃郁醇厚。

51. nadir 低谷

例：Everyone has reached his nadir in his lifetime. The thing is how you can step out of it. 每個人一生中都曾跌入穀底。重要的是你如何走出困境。

52. to denigrate 詆毀

例：Western hostility viciously denigrates the development in China. 西方的敵對勢力惡意詆毀中國的發展。

例：Almost everybody will look down upon anyone who denigrates others. 幾乎每個人都會瞧不起任何詆毀別人的人。

53. to vilify 詆毀，中傷

例：Your false statement absolutely vilified me. 你那不真實的陳述完全是在詆毀我。

54. to be resilient to 抵抗，抗壓，有韌性。

例：Young people should be resilient to any setback and whatever pressure they may face 無論面對什麼挫折和壓力，年輕人都應抵抗得住。

55. skimpy 低廉的，不足的，吝嗇的

例：This manufacturer prefers a skimpy price to attract more buyers to earn a large percentage share of its market. 這家製造商喜歡用低廉的價格來吸引更多的買主，以贏得很大的市場份額。

56. shoddy 低劣的

例：The quality of copycats looks very shoddy; even sometimes, their inferior quality may seriously impact the innovation and exploitation of the new products. 山寨產品的品質看起來很低劣，甚至有時，他們的劣等產品可能會嚴重影響新產品的創新和開發。

再比如：Nowadays, a lot of cars' quality has become shoddy due to their poor management and so called cost reduction. 如今，由於管理不善和所謂的降低成本，很多汽車的品質變得粗製濫造。

57. in the doldrums 低迷

例：Consumer data showed that buying capabilities worldwide are in the doldrums, and inflation has become worse and might be escalated to an even greater extent. 消費者資料顯示，全球購買力低迷，通脹加劇，並可能出現一定程度的升級。

58. lowlier 低三下四的，卑賤的

例：I never show any lowlier attitude towards anybody; this is my bottom line. 我從不對任何人表現出任何低三下四的態度，這是我的底線。

59. to write off 抵消，一筆勾銷

例：His significant contribution to the community wrote off his minor errors made in the past. 他對社區的巨大貢獻抵消了他過去幾年所犯的小錯誤。

60. collateral or margin 抵押品或保證金

例：The banks almost required collateral or margin for your application for funds.你申請資金時，銀行幾乎要求你提供抵押品或保證金。

61. to ward off 抵禦

例：Experts found that some specific Chinese herbal medicines can efficiently ward off COVID variants, which effectively hinder their spread.專家發現，一些特定的中草藥可以有效抵禦 COVID 變種，從而有效阻止其傳播。

62. inferno 地獄

例：The people worldwide seem to plunge into an inferno during the pandemic's peak.在疫情的高峰期，世界各地的人們似乎陷入了地獄。

63. to push back against 抵制

例：I, time by time, found people prefer to push back against some specific products made by some specific countries. What on earth is the matter? 我一次又一次地發現，人們更喜歡抵制某些特定國家生產的某些特定產品。到底發生了什麼事?

64. to spurn 抵制

例：It is incredibly challenging to spurn one's addiction to drugs due to their highly addictive nature, making it difficult for individuals to break free from their grasp. 對於那些極易上癮的毒品，要抵制它們是非常困難的，因此很多人很難戒掉。

65. to reel 顛簸，跟蹌

例：The inclement weather leaves the plane reeling in the air. 惡劣的天氣使飛機在空中顛簸。

66. apogee 巔峰，最高點

例：He reached the apogee of his career before being arrested due to his corruption. 在因腐敗被捕之前，他達到了職業生涯的巔峰。

67. to upend 顛覆

例：The fact that living together before marriage definitely upended our cognition and tradition. 婚前同居的事實無疑顛覆了我們的認知和傳統。

68. paradigm-shifting 顛覆性的

例：The global pandemic of Covid-19 brought paradigm-shifting change to humans. 新冠肺炎的全球大流行給我們人類帶來了顛覆性的轉變。

69. to brood over 惦念

例：She always broods over her family members in Europe during the pandemics. 疫情期間，她總是惦記著在歐洲的家人。

70. taint 玷污

例：This famous professor tainted his image by plagiarizing other authors' work and faking his experiments. His unethical behavior left everyone very disappointed and bewildered. 這位元著名教授通過剽竊他人作品和偽造實驗來玷污自己的形象。他的不道德行為讓大家非常失望和困惑。

再比如：A lot of manufacturers make fake brand products which absolutely tainted the market and reputation of that industry.很多製造商製造假冒品牌產品，所以他們絕對污染了市場和該行業的聲譽。

71. to tarnish 玷污

例：His behavior tarnished his fame. That's disappointing. 他的行為玷污了他的名聲，令人失望。

72. A steely smile 淡然一笑

例：When his mom asked about his wound, he gave a steely smile and reassured her not to worry. 當他媽媽問起他的傷口時，

他淡然一笑，安慰她不要擔心。

73. archetypal 典型的

例：Forcing men to pay the bride price is an archetypal bad habit of traditional Chinese custom. In this new era, we must abandon it. 強迫男人付彩禮是中國傳統習俗的典型陋習。在新時代，我們必須拋棄它。

74. to intersperse 點綴

例：The scene was adorned with a stunning array of flowers during the holiday celebration, creating a vibrant and enchanting atmosphere that filled everyone with joy and wonder. Blossoms of all varieties and colors were carefully interspersed throughout the venue, transforming it into a place of natural beauty and serenity. 在節日慶祝活動期間，場景被一系列美麗的花朵裝點得如詩如畫，營造出充滿喜悅和驚奇的生動魔幻氛圍。各種各樣色彩斑斕的花朵被精心地點綴在場地各處，將其變成了一個自然美麗和寧靜的場所。

75. garrulous 喋喋不休的

例：His wife's garrulous reprimanding sometimes completely annoyed him, which was the reason he didn't want to go back home immediately after work. 他妻子喋喋不休的斥責有時候完全讓他感到惱火，這就是他不願意工作結束後立刻回家的原因。

76. tip-top 頂級的，一流的

例：This photographer bought an expensive camera with tip-top quality. So many amateurs admired him. 這位攝影師買了一台品質頂級的昂貴相機。很多業餘愛好者都羨慕他。

77. to be slated for 定於

例：The completion of this memorial is slated for 2024. 這座紀念碑將定於 2024 年竣工。

78. bespoke 定制的

例：This travel agency can provide a remarkable bespoke journey for couples who want to spend their honeymoon outside the country. 這家旅行社可以為想在國外度蜜月的情侶提供特別定制的旅行。

79. to buck 頂住 ...壓力，激勵某人

例：His boss bucked the pressure from the board and took action to list in the stock market. 他的老闆頂住來自董事會的壓力，採取了上市的行動。

再比如：His older brother's academic success bucked his younger brother to study harder to surpass him. 他哥哥在學業上的成功促使弟弟更加努力學習以超過他。

80. to cut a mustard 達到標準，符合條件

例：All the exports were rejected by the buyers because they didn't cut the mustard due to their poor quality. 所有出口貨物因品質差，未能達到標準，因此被買家拒收。

81. discernment 洞察力，眼力

例：I appreciate his discernment in this business, predicting far-reaching returns on investment. 我欣賞他在這項業務上的洞察力，預測了廣泛的投資回報。

82. impetus 動力

例：I tried to transform the badness to a sort of impetus encouraging me to persist on to the end. 我試圖把壞事變成鼓勵我堅持到底的一種動力。

83. tailwind 動力，推動力

例：To some extent, awarding money is the unique tailwind to improve the quality of services. 從某種程度上說，獎金是提高服務品質的獨特動力。

84. to scrape together 東拼西湊

例：He scraped together enough money from his family members and relatives for the down payment of his initial purchase of a small condo. 他從家人和親戚那裡湊錢買了一套小公寓的首付款。

85. jinx 倒楣蛋兒，掃把星

例：My wife often jokes with me, saying, 'You look like a jinx who always brings me bad luck,' especially after discovering she'd received three tickets for traffic violations. 我妻子經常開玩笑說："你看起來像個掃把星，總是給我帶來黴運"尤其是

在她發現自己收到了三張交通違章罰單的時候。

86. to pry into 打聽，窺探，刺探

It is impolite to pry into others' privacy, such as their age, finances, and other personal information.打聽他人的隱私，比如年齡、財務狀況等，是不禮貌的

87. lumbering 動作遲緩的，笨拙的

例：Don't eat too much, otherwise, you are gonna weigh up and your reaction will become lumbering.不要吃太多，否則，你會變胖，你的反應會變得遲鈍。

88. judder 抖動 （多指機械方面）

例：This old car started to judder while I was driving on highway.當我在高速公路上行駛時，這輛舊車開始顫抖。

89. to tantalize 逗某人

例："Stop tantalizing me," She yelled, blinking her watery eyes to stare at him. He didn't say anything; he just turned around and walked away. "別再逗我了，"她喊道，眨著水汪汪的眼睛盯著他。他什麼也沒說，只是轉身走開了。

90. precipitous 陡峭的，險峻的

例：I stood at the bottom of the Great Wall and felt astonished about its magnificent and fantastic creation on the stretching precipitous mountains. 我站在長城腳下，驚歎於在綿延險峻的山巒上建造出如此雄偉壯麗的建築。

91. courtesy of 多虧

例：I finally accomplished this task courtesy of your outstanding efforts and dedication. 多虧了你的努力和奉獻，我終於完成了這項任務。

92. to tide over 度過

例: During the pandemic, people worldwide united and tided over this challenging moment.疫情期間，全世界人民團結一致，共渡難關。

93. to rebuff 斷然拒絕

例：My boss unreasonably required us to work extra hours

without pay; I rebuffed him by taking the risk of being fired. 我的老闆無理要求我們無薪加班； 我冒著被解雇的風險斷然拒絕了他。

94. to tut-tut 對…表示不悅，不滿
例：She attempts to attribute her husband's behavior, while he dismissively tut-tuts at her exaggeration. 她試圖歸咎于她丈夫的行為，而丈夫則對她的誇張態度表示不悅。

95. to demur at 對…表示反對
例：Mrs. Delilah has demurred at the unfair treatment. 德里拉夫人對這種不公平的待遇表示反對。

96. to matter less to 對…沒當回事
例：I quarreled with Nevaeh that day because I was too emotional, literally, it matters less to me now.那天我和內瓦赫吵了一架，因為我太情緒化了，說真的，對我來說沒當回事。

97. to feel no shame in 對…不感到羞恥
例：I am very surprised that he felt no shame in cheating on a test. 我很驚訝他在考試中作弊竟然不感到羞恥。

98. to shudder at 對…不寒而慄
例：Every person on earth shudders at the rumors of the world ending, the truth is ... 地球上的每個人都對世界末日的謠言不寒而慄，事實是 ...

再比如：So many people shudder at the collision of the asteroid with the earth.小行星與地球的碰撞讓許多人不寒而慄。

99. to be stacked against 對…不利
例：What you complained about will be stacked against you, and you might be fired. 你所抱怨的事情會對你不利，你可能會被解雇。

100. to be tut-tutting about 對…不滿
例：All the staff in this company were tut-tutting about the lowering of their salaries and the reduction of their working hours.

這家公司的全體員工都對降低工資和縮短工作時間表示不滿。

101. be iffy about 對⋯不滿意

例：My mom is iffy about their "high-quality service".我媽媽對他們的高品質服務不太滿意。

102. to be dismissive of 對⋯不屑一顧、對⋯嗤之以鼻

例：I am dismissive of all awards. 我對所有的獎項都不屑一顧。

再比如：例：The people are substantially dismissive of the meager compensation the government offered them for the severe inflation.國民對政府對嚴重的通貨膨脹的微薄補償嗤之以鼻。

103. to hold troubling implications for 對⋯產生不安的影響

例：Further devaluation of US dollars holds troubling implications for the stability of the global economy.美元進一步貶值對全球經濟穩定產生令人不安的影響。

104. to be toxic to 對⋯生危害

例：Eating anything too much, regardless of whether it's good or bad, will be toxic for your health and life. 任何東西吃得太多，不管是好是壞，都會對你的健康和生命產生危害。

105. to heap the derision on 對⋯嗤之以鼻

例：Almost all the employees heaped derision on the concept that the board advocated for constraining their appetites to adapt to the food shortage. 幾乎所有員工都對董事會提倡的"克制食欲以適應糧食短缺"的理念嗤之以鼻。

106. to sniff at 對⋯嗤之以鼻

例：He looked down upon her because he sniffed at her behavior, which was very ugly and disgusting.他看不起她，因為他對她的行為嗤之以鼻，非常醜陋和噁心。

107. to shun 躲閃，回避

例：To keep her skin looking better, The doctor told her to shun more spicy food and not to sleep to late.為了讓她的皮膚

看起來更好，醫生告訴她不要吃太多辣的食物，也不要太晚睡覺。

108. to pooh-pooh 對…嗤之以鼻、對…不屑一顧

例：At the moment, everyone seems to agree upon this advice but only one person pooh-poohed it. 目前，每個人似乎都同意這個建議，但只有一個人對它嗤之以鼻。

109. to be starry-eyed about 對…充滿幻想

例：She is still starry-eyed about her love even though she is 65 years old. 儘管她已經 65 歲了，但她仍然對自己心中的愛情充滿幻想。

110. hard-hit 對…打擊嚴重，深受打擊

例：The global economy is particularly hard-hit by all varieties of disasters. 各種災害對全球經濟的打擊尤其嚴重。

111. to be lavish in 對 …大加讚賞

例：Almost all the readers are lavish in their praise of his new book. 幾乎所有的讀者都對他的新書大加讚賞。

112. to babble at 對…喋喋不休

例：My wife babbled at me every day; I felt frustrated about it. I wouldn't even like to go back home. 我妻子每天都對我喋喋不休； 我對此感到沮喪。我甚至不想回家。

113. to do soul-searching about 對…反省

例：He does deep soul-searching about his failure in handling the issues with his son. An old saying is, "to raise them but not teach, it will be the father's fault. 他對自己在處理兒子問題上的失敗進行了反省。古語雲： "養而不教；父之過。"

114. to bridle at 對…感到不滿，憤怒，瞧不起

例：Anyone will bridle at bullying someone else. 任何人都對欺負別人感到不滿。

115. to pose a danger to …對…構成威脅

例：Ukraine's joining NATO obviously poses a danger to Russia. War seems to be unavoidable. 烏克蘭加入北約顯然對俄羅斯構成了威脅，戰爭似乎是不可避免的。

116. to be profoundly inimical to 對…極為不利

例：Trying to contact Aliens will be profoundly inimical to humans. 試圖與外星人接觸會對我們人類造成極大的傷害。

117. to pin high hopes on 對 … 寄予厚望

例：Almost all the Chinese parents pinned high hopes on their children, especially for better jobs and higher salaries. 幾乎所有的中國父母都對自己的孩子寄予厚望，尤其是對更好的工作和更高的薪水寄予厚望。

118. to be cagey about 對…謹慎

例：During the interview, he was cagey about disclosing his privacy and his family's information. 在採訪中，他對自己的隱私和家事表現得很謹慎。

119. to gasp at 對…驚歎

例：He rarely talked more about his research; however, many of his colleagues gasped at his magnificent achievement years later. 他很少談論自己的研究；然而，多年後，他的許多同事對他的輝煌成就驚歎不已。

120. to feel disillusioned with 對…絕望

例：One of my friends' girlfriends often sneakily stole his money; he thoroughly felt disillusioned with her behavior and decided to leave her. 我一個朋友的女朋友經常偷偷地偷他的錢，他對她的行為徹底失望了，決定離開她。

121. to yammer about 對 …嘮叨

例：Never ignore your parents' yammering about you; almost everything they say is for your own good. 永遠不要忽視你父母對你的嘮叨，他們說的幾乎所有話是為你好。

122. to waver 動搖，猶豫

例：He wanted to expand his business across the nation. However, considering the higher cost, he started to waver in his decision. 他想把事業擴大到全國，但考慮到費用較高，他的決心開始動搖了。

123. to have/has little incentive to 對…沒什麼積極性

例：I earned less in this company, so I have little incentive to accomplish any projects. 我在這家公司掙錢太少，所以，對完成任何項目都沒有積極性。

124. that's not much use for 對…沒有多大用

例：That's not much use for improving his academics even though he invested tremendous energy into and did copious homework . The critical issue was resulted from his ways of studying. 儘管他投入了巨大的精力，做了大量的家庭作業，但這對他的學習成績提高並沒有多大作用。關鍵問題是由他的學習方法引起的。

125. to be touchy about 對…敏感

例：Perhaps he is very touchy about being looked at by others, which makes him so shy or even nervous. 也許他對被別人看著很敏感，這讓他很害羞，甚至很緊張。

126. to be ambiguous about 對…模棱兩可

例：Chloe is ambiguous about her promise to release her essay at the end of this month. 克洛伊對她在月底發表論文的承諾模棱兩可。

127. to seethe at 對…惱火

例: He didn't know how to talk to the others adequately, so people seethed at his attitude and aggressive expression. 他不知道如何與別人充分交談，所以人們對他的態度和咄咄逼人的表情感到惱火。

128. to be coy about 對…閃爍其詞

例：He boasted about helping me find a job, but half a year passed, and whenever I followed up, he was always coy about it. That really disappointed me. 他

吹噓說幫我找了份工作，但半年過去了，只要我跟他核實，結果他總是對此閃爍其辭，這讓我很失望。

129. to be unfathomable to 對 ...深不可測

例：The discovery of Aliens living on the other planets among the galaxy are unfathomable to humans.探索生活在銀河系其它行星上的外星人對我們人類來說是深不可測的。

130. to bode ill for 對···是不祥之兆

例：Much money was poured into real estate, which came from the seniors' retirement funds and boded ill for those older adults under the current sloppy market. 大量資金湧入房地產市場，這些資金來自老年人的退休基金，在當前低迷的市場環境下，這對老年人來說是不祥之兆。

131. to impose tight controls on 對···實施了嚴格的控制

例：Due to the severe spreading of Omicron, the government imposed tight controls on any seafood imported from abroad.由於歐米克隆的嚴重傳播，政府對任何從國外進口的海鮮實行嚴格控制。

132. it is congenial for 對···是適宜的

例：It is congenial for the couple to consider divorce if they have been quarreling with each other endlessly for almost everday.如果這對夫婦每天整天爭吵不休，考慮離婚是適宜的。

133. to wink at 對···使眼色，對···視而不見

例：I sensed John was not honest because he winked at his partner during the negotiation.我感覺到約翰不誠實，因為他在談判中對他的搭檔使眼色。

再比如：You can't wink at his ugly behavior.你不能對他的醜陋行為視而不見。

134. to keep tight-lipped about 對···守口如瓶

例：I appreciate his personality, he keeps tight-lipped about everything you tell him. 我欣賞

他的性格，他對你告訴他的一切都守口如瓶。

135. to pose an unprecedented challenge to 對⋯提出挑戰

例：The upcoming economic downturn posed an unprecedented challenge to all the countries in the world.即將到來的經濟衰退對世界各國帶來了前所未有的挑戰。

136. to waffled about 對 ⋯問題含糊其辭

例：The president waffles about details of how to guarantee medical insurance for every American. 總統對如何保證每個美國人都有醫療保險的細節講得含糊不清。

137. to entertain any doubt about 對⋯心存懷疑

例：I never entertained any doubt about his motives because he showed everyone that he was honest. Finally, I was deceived by him.我從沒對他的動機心存懷疑，因為他向所有人展示的他是最誠實的人，最後我被他欺騙了。

138. to be agog for 對⋯興奮不已

例：All the kids are agog for visiting Disney World.所有的孩子都為參觀狄斯奈樂園而興奮不已。

139. to be gleeful at 對⋯幸災樂禍

例: His secretary was gleeful at his arrest due to his corruption. Later on, she was also fired by the board.他的秘書對他因腐敗而被捕幸災樂禍。後來，她也被董事會解雇。

140. to view... with mirth 對⋯幸災樂禍

例：My wife doesn't get along well with my mom, and they often quarrel. One day, when my mom got sick, my wife viewed her sickness with mirth. However, my mom still showed a open heart towards her. 我的妻子和我媽媽相處得不好，經常爭吵。一天，我媽媽生病了，我妻子對此幸災樂禍。然而，我媽媽仍然對她表現得很包容。

141. to be clueless about 對…一竅不通

例：I am absolutely clueless about picture drawing. 我對畫圖一竅不通。

142. to have no inkling of 對…一無所知

例：I knew a poor young lady who was fired after lunchtime, and she had no inkling of it until in the morning. 我認識一位元可憐的年輕女士，她在午飯後被解雇了，而她甚至在早上都對此一無所知。

143. to be not much use for 對…用處不大

例：Just listening to recordings to learn a language is not much use for new language learners. 對於語言學習者來說，僅僅通過聽錄音對學習一門語言用處不大。

144. to be venomous about 對…有惡毒

例：Some men are outlandish; their attitudes are venomous about beautiful women. I guess they got hurt, or they have schizophrenia. 有些人很古怪；他們對美女的態度往往是惡毒的。我猜他們受傷過，或者他們患有精神分裂症。

145. to have a bearing on 對…有影響

例：The new policy will have a bearing on people purchasing properties. 新政策將對人們購買物業有影響。

146. to rave about 對…讚不絕口

例：This man raved about her kindness and the incredible support she offered during his difficult financial situation in the past. 這個人對她的善良和在他過去財務困難時所提供的巨大支援讚不絕口。

147. to wreak havoc on 對…造成嚴重破壞

例：Each year, typhoons wreaked havoc on the Philippines. 每年，颱風在菲律賓造成嚴重破壞。

148. to be crucial to 對…至關重要

例：Cooperation among different departments will be crucial to the accomplishment of this project. 不同部門之間的合

作對完成這個專案是至關重要的。

149. to be obsessed with 對⋯著迷
例：Willow often goes to the outskirts with her boyfriend for a picnic. She is obsessed with fishing. 威洛經常和她的男朋友去郊外野餐。她對釣魚很著迷。

150. to be complacent about 對 ...自滿
例：I always remind my son to avoid being complacent about his academic achievement.
我總是提醒兒子不要對自己的學業成績自滿。

151. to turn a blind eye to 對⋯視而不見， 睜一隻眼，閉一隻眼
例：The local police turned a blind eye to violence.當地員警對暴力事件視而不見。

152. to have scruples about 對⋯有顧慮
例：Juan finally abandoned his willingness to go abroad because he had a lot of scruples about his family. He is too nostalgic.胡安

最終放棄了出國的意願，因為他對家庭有很多顧慮。他太懷舊了。

153. to round on sb. 對某人大發雷霆
例：My boss suddenly rounded on me, and I felt bewildered at what was happening. Later, I got to know he was frustrated about my refusal of appearing at his party.我的老闆突然對我大發雷霆，我不知道發生了什麼事。後來，我知道他對我拒絕出席他的聚會感到沮喪。

154. to be dear to sb. 對某人珍貴
例：All of these pictures taken for my dad are dear to me, especially after he passed away. 所有這些為我爸爸拍攝的照片對我來說都是珍貴的，尤其是在他去世後。

155. to prod 敦促
例：The UN prods all countries involved in conflicts to remain calm, as this is the best way for justice, and unity to return.聯合國敦促所有捲入衝突的國家保持冷靜,以換取正義和團結。

156. blunt 鈍了

例：My mom sharpens the kitchen knives because they are too blunt to cut anything.我媽媽正在磨菜刀，因為它們太鈍了，什麼東西都切不了。

157. fickle 多變的，反復無常的

例：This commander kept his cool while facing a fickle situation.面對多變的形勢，這位指揮官保持了冷靜。

例：This guy is so fickle, it is hard to get along with him.這哥們兒反復無常，很難和他相處。

158. to claw back 奪回，收回，追回，彌補等

例: We can claw back some of our advantages in the market thanks to our adjustment of the production of our products. 通過調整產品生產，我們可以在市場上奪回一些優勢。

再比如：In ancient China, it was hard for the emperor to claw back his order as soon as he had issued it. 在中國古代，皇帝下了命令就很難收回。

159. juicy 多汁的，活力的，生動有趣的，妙趣橫生的；報酬豐厚的；<非正式>充滿誘惑的，吸引人的。當然，這個詞有很多意思，比如：某東西值很多錢，生動有趣的，妙趣橫生的。我們這裡重點說它多汁的用法。

例：The steak in this restaurant is very tasty, juicy and tender. 這家餐廳的牛排非常美味，多汁、嫩滑。

160. to have plenty going for 對…大有裨益、大有好處。

例：Eating a wider variety of vegetables and engaging in mild, proper exercise have plenty going for them when it comes to improving your health, helping to strengthen your immune system and lowering your chances of developing cancer. 多吃各種蔬菜並進行適量的溫和運動對你的健康大有裨益，有助於增強免疫系統並降低患癌症的風險。

161. deadweight loss 打水漂兒、無謂損失

例：Prepaying for any service can result in deadweight loss to some extent, as stores may unexpectedly declare bankruptcy. 預付任何服務可能會在某種

程度上導致打水漂兒，因為商店可能會突然宣佈破產。

E

1. miscreant 惡劣的
例：Some countries in this world exhibited miscreant behavior, plunging the entire world into catastrophe 世界上一些國家的不法行徑使整個世界陷入了災難之中 。

2. wretched 惡劣的，討厭的
例：His wretched conduct repelled those around him. 他的惡劣行為讓周圍的人都感到很厭惡。

3. inclement 惡劣天氣
例：Inclement weather led to the cancellation of all flights, stranding hundreds of thousands at the airport. 惡劣天氣導致所有航班被取消，數十萬人被困在機場。

4. pebbles 鵝卵石
例：I walked along the pebbled street, pondering my future, filled with both perplexity and hope. 我走在鵝卵石鋪就的街道上，

思索著未來的生活，心中充滿了困惑與希望。

5. to throttle 遏制、扼殺
例：A series of regulations were rolled out to throttle the expansion of monopolies and rein in harmful competition。一系列法規相繼出臺，以遏制壟斷的擴以及惡性競爭。

6. rancorous 惡意的
例：I understood that your disagreement with us was not rancorous. 我明白你和我們之間的分歧並沒惡意。

7. maliciously 惡意地
例：She has a habit of maliciously gossiping about others behind their backs. 她有在背後惡意議論他人的習慣。

8. to scotch 遏制
例：The government should step in to scotch the random use of medications for COVID treatment

政府應該介入，遏制隨意使用藥物治療新冠病毒的行為。

9. to snuff out 遏制, 扼殺
例：The US government tried to snuff out inflation by raising interest rates, but nobody knows whether it will be effective 美國政府試圖通過提高利率來遏制通貨膨脹，但沒人知道這是否會有效。

再比如： The improper policy snuffed out the prosperity of the property market 不當的政策扼殺了房地產市場的繁榮

10. hoax 惡作劇
例：I received many calls from unknown numbers and thought they were hoaxes. 我接到了許多來自陌生號碼的電話，我以為那些電話是惡作劇。

11. vice 邪惡（ 看到這個詞，大多都會想到副的， 比如副部長 vice ministry, 副主任 vice director 等等。其實它還有另外一個意思就是邪惡。）
例： We must encourage kindness and eradicate vice 我們必須揚善， 除惡。

12. to tamp... spread 遏制…的傳播
例： This suggests that Israel's high vaccination rate will do little to tamp down Omicron's spread 這表明以色列的高疫苗接種率對遏制奧密克戎 的傳播作用不大。

F

1. to dither 發抖，顫抖
例： Landon gave a speech in front of 100 million people via the internet. He was so nervous, excited, and emotional that almost everyone could feel his whole body was trembling uncontrollably. dithering. 蘭登通過網路向一億人發表了演講。他緊張、激動、情緒激烈，幾乎所有人都能感受到他全身都在不由自主地發抖。

2. to dole out 發放
例：During the lockdown, many governments doled out money to help their citizens get through

difficult times. 在封鎖期間，許多政府發放資金以幫助公民渡過難關。

3. to chafe at 發火
例：The salesman remained silent as his client chafed at him, trying to avoid escalating the situation. anger.這個推銷員在客戶對他發火時保持沉默，以避免事態升級。

4. to fume about 憤怒，生氣
例：This famous actress literally stole something from a convenience store in Hawaii, causing many of her fans to fume over her disgraceful behavior. 這位著名女演員竟然在夏威夷的一家便利店偷東西，許多粉絲為她這種醜陋的行為感到憤怒。

5. sobering 發人深省的，耐人尋味的
例：My dad passed away, yet his sobering conversations with me have remained in my mind forever 我父親去世了，但他曾對我說的那些發人深省的話語永遠留在了我的腦海中。

6. to blast off 發射升空

例：The space shuttle will blast off from Cape Canaveral, Florida, on a journey of around 150 million kilometers to the Sun to uncover the secrets of its mysterious atmosphere 這架太空梭將從佛羅里達州的卡納維拉爾角發射，踏上一段約 1.5 億公里的旅程，前往太陽，揭示其神秘大氣的奧秘。

7. prosaic 乏味的，平淡無奇
例：The content he wrote was quite prosaic
他所寫的內容十分乏味，缺乏想像力。

再比如：When I was a kid, I always felt the world was beautiful. But now that I've grown up, I've come to realize it's actually prosaic and dull. 小時候，我總覺得這個世界很美好。可現在長大了，我才發現它其實平淡無奇、無聊至極 。

8. to stunt 發育遲緩
例：In impoverished areas, infants are seriously stunted in their growth. 在貧困地區，嬰兒發育嚴重遲緩.

9. visceral 發自內心的

例：He showed visceral emotion upon hearing the truth of this story. 當他聽到這個故事的真相時，表現出了發自內心的情感。

10. to rejoinder 反駁

例：My rejoinder is simple: why can't you forgive her, since she has already apologized for her improper behavior? 我的反駁很簡單：既然她已經為不當行為向你道歉，為什麼你不能原諒她呢？

11. bed-hopping 反復無常的

例：I loathe unpredictable, bed-hopping people—no matter who they are. 我討厭那些反復無常的人，無論他們是誰。

12. introspection 反思

例：I made mistakes, but I immediately turned to introspection to avoid repeating them in the future 我犯了錯誤，但我立刻進行了反思，以避免將來重蹈覆轍。

13. cumbersome 繁瑣的

例：The visa application procedure became cumbersome due to the increasing volume of applications. 由於申請數量不斷增加，簽證申請流程變得繁瑣起來。

14. to change beyond recognition 翻天覆地的變化

例：The technology bestowed by aliens changed human life beyond recognition. 外星人賜予的科技讓人類的生活發生了翻天覆地的變化。

15. to mirror 反映

例：Despite disliking this novel, I acknowledge that it mirrors the author's experiences and emotions. 儘管我不喜歡這本小說，但它確實反映了作者的經歷和情感。

16. twitchy···煩躁不安的，焦躁不安的

例：I tried to avoid shopping on weekends because the crowded scenes made me feel twitchy. 我儘量避免在週末購物，因為如此擁擠的場面讓我煩躁不安。

再比如：The impending final exam made him feel twitchy and anxious all day long. 臨近的期

末考試讓他整天都感到焦躁不安。

17. onerous 繁重的, 過重的
例：No matter where you live on earth, your kids may face onerous homework every day.無論你住在地球的哪個地方，你的孩子每天都可能面臨繁重的作業。

再比如：He borrowed a lot of money, making his debt too onerous for him to afford. 他借了很多錢，以至於他的債務過重超出了他的承受能力。

18. to stymie 失去、妨礙
例：His arrogance stymied both his cooperation with colleagues and his opportunity for promotion to team leader.
他的傲慢阻礙了與同事的合作，也讓他失去了晉升為團隊領導的機會。

19. to fart 放屁
If you start farting more frequently, you might need to be alert to potential liver problems. It's best to see a doctor for further diagnosis. 如果你開始頻繁放屁，可能需要警惕肝臟問題。

最好去看醫生進行進一步診斷。

20. to slacken 放緩
例：The coronavirus seriously slackened the development of the global economy. 新冠肺炎疫情嚴重放緩了全球經濟發展。

21. to break up 放假
例：This summer, schools will break up earlier than ever before, even though they usually do so in July. 今年夏天，學校將比以往任何時候都提前放假，儘管一般情況下是在七月份。

22. to forgo 放棄
例：Cole forgoes all his spare time to volunteer and serve the local seniors. 科爾放棄了所有的業餘時間自願，去為當地的老年人服務。

23. to back down 放棄
例：My son has been enrolled at the University of Toronto; however, he wanted to back out because he was concerned that lower scores given by professors might affect his application for the master's degree program. It seems these are just rumors spreading across the internet. 我兒子已經被多

倫多大學錄取；然而，他想放棄，因為他擔心教授給出的低分可能會影響他申請碩士學位課程。看來這些只是網路上的謠言。

再比如：I hope you never back down from your hope of finding your daughter, who went missing many years ago. 我希望你永遠不會放棄尋找多年前失蹤的女兒的希望。

24. to forsake 放棄
例：The divorce left him in pain, as he lost his job and had to forsake custody of his kids 離婚讓他痛苦不堪，他失去了工作，不得不放棄孩子的監護權。

25. to spurn 放棄
例：To save her son's life, this mother never spurned her last chance to donate part of her liver to him. 為了挽救兒子的生命，這位母親沒有放棄最後的機會，將自己的部分肝臟移植給他。

26. to relinquish 放棄 （很勉強地）較正式

例：I have to relinquish my suggestion to my son regarding his course selection. 我不得不放棄給兒子提有關選課的建議。

27. to let up 放鬆
例：We can't let up this project despite many difficulties on the way to completion. 儘管完成這個項目還有許多困難，我們也不能放鬆。

28. to scrap 放棄，廢棄
例：The local government rolled out a newly designed license plate for vehicles, but it later found that it was difficult to clearly identify. As a result, all of them had to be scrapped. 當地政府推出了新設計的車牌，但後來發現這種車牌難以清晰識別，因此所有車牌都不得不被廢棄。

再比如：She dedicated herself to cancer treatment research for 20 years, but now she feels exhausted and wants to scrap it. 她在癌症治療研究上奉獻了20年，但現在她感到筋疲力盡，想要放棄這項工作。

還比如：The marketing strategy seemed unrealistic, so the board decided to scrap it and devise a new one 行銷策略看起來不切實際，因此董事會決定廢棄它，並制定一個新的策略。

29. to leave sb. on the loose 放任某人，讓某人無所事事

例：She left her son on the loose, and as a result, he struggled to accomplish anything successfully, including managing his own life. This is undeniably a tragic situation. 她自由放任自己的兒子，結果他在任何事情上都難以成功，甚至無法管理自己的生活。這無疑是一個悲劇的局面。

再比如： The boy became so absorbed in gaming that he was left at a loose end, and as a result, he flunked a couple of subjects this semester. 這個男孩沉迷于遊戲，導致他感到迷茫。這個學期，他掛了幾門課。

30. to wind down 放鬆

例：Since today is a holiday, I plan to wind down and take a leisurely stroll 今天是假日；想放鬆一下，到處逛逛。

31. to unwind 放鬆，展開

例：I'm trying to unwind after a long day at work. 我今天工作了一整天，想放鬆一下。

32. to denigrate sb. 誹謗，貶低某人

例：The private lives of many movie stars have been exposed, and without distinguishing between truth and falsehood, some people denigrate them. This denigration not only affects the celebrities but also causes suffering for their lives and families. 許多電影明星的隱私被公開，一些人在不分辨真假的情況下誹謗這些明星。這種誹謗不僅影響了這些名人，還給他們的生活和家庭帶來了苦難。

33. libelous 誹謗性的

例： Some expressions in his speech were libelous, which fundamentally tarnished my reputation 他演講中的一些言論是誹謗性的，嚴重破壞了我的聲譽。

34. to be strikingly frightened of 非常害怕

例：I am strikingly frightened of my mom getting Covid-19, especially since she is over 80. 我非常害怕我媽媽感染新冠，尤其是她已經超過 80 歲了。

35. meticulous 非常細緻入微

例：My mother possesses the admirable quality of being incredibly meticulous in every aspect of her life, showing genuine concern for even the smallest details. 我母親具備一個令人欽佩的品質，那就是在生活的每個方面都非常細緻入微，她對每一個小細節都充滿關心。

36. to hurtle 飛馳而過，猛衝

例：I saw some of the drivers hurtling around us. It seemed like they were racing, which was very scary and dangerous. 我看到一些司機在我們周圍飛馳而過。看起來他們在賽車，這非常可怕和危險。

37. to rescind sth.... 廢除，取消

例：The government made a decision to rescind the ban on wearing mask in all public places. 政府決定廢除在所有公共場所戴口罩的禁令。

再比如：They signed a sales agreement days ago; regretfully, it was unreasonably rescinded by the client, so we will consider applying a penalty. 他們幾天前簽署了銷售協定，但遺憾的是，客戶無理撤銷了該協定，因此我們將考慮施加罰款。

38. tosh 廢話

例：His speech was fraught with much tosh, which was both unrealistic and hollow 他的演講充滿了廢話，完全不切實際且空洞無物。

39. verbiage 廢話

例:He filled his letter with so much verbiage that I couldn't make it to the end. Frustrated, I gave up and stood by the window, unconsciously staring outside. 他在信中充滿了過多的廢話，讓我無法讀到最後。我感到厭煩，放棄了，站在窗邊無意識地望著外面。

40. piffle 廢話，胡扯
例：The entire speech is piffle. Nobody would like to listen to it. 整個演講都是廢話，沒有人願意聽。

再比如:What he explained from the very beginning was piffle, lacking any facts to support it 他從一開始所解釋的就是在胡扯，缺乏任何事實來證明。

41. irrational 不理性的，不合邏輯的，荒謬的
例：There is irrational consumption among young people, and we must guide them to spend wisely. 年輕人中存在不理性的消費，我們必須引導他們以明智的方式消費。

42. derelict 廢棄的
例：After this young man declared bankruptcy, he had to move from his luxury mansion to a derelict house. He suddenly became mature enough to confront his current situation. 這個年輕人宣佈破產後，不得不從豪宅搬到一所廢棄的房子裡。 他突然變得足夠成熟，可以面對現在的處境。

43. whizzy 飛速發展的，出色的
例：In China, the whizzy 5G technology is all the rage, with download speeds faster than ever and improved efficiency. 在中國，飛速發展的 5G 技術非常流行，提供著前所未有的超快下載速度和更高的效率。

44. fecund 肥沃的，生育能力強
例：Thailand has vast and fecund lands, which yield tremendous amounts of rice for export worldwide every year. 泰國擁有廣闊而肥沃的土地，每年收穫大量稻米出口到世界各地。

再比如：The men in the Middle East are often considered fecund, known for their strong reproductive capabilities.中東的男性通常被認為是多產的，以他們強大的生育能力聞名

45. to chill 非正式： 放鬆，讓人心寒
例：After a long day of work, we chilled at a bar on King St, enjoying a couple of beers .在長

時間的工作後，我們一起在
國王街的酒吧裡放鬆，喝了
幾瓶啤酒。

再比如：Her statement chilled
me to the core 她的話使我心
寒。

46. contraband 非法買賣的
例：In China, the law stipulates
the prohibition of contraband
transactions involving
endangered wild animals or birds.
在中國，法律規定禁止非法
買賣瀕危野生動物或鳥類

47. unravel 分崩離析、無與
倫比的
例：During the pandemic,
people became panic, and the
situation became unraveled
worldwide.疫情期間，人們變
得恐慌，全球局勢變得分崩
離析。

再比如：She achieved
unrivaled praise among her
colleagues. So many people
admired her. 她在同事中獲得
了無與倫比的讚揚。很多人
都欽佩她。

48. offshoot 分店，分支機搆

例：This bubble tea store is very
popular locally. The owner now
plans to expand the business by
launching offshoots across the
country. 這家奶茶店在本地非
常受歡迎，店主現在打算在
全國範圍內開設分店，擴大
經營規模。

49. to trickle down 分給
例：My boss is very generous;
he constantly lets benefits trickle
down to his employees. 我的老
闆很慷慨；他不斷地把福利
分給員工。

50. to incense 憤怒, 激怒
例： When his wife angrily told
him she would refuse to live with
his parents, he was absolutely
incensed. 當他的妻子氣憤地
告訴他說她拒絕和他的父母
一起生活時，他感到非常憤
怒。

再比如：He was incensed by
someone's accidental misspelling
of his name, believing the
mistake was a sign of disrespect.
他對有人不小心拼錯了他的
名字感到憤怒，因為他認為
這個錯誤不尊重他。

51. divergent 分歧的

例：Sometimes, it's quite common for spouses to have divergent views on an issue 有時，夫妻之間在一個問題上有不同的觀點，似乎是很常見的。

52. to be widely scattered 分佈各處

例：New immigrants are widely scattered throughout the country. 新移民廣泛分佈在全國各處。

53. to divvy up 分配

例：After his parents accidentally passed away, the family members legitimately divvied up their savings. 他的父母意外去世後，所有家庭成員合法地分配了他們的積蓄。

再比如：I wouldn't like living in condos because the maintenance costs, especially repairs, have to be divvied up among all the residents. 我不喜歡住在公寓裡，因為維修費用，尤其是修理費用，必須由所有住戶分攤。

54. vibes 氛圍

例：One of my friends often tells me he prefers the vibe of western-style restaurants, so he goes there for dinner every weekend. 我有個朋友常說他更喜歡西式餐廳的氛圍，所以每個週末都去那兒吃晚飯。

55. to parse 分析

例：I remember that when I was in high school, our teacher often led us to parse articles in terms of the author's style, such as word choice and expressions, teaching us to mimic their writing techniques. This approach had a profound impact on my writing later on. 我記得在高中時，老師經常引導我們從作者的風格角度解析文章，比如用詞和表達方式，教我們模仿他們的寫作技巧，這對我後來的寫作產生了深遠的影響。

56. to drift into 紛紛湧入

例：With launching the war between Russia and Ukraine, a large amount of Ukrainians drifted into the neighboring countries, like Poland, Czechoslovakia, Germany, etc... 隨著俄烏戰爭的爆發，大批

烏克蘭人湧入波蘭、捷克斯洛伐克、德國等鄰國。

57. blandishment 奉承
例：I can instantly sense when someone is full of blandishment, trying to win my favor just to ask for help or personal gain. 我能立刻察覺出某人滿嘴奉承，只是為了向我求助或謀取利益。

58. to fawn over 奉承
例：I look down on people who fawn over their bosses or leaders. 我看不起那些對老闆或上司阿諛奉承的人。

59. to flatter 奉承，獻媚
例：I have no respect for people who flatter those in power just to gain advantages. 我看不起任何奉承地位高的人，或能給他們帶來好處的人。

60. hush money 封口費
例：He comes across as a hero for exposing counterfeit products made by certain manufacturers who tried to bribe him with hush money — which he ultimately refused. 他看起來就像一位英雄，揭露了一些廠商製造的假冒產品，而這些廠商試圖用封口費賄賂他，最終被他拒絕了。

61. off-the-wall 瘋狂的，異乎尋常的
例：His performance was completely off-the-wall — no one could understand what he was singing, but he seemed intoxicated by his own voice. 他的表演完全瘋狂，沒人聽得懂他在唱什麼，但他似乎陶醉在自己的歌聲中。

62. bumper 豐盛的
例：She prepared a bumper dinner for us, with dishes filling the entire table 她為我們準備了滿桌子的豐盛晚餐。

63. substantial （飯菜）豐盛的
例：My mom has prepared a substantial dinner for us tonight, Hurry up, let's go. 我媽今晚給我們準備了一頓豐盛的晚餐，快點，我們趕緊走吧！

64. to overrule 否決
例：This world is cruel but undeniably realistic. The truth is, wealthy people often have the

power to overrule the opinions and suggestions of the poor, simply because they hold the right to speak. My question is: is that fair? 這個世界是殘酷的，但也非常現實。事實是，富人往往能夠否決窮人提出的意見和建議，因為他們掌握話語權。我的問題是：這公平嗎？

65. to repudiate 否認
例：The local government repudiated the rumor of a school shooting that allegedly left thirteen people dead 當地政府否認了關於一起校園槍擊事件的謠言，據稱事件造成十三人死亡。

再比如：With the rapid development of the internet, all parents must stay vigilant and repudiate any unhealthy content that could negatively affect their children 隨著互聯網的迅速發展，所有家長都必須警惕並堅決抵制任何可能影響孩子的不良內容。

66. to exact one's own toll 付出某人代價

例:His wrong behavior eventually exacts its own toll 他的錯誤行為最終要付出代價。

67. to foot the bill 負擔費用，支付帳單
例 ： Inflation right now is outrageous and keeps getting worse. My income can barely foot the monthly bills. 現在的通貨膨脹簡直離譜，而且還在不斷惡化。我的收入連每月的帳單都快負擔不起了。

68. turgid 浮誇的
例：I don't appreciate his writing style; it comes across as turgid and abysmal, making the content difficult to grasp. The excessive ornateness and complexity only further obscure understanding.我不欣賞他的寫作風格；顯得浮誇晦澀，讓人難以理解內容。過於華麗和複雜的表達反而讓理解變得更加困難。

69. superficial 膚淺的
例：Many girls don't realize that guys often abhor superficial behavior in women. 很多女生沒意識到，男生往往厭惡女人膚淺的行為 。

70. frivolous 膚淺的，輕浮的，愚蠢輕浮的

例：I read that novel, but I found its content was completely frivolous, with an unrealistic plot 我讀了那本小說，但覺得它的內容非常膚淺，劇情也不現實。

再比如： The behavior of the young, educated woman may appear frivolous in public, potentially leading to negative consequences or repercussions. 作為一名受過教育的年輕女性，她的行為在公眾面前顯得輕浮，可能會引發負面影響。

71. to sire someone 撫養某人，原意是成為…的父親

例： Richard saved a little girl who had lost her parents, and though not her biological father, he longed to sire her a new future filled with love and care 理查救了一位失去父母的小女孩，儘管不是她的親生父親，但他願意撫養她，為她開創一個充滿愛與關懷的新人生。

72. sideline 副業

例 :As you know, inflation is severe. Prices are skyrocketing, and anyone with just one job can barely afford to live in this city. What's your sideline? 你也知道，現在通貨膨脹很嚴重，所有東西的價格都在瘋狂上漲。一個人只靠一份工作根本負擔不起在這座城市生活。你有沒有副業啊？

73. well-heeled 富有的

例： He married a well-heeled woman, and in a single night, he transformed into a tycoon 他與一位女富婆結婚，在僅僅一夜之間，他就變成了富翁。

74. affluent 富有的，富裕的

例： Which city in China is the most affluent one? The answer is "Shanghai". 中國哪個城市最富裕？答案是"上海"。

75. debt-ridden 負載累累，債臺高築，債務纏身

例：He was trapped in a debt-ridden situation, and no one was willing to lend him a hand 他陷入了負載累累的困境，沒有人願意幫他一把。

G

1. to polish 改進，潤色
例：Sawyer polished his essay to meet his professor's requirements. 索耶改進了他的論文以符合教授的要求。

2. to ameliorate 改善
例：You can't change your fate, but you can ameliorate it to a certain extent. 你不能改變你的命運，但你可以在一定程度上改善你的命運。

3. to turf out 趕出去
例：It is said that hundreds of thousands of people were turfed out of that country during the pandemic, which is both tragic and absurd 據說在疫情期間，成千上萬的人被趕出了那個國家，這既令人悲哀又荒唐。

再比如：After a severe quarrel with his dad, he was turfed out of his home.在與父親大吵一架後，他被趕出了家門。

4. feel queasy 感到噁心

例：I felt queasy while watching all the bloody scenes in the movie. 看電影裡那些血腥場面時，我感到一陣噁心。

5. to be (feel) thrilled 感到激動
例：We parted ways when I was just a little boy. Now that we've grown up and reunited today, I feel a bit thrilled. 我們在我還是個小男孩的時候分別了，現在我們都長大了，今天再次相見，我感到有點激動

6. to cringe 感到難為情，感到難堪，畏縮
例：I cringed when I recall what I made mistakes.當回想起我所犯的錯誤時，我感到難為情。

7. nonplussed 尷尬的,不知所措
例：As soon as someone mentioned his divorce, he instantly felt nonplussed. 一提到他離婚，他就立刻感到尷尬。

8. squeaky clean 乾乾淨淨的

例：Considering the room was squeaky clean, he decided to rent it.考慮到房間乾乾淨淨，他決定租下它。

9. brisk 乾淨俐落的

例：I appreciate the team leader for making a short, brisk speech. Its content definitely made sense. 我感謝隊長發表了一次乾淨俐落的講話，內容確實有意義 。

除此之外，它還有很多意思： 輕快的，生氣勃勃的；興隆的，紅火的；涼爽的，清新的：麻利的

10. to meddle 干涉

例：I advise parents to avoid meddling in their children's marriage, and especially in their personal lives. 我給所有父母的建議是，不要干涉孩子的婚姻，尤其是他們的個人 生活。

11. parched 乾燥的，炎熱的

例："With the deterioration of the global climate, droughts have become routine, and the soil has turned parched. Climate change is threatening each one of us. 隨著全球氣候惡化，乾旱已成常態，土壤也變得乾燥。氣候變化正威脅著我們每一個人。

12. to shoo away 趕走

例：One day, I saw many wild animals around my house, like raccoons, foxes, and geese, so I had to shoo them away.有一天，我看到我家周圍有很多野生動物，像浣熊、狐狸和鵝，我不得不把它們趕走。

13. had barely...when 剛⋯就⋯

例：This driver had barely passed the intersection when a severe traffic accident occurred behind him. 這名司機剛駛過十字路口，後方就發生了一起嚴重的交通事故。

14. hefty 高大健壯的

例：Men born in the northern regions, relatively, are heftier than southerners 相對而言，出生在北方地區的男人比南方人更高大健壯。

15. enigmatic 高深莫測的，神秘的

例：Her appearance on stage seems enigmatic due to her long disappearance, as if she had evaporated 她的亮相顯得高深莫測，因為她已經消失了很長一段時間，仿佛她已經蒸發了。

再比如：This guy looks enigmatic; very few people can read him. 這個人看起來神秘莫測，很少有人能看透他。

16. geek 高手(在某領域）

例：Waylon is a gaming geek, completely intoxicated by the virtual world. 韋倫是個遊戲高手，沉醉于虛擬世界。

17. blustering 氣勢洶洶的

例：His blustering attitude towards me definitely leaves me flustered. 他對我氣勢洶洶的態度讓我感到不知所措。

18. decorous 高雅的

例：No matter what she wears, she always looks decorous and composed. 無論她穿什麼，她總是顯得高雅而沉穩。

19. to foul up 搞砸，搞糟

例：His negligence fouled up the implementation of the marketing plan, resulting in a significant loss for the company — so he was fired. 由於他的疏忽，行銷計畫的執行被搞砸了，導致公司遭受重大損失，最終他被解雇。

20. furore 公憤

例：Spitting in a public place can cause a furore. 在公共場所隨地吐痰會引起公憤。

21. sundry 各式各樣的，雜的

例：James shows strong experience in communicating with sundry people from all fields. 詹姆斯在與各行各業的人士溝通方面展現了豐富的經驗。

22. to infringe upon 給 ...帶來痛苦

例：The war launched by Russia has inflicted great suffering upon the Ukrainian people. 俄羅斯發起的戰爭給烏克蘭人民帶來了巨大痛苦。

23. to cast a pall over 給…蒙上陰影

例：Her divorce cast a pall over her career, distracting her to the point of despair. 她的離婚給她的事業蒙上了陰影，令她陷入了絕望。

24. to suckle 給…餵奶

例：The baby has started crying; I guess you'll probably need to suckle him. 孩子開始哭了，我猜很可能你得給他餵奶。

25. to be yoked to 跟…扯上關係

例：Despite his celebrity status in the country, I'd still be hesitant to be yoked to him. 儘管他在國內是名人，我仍然不願意與他扯上關係。

26. a junket tour 公費旅遊

例：The local government prohibited their cadres from going on a junket to curb this kind of misbehavior. 當地政府禁止他們的幹部進行公費旅遊，以遏制這種不當行為。

27. latrine 公共廁所

例：I urgently went to the latrine because of my stomach pain; I could no longer hold it. 肚子痛，急忙上公共廁所； 我再也憋不住了。

28. to solidify 鞏固

例：In the fierce competition, this manufacturer aimed to solidify its marketing monopoly but ended up being eliminated due to a lack of innovation. 在激烈的競爭中，這家製造商試圖鞏固其市場壟斷，但由於缺乏創新，最終被淘汰。

29. overt 公開的

例：This professor issued a covert letter to clarify the rumor that he had plagiarized someone else's thesis. 這位教授發佈了一封公開信，澄清了他抄襲他人論文的謠言。

30. blatant 公然的，喧囂的，華麗的

例：Given his publicly blatant discrimination against a vulnerable group, he was condemned and forced to step down. 鑒於他公然對弱勢群體的明顯歧視，他受到了譴責，並被迫辭職。

31. to embolden sb to do sth 鼓勵某人去做某事。

例: William encourages his son to face any challenges on his path to success. 威廉鼓勵他的兒子面對通往成功道路上的一切挑戰。

很多人會問我能不能用 encourage 呢？當然可以，但意思略有不同。encourage 是在精神上鼓勵某人去做事，給予對方更多的是激勵與希望。而 embolden 則強調某人站在背後給其壯膽，所給予的是鼓舞。當然，兩者都有鼓勵的意思，只是含義略有不同。

32. to be in cahoots 勾結在一起

例：No matter the country, officials are always in cahoots, while ordinary people are left to suffer. 無論哪個國家，官員總能勾結在一起，而普通百姓總是身陷困境。

33. stodgy 古板的

例：His design feels a bit stodgy, lacking innovation and creativity. 他的設計看起來有些古板，缺乏創新和創意。

34. trough 谷地

例: In 2022, his career hit a trough, and he struggled to make a living. 在 2022 年，他的事業跌入低谷，生活變得艱難。

35. to peg 固定（匯率）

例：I want to exchange some money for US dollars today, but since the rate isn't pegged, it could go up or down. 我今天想兌換一些美元，但因為匯率沒有被固定，可能會上下波動。

36. to drum up 鼓起

例：It would be best if you drummed up your strength and encouragement to fight back while being bullied .當你被欺負的時候，你必須鼓起你的力量和勇氣去反擊。

37. forlorn 孤獨的

例：Most seniors feel forlorn after officially retiring, especially when their children have moved far away 大多數老年人在正式退休後會感到孤獨，尤其是當他們的孩子遠離自己時。

38. wacky 古怪的

例：Tom impressed me with a wacky behavior. 湯姆以他古怪的行為給我留下了深刻印象。

39. to gauge 估計，判斷

例：it is hard to gauge what the weather will be like next week. 很難估計下星期的天氣如何。

40. patron 顧客，贊助人

例：Patrons living in the luxury hotel can take the food away, however, ordinary customers can't. 住在豪華酒店的顧客可以帶走食物，但普通顧客不能這樣做。

41. to nudge 鼓勵，勸說

例：The government enacted a new law to nudge women into having more children. 政府頒佈了一項新法律，鼓勵婦女生更多的孩子。

42. insular 孤僻的；與世隔絕的

例：I prefer to be friends with open-minded and optimistic people rather than those with insular instincts and traits. 我更喜歡與思想開明、樂觀的人做朋友，而不是那些有著孤僻本能和特點的人。

43. to pluck up the courage to 鼓起勇氣 ...

例：After quarreling with Raelynn, I plucked up the courage to call her and apologize, and she finally came back to me. 與 Raelynn 雷琳爭吵後，我鼓起勇氣給她打電話道歉，最終她回到了我身邊。

(pluck 這個詞的含義非常多，有掐，捏，摘，拔，夾，拉，奪等等含義，是典型的一詞多義。如果專門講這個詞，估計要好幾頁，這裡只是選用它最常用的一種，如果大家對其更多含義和使用方法感興趣，可以進一步查字典詳細瞭解。

44. to summon up the courage to 鼓起勇氣做

例：He lost almost everything but still summoned the courage to restart his business. After a few years, he raked in tremendous rewards through his effort and persistence. 他幾乎失去了一切，但仍然鼓起勇氣

重新開始自己的生意。幾年後，他憑藉努力和堅持賺得了豐厚的回報。

45. to buoy 鼓舞，支持

例：He lost everything due to his bankruptcy; however, his friends and relatives are trying to buoy his spirits and help him get through it. They hope he can start over from scratch. As the old saying goes, 'Where you fell, you must rise again.由於破產，他失去了一切；然而，他的朋友和親戚正在努力鼓舞他的士氣，幫助他度過難關。他們希望他能從頭開始。正如古話所說：'哪裡跌倒，哪裡站起來 '。

46. willful 故意的

例：Engaging in willful food wastage can be considered morally reprehensible and, to some extent, a criminal act. 故意浪費食物可以被視為道德上的可恥行為，在某種程度上，這也可以視為犯罪行為。

47. opinionated 固執己見的

例：He often told his son to avoid being opinionated, as it would allow him to make tremendous progress 他常常告訴兒子要避免過於固執己見，因為那樣可以取得巨大的進步。

48. to festoon 掛滿彩燈

例：During the Spring Festival in China, you can see the streets festooned with various flowers and colorful lights, creating a vibrant holiday atmosphere 在中國的春節期間，街道上到處掛滿五彩斑斕彩燈，和各式各樣花卉，彌漫著濃厚的節日氣氛。

49. quirk 怪癖

例：He has a quirk, such as brushing his teeth four times a day. However, experts have confirmed that frequent mouth cleaning may not be healthy for your teeth.他有一個怪癖，比如每天刷四次牙。然而，專家已經確認，頻繁刷牙可能對牙齒健康不利。

再比如：His colleagues were bewildered by his quirk of wearing a jacket in the heat of summer. 他的同事們對他在

炎熱的夏天穿著夾克的怪癖
感到困惑。

50. to decommission 關閉
例：The local government was
forced to decommission the
nuclear power plant near the lake
due to strong public protest. 由
於市民的強烈抗議，當地政
府被迫關閉了湖邊的核電
站。

51. linchpin 關鍵
例：TSMC controls the linchpin
technology for producing two-
nanometer chips. 台積電掌握
著製造兩納米晶片的關鍵技
術。

52. pivotal 關鍵的
例：Ostensibly, it seems like you
have many friends. However,
when you're at a pivotal moment
in life, none of them can be found.
That's why I often tell my so-
called 'friends' that there are no
genuine friendships in this world.

Friendship, in reality, is a
relationship based on benefits —
people are willing to be your
friend only when you can offer
them something. Otherwise, they
disappear. And vice versa.

I understand some may
reprimand me for being cynical or
biased. But someday, when
you're my age, you'll understand
everything.
表面上看，你好像有很多朋
友。但當你真正處於人生關
鍵時刻時，卻一個也找不
到。這就是為什麼我經常對
我的'朋友們'說，世上根本沒
有真正的友誼。

朋友的定義，其實就是利益
關係——只要你能帶來好
處，他們才願意做你的朋友
。否則，一個都不會留下。
反之亦然。

我知道有人可能會責備我偏
激，但等你到了我這個年
紀，你就會明白一切。

53. to instill 灌輸
例：A key part of school
education should be to instill in
young children the values of
respecting elders and practicing
thrift habits that will benefit them
throughout their lives.
I felt deeply pained when I saw a
child throw away all four pieces of
bread and vegetables from a
burger, keeping only the meat.
學校教育中一個重要的部分
應該是向孩子們灌輸尊敬長

輩和勤儉節約的觀念，這些
習慣將使他們終生受益。

當我看到一個孩子把漢堡裡
的四片麵包和蔬菜全扔進垃
圾桶，只吃了裡面的肉時，
我感到非常痛心。

54. to sour the relationship 關係變差
例：The escalation of the controversy between the two countries soured their relationship and stymied both economies. 兩國爭端的升級使彼此的關係變差，並阻礙了兩國的經濟發展。

55. to keep tabs on 關注
例：The whole world has been keeping tabs on the Russia-Ukraine war, which has lasted for over a year. Yet, no one knows how or when it will end. 全世界都在密切關注俄烏戰爭，這場戰爭已經持續了一年多，但沒有人知道它將如何或何時結束。

56. subterfuge 詭計
例：He often remains silent, but once he speaks, he can instantly see through the other party's subterfuge 他常常沉默不語，但只要一開口，便能一眼識破對方的詭計。

57. ruse 詭計
例：He is brilliant and can come up with a lot of cunning ruses. 他很聰明，詭計多端。

58. eerily 詭異地
例：This picture eerily depicted something related to aliens or nonhumans, causing some experts to be horrified. 這張圖片詭異地描繪了一些與外星人或非人類有關的東西，這讓一些專家不寒而慄。

59. cudgel 棍棒
例：In Canada, if you grab a cudgel to beat someone, you can still be sued just as if you were using a weapon like a gun. 在加拿大，如果你拿起棍棒毆打某人，你將面臨與使用槍支等武器相同的訴訟。

60. overwrought 過度緊張的
例：I am mentally overwrought today; I need to take a break. 我今天精神過度緊張；我得休息一下。

61. to overegg 過分地做 …
例：Their behaviors are too overegged. 他們的行為太過分了。

62. finicky 過分繁瑣的
例：I was bewildered by why some of the welfare application procedures were so finicky, but later, I learned they never really wanted you to get it. 令我很困惑的是為什麼有些福利申請程式過分繁瑣，後來我知道他們壓根兒就不希望你得到它。

63. to be cocksure about 過分自信
例：Nowadays, many girls are very cocksure about their looks, often boasting in public about how pretty they are. Unfortunately, I can't bring myself to flatter them. 現在很多妹子都過分自信自己的顏值。 他們總是在公共場合吹噓自己長得漂亮。 可惜我著實不敢恭維。

64. oblique 拐彎抹角的，隱晦的
例：He conversed with one of his clients and discerned an oblique complaint about the sluggishness of their service response 他與其中一個客戶交談時，察覺到客戶在拐彎抹角抱怨服務反應慢的問題。

65. hunky-dory 搞定一切
例：He boasted that everything he did would be hunky-dory, but in reality, he made things worse. 他吹噓說自己做的事情都能搞定一切，但實際上他弄得一團糟。

66. to chuckle 咯咯笑
例：When I asked her if she loved me, she always chuckled and remained silent. 當我問她是否愛我時，她總是咯咯笑著不言語。

67. staid 古板的，保守的，陳舊的 嚴肅的
例：The application procedure for studying at the university is too rigid to complete. Unfortunately, I have to give up on it. 大學的申請程式過於古板，難以完成。不幸的是，我不得不放棄。

68. to put on the back burner 擱置

例： The further expansion of this company has been put on the back burner due to the challenging situation following the outbreak of the pandemic 由於疫情爆發後的困境，這家公司進一步擴展的計畫已被擱置。

69. to slam on 給 …帶來猛烈衝擊

例：The pandemic slammed on the global economy, and no country was spared from its effects 疫情給全球經濟帶來猛烈衝擊，沒人能逃脫其影響。

70. caveat 告誡

例：Vendors often posted caveats in the store stating no refunds or exchanges, which made me uncomfortable. Almost made me decide never to return to that store again. 商販經常在店裡貼告誡，不退不換，讓我很不舒服。 差不多，我不會再去那家店了。

71. to tinker with 改裝、修修補補

例：Some Mercedes-Benz cars have been tinkered with using AMG technology.一些梅賽德斯-賓士汽車被用 AMG 技術進行過改裝。

再比如：In our local area, it's hard to find someone willing to tinker with small house repairs, as they tend to look down on earning a small amount of money and always prefer chasing big projects that bring in more profit. .
在我們當地，很難找到願意修修補補房子的人，因為他們看不起掙小錢，總是想接大工程賺大錢。

72. to give sb. a leg up 給某人幫助和支持

例：During his studies, his parents gave him a significant leg-up; otherwise, he wouldn't have been able to afford his tuition fees and accommodation.
在求學期間，他父母給了他很大的幫助，否則他無法負擔學費和住宿費用。

H

1. flagrant 駭人聽聞的
例：We often hear about teachers sexually assaulting their students, which is a flagrant violation of both ethics and humanity. Don't those teachers have daughters around the same age as their victims? 我們經常聽到老師性侵學生的事情，這是對道德和人性的公然違反。實在駭人聽聞。那些老師的女兒不是和受害者年齡相仿嗎？

2. nebulous 含糊其辭的
例：His nebulous explanation led to a delay in the implementation of the contract. The company's board will further discuss how to handle the situation. 他含糊其辭的解釋導致合同的執行延遲。公司董事會將進一步討論如何處理。

再比如：例：Due to his psychological issues, his cognition has become increasingly nebulous. 由於心理問題，他的認知變得越來越模糊不清。

3. to insulate 含沙射影的，旁敲側擊
例：He insinuated that someone had stolen his watch.他含沙射影地說有人偷了他的手錶。

4. parsimonious 寒酸的
例：I reminded him to bring this small gift when visiting his professor, though it does look rather parsimonious.我提醒他帶上這份小禮物去看望他的教授，雖然看起來有些寒酸。

5. without blushing 毫不臉紅
例：He often deceived his wife without blushing, coming up with numerous excuses and stories. 他經常毫不臉紅地欺騙妻子，編造了許多藉口和故事。

6. pugnacious 好鬥的
例：Boys tend to be more pugnacious than girls because it is an instinct inherent in humans. 男孩比女孩更具好鬥性，因為這是人類的本能。

7. unscathed 毫髮無損的
例：No cities on earth can escape unscathed by the pandemics.地球上的任何城市都無法在大流行面前毫髮無損的。

8. moat 壕溝
例：There is no moat too wide to cross, and no difficulty too great to overcome. I always remind myself to persist in doing what I love, for I believe I can ultimately achieve my goal. 沒有不能逾越的壕溝，沒有不能克服的困難。 我時常提醒自己堅持做自己喜歡的事情，因為我相信最終可以實現自己的目標。

9. posh 豪華的，時髦的
例：As of today, a posh courtyard house in Beijing is worth more than 100 million dollars. 截至今天，北京的豪華四合院值得超過 1 億美元。

10. swanky 豪華的，時髦的
例：She recently changed jobs and was hired by a prestigious company. She also moved into a swanky condo, and many of her colleagues admired her. 她最近換了工作，被一家著名企業聘用，並搬進了一套豪華公寓，許多同事都羨慕她。

11. to howl 嚎叫，憤怒
例：After her husband passed away, she felt lonely, so she moved to a mountain village. Sometimes, she would feel scared when hearing the wolves howling at night, but she has since gotten used to it, and everything now feels like a routine. 丈夫去世後，她感到孤獨，於是搬到了一個山村。有時候，夜晚聽到狼嚎叫，她會感到害怕，但她已經習慣了，現在一切對她來說都習以為常。

12. to eviscerate 耗盡
例：After enduring such horror and misery, her spirit and energy have been completely eviscerated. 經歷了這場恐怖與痛苦之後，她的精神和活力已被徹底耗盡。

13. unreservedly 毫無保留地
例：In this world, only your parents can help and support you unreservedly.在這個世界上，

只有你的父母可以毫無保留地幫助和支持你。

14. estuary 河口，江口
例：Yellow River estuary 黃河河口 Yangzi River estuary 長江江口 以此類推，所有江河湖海的出入口都可以使用 estuary.

15. rational 合理的
例：Executing all the principal offenders and their accomplices involved in human trafficking, with death penalties for their crimes regardless of their ages, seems rational. 對所有參與人口販賣的主犯和從犯執行死刑，無論其年齡如何，看起來是合理的。

16. to bandy words with sb. 和某人頂嘴
例：Her son is always bandying words with her, clearly, he's been overly indulged. 她的兒子總是與她頂嘴。顯然，顯然是被慣壞了。

17. sought-after 很吃香的，最受青睞的
例：This entrepreneur brought us a large number of orders, making him a highly sought-after client. 這位元企業家為我們帶來了大量訂單，因此成為了很吃香的客戶。

18. it is tempting to think that... 很容易讓人們想到 ...
例：I saw many people being robbed in broad daylight — it is tempting to think that this place is unsafe. 我看到很多人在光天化日之下被搶劫，很容易讓人想到這個地方不安全。

19. windfall 橫財，意外之財
例：His uncle won a 17 million lottery last year. Unfortunately, he failed to manage the windfall and spent it all within a short period of time , some of it was even taken by scammers. 他叔叔去年中了 1700 萬的彩票，但遺憾的是沒能好好管理這筆橫財，短時間內就花光了，其中一部分還被騙走了。

20. to span 橫跨
例：Bullet trains spanning 20 provinces across the country have created numerous job opportunities and boosted local economies. 橫跨全國 20 個省份的高鐵不僅創造了大量就

業機會，也帶動了當地經濟的繁榮。

21. to sprawl over 橫跨，延綿，覆蓋

例：The Great Wall of China stretches 21,196 kilometers, spanning 15 provinces across the country. 中國的萬里長城全長 21,196 公里，橫跨全國 15 個省份。

22. a smash hit 轟動

例：The exposure of the scandal involving the massacre of civilians during the Russia–Ukraine war became a smash hit in global media. 有關俄羅斯與烏克蘭戰爭中屠殺平民醜聞的曝光在全球媒體上引發了轟動。

23. to con 哄騙

例：Recently, many seniors were conned by scammers over the phone into transferring large amounts of money, some of which could have been their life savings or hard-earned coins. 最近，許多老年人通過電話被哄騙，向詐騙分子轉帳了大筆錢款，其中一些可能是他們的畢生積蓄或辛苦掙來的錢。

24. one flood too many 洪水氾濫

例：In the summer, the southern part of Bombay faces one flood too many, as heavy rains rapidly inundate the area. 在夏季，孟買南部洪水氾濫，暴雨迅速淹沒了該地區。

25. fat book 厚厚的書

例：He wrote a fat book describing his experience with the renovation of the atomic bomb. 他寫了一本厚厚的書，描述了自己參與原子彈改造的經歷。

26. contrite 後悔的

例：I often heard someone say he was not contrite about missing opportunities or making mistakes. In fact, after dealing with him, I finally understood that this kind of person actually cares deeply about everything. 我經常聽到有人說他不會因為錯過機會或犯錯感到後悔。其實跟這種人打過交道後，我終於明白了，他對一切都很在乎。

再比如：I knew a guy who boasted that he would never be contrite, regardless of what wrong he did. 我認識一個人吹噓說，無論他做錯了什麼，都不會後悔。

27. to feel chill to the bone 後背發涼
例：He accidentally fell from the 10th floor of the building. Though he survived, he was left feeling chilled to the bone. 他不小心從大樓的 10 樓摔下，雖然他活了下來，但仍感到後背發涼。

28. cheeky 厚顏無恥的
例:Some online trolls are cheeky enough to attack people who express divergent views. Their ugly behavior left me feeling disgusted. 網上一些噴子厚顏無恥地攻擊持不同觀點的人，他們的醜陋行為讓我感到噁心。

29. brazenly 厚顏無恥地
例：This guy gave the waitress a hard time, yet he brazenly complained about being treated unfairly. 這個人刁難這個女服務員，而他卻厚顏無恥地抱怨自己受到了不公平的對待。

30. to crank out 胡亂做、粗製濫造
例：In an article, he cranks out a boastful account of how he made a lot of money from the stock market. 他在一篇文章中胡亂寫了一通，吹噓他如何從股票市場賺了很多錢。

再比如：It is said that robots controlled by AI technology can crank out anything within a few seconds, significantly increasing product output, allowing manufacturers to rake in profits. 據說，受人工智慧技術控制的機器人可以在幾秒鐘內粗製濫造任何東西，這大大提高了產品產量，使製造商能夠賺取豐厚的利潤。

31. elision with the rights of 忽略了 ...的權利
例：This novel fully exemplifies its elision with the rights of women in the countryside. To put it bluntly, it's full of male chauvinism. 這本長篇小說充分表明了其忽略農村婦女的權力。說白

了，就是充斥著大男子主義的內容。

32. to woolgather 胡思亂想,心不在焉

例：After breaking up with his girlfriend, he was too distracted to work. He was so woolgathered that he couldn't complete his monthly quota and ended up getting fired. 和女友分手後，他無心工作，整日胡思亂想，心不在焉，無法完成月度指標，最終被解雇了

33. twirling 弧旋的，旋轉的

例：If you launch a twirling ping-pang ball, the other party will fail to return it.如果你發起一個弧旋球，對方就接不住的。

34. drivel 胡言亂語

例：She was often insulted and attacked online, and her mom persuaded her to ignore all that drivel. 她經常在網上受到侮辱和攻擊，媽媽勸她無視那些胡言亂語。

35. to shell out 花（錢）

例：To get a luxury watch, he had to shell out all his savings. 為了購買一隻豪表，他不得不花光了所有的積蓄。

36. to channel one's grief into hard work 化悲痛為力量

例：A young doctor passed away, it's a great loss for all of us. However, we should channel our grief into hard work to carry on his dream. 一位年輕的醫生離世了，這是我們巨大的損失。然而，我們應當化悲痛為力量，努力工作，實現他的夢想。

37. to chop up complexity to simplicity 化繁為簡

例：We must advocate chopping up complexity into simplicity the moment we attempt to solve tough issues. 一旦我們試圖解決棘手問題，就必須提倡化繁為簡。

38. slick 花裡胡哨的

例：So far a lot of websites have slick designs but very hollow content. .到目前為止，很多網站的設計花裡胡哨的，而內容卻非常空洞。

（slick 當然還有很多形容漂亮的意思，比如：華而不實

的 ,最好的 ,熟練的， 聰明的 ,靈巧的,光滑的,花言巧語的,很棒的.)

39. to take up time 花時間，佔用時間

例：I know it may take up your time, but I had to try to persuade you to reconsider our relationship. I can't bear breaking up with you because I love you so much.我知道這可能花了你的時間，但我還是想努力勸你重新考慮我們的關係。因為我太愛你了，真的無法承受分手。

40. to be about to go up in smoke 化為烏有，白費了，付諸東流

例：All the pictures I took over the past years were destroyed due to a malfunction in my laptop's hard drive, so all my efforts are about to go up in smoke. 由於筆記型電腦硬碟故障，過去幾年我拍的所有照片都化為烏有，我的努力也將付諸東流。

41. to be nostalgia for 懷念

例：I am always nostalgia for my old classmates, teachers, and professors.我總是懷念我的老同學、老師和教授。

42. to cast doubt on 懷疑

例：George claimed that he intended to donate around 1 million dollars. Unfortunately, a long time passed, and he took no action. As a result, many people began to doubt his sincerity and honesty. George 聲稱他打算捐贈約 100 萬美元，但不幸的是，過了很長一段時間，他沒有採取任何行動，因此許多人開始懷疑他的真誠和誠實。

43. to whoop 歡呼， 大聲呼叫

例：So many people whopped on the spectator stands while watching the soccer finals. 許多人在觀看足球決賽時在看臺上歡呼。

44. to caper 歡呼雀躍

例：The crowd began to caper upon learning that their team had won the championship. Excitement filled the air as fans leaped and danced, celebrating the victorious moment together. 人群在得知他們的球隊贏得

冠軍後開始歡呼雀躍。興奮
的氣氛彌漫在空氣中，球迷
們跳躍舞動，共同慶祝這勝
利的時刻。

45. respite 緩解

例：The heavy rain is no respite
for the drought at all. 這場大雨
根本不能緩解乾旱。

再比如：This new medicine
can instantly provide respite from
his cancer pain. 這種新藥能立
刻緩解他的癌痛。

46. to allay 緩解，減輕

例：Her teacher tried to allay
her students' anxiety, especially
during the university entrance
examinations each year. 她的
老師試圖緩解學生的焦慮，
尤其是在每年的高考時。

再比如：例：It is said that the
restricted disclosure about aliens
living on the moon is meant to
allay the fears of humans on
Earth, as the world would be
thrown into turmoil if everyone
knew the truth. 據說，限制公
開外星人居住在月球上的事
實是為了減輕我們生活在地
球上人類的恐懼，因為，一

旦大家知道這一事實，整個
世界將陷入混亂。

47. ludicrous 荒唐可笑的

例：Everyone seems to take it
as ludicrous when mentioning AI
will supplant our human beings.
當提到人工智慧將取代我們
人類時，每個人似乎都認為
這很荒唐可笑。

48. to balk at 回避

例：My question is, why do you
always try to balk at my point? 我
的問題是為什麼你總是回避
我的觀點。

49. to parry 回避，躲避

例：During the conference, he
tried to parry the sensitive
questions to mislead the public in
the wrong direction. 在會議期
間，他試圖回避敏感問題，
誤導公眾誤入歧途。

50. to sidestep 回避，躲避

例：I don't understand why you
sidestepped my question. Please
answer me directly. 我不明白你
為什麼回避我的問題，請直
接回答我。

再比如：He admitted the mistakes he made but sidestepped the key ones.他承認自己犯下的錯誤，但回避了關鍵的錯誤。

51. to shy away from 回避，躲避，羞於

例：This president made so many mistakes so he tried to shy away from giving a public speech.這位元總統犯了許多錯誤，所以他試圖避免發表公開演講。

52. to scupper 毀掉

例：Material of inferior quality can certainly scupper your product. Sooner or later, your sales and market will stagnate. 劣質材料肯定會毀掉你的產品。遲早，你的銷量和市場將停滯不前。

53. to mutilate 毀壞

例：After a catastrophic car accident, his face was completely mutilated. 在一場災難性的車禍後，他的臉完全毀容。

54. profligacy 揮霍

例：Almost all seniors, at the age of around 70-80, can't understand young people's profligacy and their attitudes toward life. 幾乎所有 70 到 80 歲的老年人都無法理解年輕人揮霍無度的行為和他們對生活的態度。

55. to splurge 揮霍

例：When I saw so many young people gathering in bars to party, I felt they were splurging their youth and life. 當我看到這麼多年輕人在酒吧裡聚集狂歡時，我覺得他們在揮霍自己的青春和生命

56. be extremely reticent about 諱莫如深

例：He was extremely reticent about his background and experiences; no one in the office knew what had happened to him. 他對自己的背景和經歷諱莫如深，辦公室裡沒人知道曾經在他身上發生過什麼。

57. kickback 回扣

例: There is a corrupt practice in hospitals where doctors often try to get kickbacks from pharmaceutical manufacturers for the prescribed medicines. 醫院中存在一種腐敗現象，醫生

通常會從處方藥中向製造商收取回扣。

58. obscure 晦澀難懂的
例：Almost all the students complained about the professor's obscure lecture. 幾乎所有的學生都抱怨教授講的課太晦澀難懂。

59. elusive 晦澀難懂的
例：His speech is elusive, shrouded in layers of ambiguity and unpredictability, leaving listeners confused and unable to grasp its meaning. 他的演講晦澀難懂，籠罩在層層模糊和不可預測之中，聽眾感到困惑，無法理解其含義。

60. arcane 晦澀難懂的，神秘的
例：The article he wrote seems too arcane to be understood by many readers. 他寫的文章似乎過於晦澀，難懂，許多讀者難以理解。
再比如： Their tradition seems arcane, historical, and sacred. 他們的傳統似乎是神秘的，歷史的和神聖的。
His writing style is very arcane; only a few people can understand him. 他的寫作風格非常晦澀，只有少數人能理解他。

61. to wield 揮舞（棍棒或手中的權力）
例：Nathan wielded a steel rod and randomly attacked people walking on the street. He was immediately arrested by the police. 南森揮舞著一根鋼棍，隨機襲擊街上的行人。警方立即將他逮捕

62. to hark back to 回想起，回憶起
例：At his final moment on the way to the execution ground, he harked back to his unforgettable moments spent with his wife, children, and parents as well. 在走向刑場的最後時刻，他回想起與妻子、孩子和父母度過的難忘時光。

63. jocular 詼諧的，幽默的
例：Men's jocular style of conversation can mesmerize women. 男人詼諧的談話風格可以讓女士們著迷。

64. leeway 迴旋餘地
例：Never promise anyone 100%; instead, give yourself

more leeway. 永遠不要向任何人承諾 100%； 相反，你必須給自己更多的迴旋餘地。

65. mayhem 混亂
例：The situation in the middle east is mayhem with all parties involved in the regional conflicts. 中東局勢一片混亂，所有各方都捲入了地區衝突。

66. to conjure out of thin air 橫空出世
例：Nowadays, so many "black technologies" seem to be conjured out of thin air, leaving people puzzled about how and where they originated. 如今，許多"黑科技"仿佛橫空出世，讓人們不禁感到困惑，不知道它們是如何以及從哪裡來的。

67. shambolic 混亂不堪的
例：Due to the shambolic management, the company was embroiled in heavy debt and almost declared bankruptcy. 由於管理混亂不堪，這家公司負債累累，幾乎宣告破產。

再比如：Due to the emergency, a shambolic situation unfolded at the airport. 由於緊急情況，機場發生了混亂局面。

68. desultory 混亂的，無條理的
例：Given the desultory management in the company, Rowan decided to quit as a form of protest. 鑒於公司管理混亂，羅文決定辭職以示抗議。

69. to obfuscate 混淆
例：The spokesperson of the company obfuscated the facts to prevent the investigation from progressing. 這家公司的發言人混淆了事實，以 阻止調查的進行。

70. to procure 獲得
例：It was quite hard to procure food, especially during the pandemic lockdown. 尤其是在疫情封鎖期間，獲取食物變得非常困難。

71. to reap 獲得
例：Thanks to his tremendous exertion, he reaped a promotion to become CEO of this company. 由於他的努力，他獲得了晉升，成為這家公司的 CEO。

72. to derive from 獲得

例：Who will derive the most benefit from the friendly relationship between China and the US? Undoubtedly, it is America. 誰會從中美之間的友好關係中獲得最大的利益？ 毫無疑問,應該是美國。

73. bane 禍根

例：Arrogance is the bane of your failure. 傲慢是你失敗的禍根。

74. to go viral 火了，走紅 、瘋狂傳播

例：His remarkable performance went viral after being shared online. 他的特別表演在網上發佈後迅速火了起來。

再比如： The news that a little boy saved the lives of five dogs went viral last weekend. 上週末，一個小男孩救了五條狗生命的消息在網上瘋傳。

75. snappier 活潑的

例：I adore her snappier personality and amiable characteristics.我喜歡她活潑的性格及和藹可親的特點。

76. to stoke it up 火上澆油

例：He is outraged; please don't stoke it up. 他在氣頭上，就不要火上澆油了。

77. pandemonium 混亂

例：Pandemonium erupted as Michael Jackson entered the stadium; the audience went wild. Emotions ran high, and everyone cheered and applauded enthusiastically. 當邁克爾·傑克遜進入體育場時，場面一片混亂，觀眾們瘋狂歡呼。情緒激動，所有人都熱情地為他喝彩和鼓掌。

78. ramification 後果

例:His offensive speech and behavior caused serious ramifications among young people.他的冒犯性言論和行為在年輕人中造成了嚴重後果。

再比如：Juvenile offenders who exploit legal loopholes to commit crimes often fail to consider the ramifications of their actions. 那些利用法律漏洞犯

罪的未成年罪犯，往往沒有意識到自己行為的嚴重後果。

79. to concur with 和 ...意見一致

例：I concurred with my brother on taking care of our mother and ensuring she lives a comfortable and happy life. 我和我哥哥意見一致，要照顧好我們的媽媽，確保她生活得舒適和幸福。

80. to deplete 耗盡

例：The prosperity of his business gradually depleted his health; in the end, his wealth couldn't save his life. 生意興隆耗盡了他的健康，他的財富也救不了他的命。

再比如：Constant quarreling with her depleted his patience, and he eventually decided to file for divorce. 與妻子不斷的爭吵耗盡了他的耐心，他最終決定離婚。

81. to scramble to 慌亂，手忙腳亂做 ...

例：Kids are very naughty. Sometimes, when they see their teacher entering the classroom, they immediately scramble back to their seats. 孩子們很調皮，有時候一看到老師走進教室，就立刻慌亂跑回自己的座位。

再比如：The scramble for custody of his children left him exhausted and deeply depressed. He swore never to marry again, as the experience had struck him to the core. 為了爭奪孩子的撫養權，他身心俱疲，情緒低落。他發誓再也不結婚了，因為這段經歷對他打擊太大了。

82. to jumble up 混在一起，摻和在一起

例：Please try not to jumble up dark-colored clothes with white or light-colored ones when using the washing machine. 使用洗衣機時，請儘量不要把深色衣物和白色或淺色衣物混在一起洗。

83. to hoover up 獲得，奪得、賺了一大筆（錢）

例：This institute hoovered up a large amount of funding to further research the most effective treatment for cancer.

這個研究所獲得了大量資金，用於進一步研究最有效的癌症治療方法。

再比如：To hoover up the big prize, she dedicated herself fully to this research, knowing it could earn her one million dollars. 為了贏得大獎，她全身心投入這項研究，因為她知道這將為她帶來一百萬美元。

還有：He suddenly hoovered up a tremendous amount of money by playing the lottery; he didn't know how to spend it and also couldn't ease up eating and sleeping well. 他靠買彩票一下子吸了一大筆錢，不知道怎麼花，也寢食難安。

84. sluggish 緩慢的
例：The sluggish car impeded traffic during rush hour. 那輛車行駛緩慢，在高峰時段阻礙了交通。

J

1. sheer 極 (表示強調）
例：Recently, scientists invented a sheer, lightweight paper that is solid, super thin, and nontransparent, which could have significant implications for the printing industry. 最近，科學家們發明了一種極輕的紙，其特點是結實、超薄和不透明，這對印刷行業可能具有重要意義。

2. to trounce 擊敗，痛打
例：Her attitude toward a good person and a bad one is starkly different, and she ruthlessly trounced her enemies. 她對好人和壞人的態度截然不同，並且她無情地擊敗了她的敵人。

3. to topple 擊敗，戰勝
例：This company toppled its competitors in the fierce competition, thanks to its highly effective marketing plan. 憑藉極具成效的行銷計畫，這家公司在激烈的競爭中擊敗了同行。

4. to huddle around/together 擠成一團

例：So many people are huddling together for COVID-19 tests, and I'm really concerned about the risk of them getting infected. 這麼多人擠成一團做新冠病毒檢測，我很擔心他們會被感染。

5. humungous 極大的，巨大的

例：The discovery of life on Mars had a humungous impact on humanity. 火星上生命的發現對人類產生了極大的影響。

6. blisteringly 極熱、極冷等

例：This summer has been blisteringly hot and unbearably humid, leading to numerous heat-related deaths. 今年夏天極度炎熱，濕度極高，導致許多人因高溫喪生。

7. to elicit 激發，引發

例: Overall, she elicits positive energy, which draws people to her and makes everyone want to be close to her. 總的來說，她激發出正能量，吸引著大家靠近她。

再比如：The increasing number of cases involving the sudden disappearance of young people has elicited widespread concern in society. 越來越多關於年輕人突然失蹤的案件在社會上引發了廣泛的關注。

8. scarcely day, month, year without sb doing sth 幾乎 ...都做 ...

例：Scarcely a year goes by without men or women, young or old, dressed in colorful clothes, participating in this ceremony to celebrate their holiday. 幾乎每年都有男女老少穿著五顏六色的衣服，參加這個儀式來慶祝他們的節日。

9. on the cusp of 即將步入⋯、處在風口浪尖上

例：People born in the 60s may soon be on the cusp of retirement. 60 年代出生的人可能很快就要迎來退休年齡。

10. imminent 即將到來，迫在眉睫

例：More small earthquakes are occurring frequently, indicating that a bigger one is imminent. 小

地震頻繁發生表明大地震即將來臨。

11. on the horizon 即將到來

例：Humanity's move to other planets is on the horizon. 我們人類移居到其他行星的時代即將到來。

12. in the offing 即將來臨

例：With the deterioration of the pandemic, a global food shortage may be in the offing.隨著疫情的惡化，全球糧食短缺可能即將來臨。

13. outgoing 即將離任的

例：As the outgoing chairman of the board, he delivered a touching and impressive speech. 作為即將離任的董事會主席，他發表了非常令人感動和令人印象深刻的演講。

14. steep 急劇的，過高的

例：The war between Russia and Ukraine led to a steep increase in gas prices. 俄烏戰爭導致天然氣價格急劇上漲。

再比如：Buyers fear steep prices because their salaries are insufficient to afford them. 買家擔心過高的價格，因為他們的工資無法負擔。

除此之外，Steep 還有很多意思，比如：陡峭的，深度浸泡的等。

15. breakneck 極快的，非常危險的,飛快的等

例：Olivia got injured in a car accident, so I had to rush her to a nearby hospital at breakneck speed.奧莉維亞在一場車禍中受傷，所以我不得不以極快的速度將她送往附近的醫院。

16. amass 積累，積攢

例：Gabriel amassed a large collection of novels to read. 加布裡埃爾積累了大量的小說來閱讀。

17. serendipitously 僥倖地

例：Serendipitously, his daughter dodged the disaster that led to the murder of the entire family, as she happened to be at her uncle's house. 僥倖地是，他的女兒躲過了導致全家人被殺的災難，因為她恰好在她叔叔家。

18. to be embroiled in 捲入
例：The whole world is embroiled in the pandemic. 當前，整個世界捲入疫情。

19. to rile 激怒
例：In this civilized community, his coarse language riled me. I don't believe anyone could accept it.在這個文明的社會裡，他粗俗的語言確實激怒了我。我相信沒人能接受。

20. to stoke 激起
例：His rudeness stoked public outrage. 他的粗魯行為激起了公憤。

再比如：The excitement stoked by his enrollment at the University of Toronto led to his insomnia. 由於他被多倫多大學錄取而激起的興奮，導致了他的失眠。

21. to spur 激起（加速，促進，鼓勵等）
例：Her wrong decision spurred an outcry from the entire staff. 她錯誤的決定激起了全體員工的強烈反應。

22. dire 極其嚴重的
例：This summer, large swarms of locusts attacking the continent will worsen the already dire food shortage in many countries. 今年夏天，大量蝗蟲襲擊大陸，將加劇許多國家本已極其嚴重的糧食短缺。

23. intractable 棘手的
例：After the pandemic, we will face many intractable economic problems. 疫情過後，我們將面臨許多棘手的經濟問題。

24. ticklish 棘手的
例：Seniors, especially those without children, often feel lonely and helpless when faced with difficult issues that are hard to handle.老年人，尤其是沒有孩子的，面對難以處理的棘手問題時，常常感到孤獨和無助。

25. to tangle 糾纏，混亂
例：The regional conflicts almost resulted from how frequently they tangled with each other. 地區衝突幾乎是由於他們頻繁相互糾纏所導致的。

26. thorny issue 棘手的問題

例： Improving traffic in the city seems to be a thorny issue. 改善城市交通似乎是一個棘手的問題。

27. to let bygones be bygones 既往不咎

例:Due to their unique relationship, her boss will let bygones be bygones 由於他們獨特的關係，她的老闆會既往不咎。

28. wrenching 極為痛苦的

例： He went through a wrenching experience in losing overweight, he finally succeeded. 他的減肥經歷了極為痛苦過程，終於成功了。

29. mascot 吉祥物

例： The panda, a mascot of China and a living fossil, attracts tens of millions of people from around the world to visit it in zoos each year. 大熊貓是中國的吉祥物，也是一個活化石，每年吸引全球數千萬遊客到動物園參觀。

30. to be in sore need of 急需

例： During the board meeting, I told the investors that we would be in sore need of a significant amount of money for our marketing expansion.在董事會上，我告訴投資者，我們的市場擴展急需大量資金。

31. backlog 積壓的貨物，積壓的工作

例： This company is in despair due to a lack of funds and a backlog in its stock. 由於資金短缺和庫存積壓的貨物，這家公司陷入了困境。

32. consummate 技藝精湛的、卓越的

例： She is a consummate dancer, although very few people know her. 她是一位技藝精湛的舞者，儘管很少有人認識她。

再比如： Teresa Teng is the most consummate singer in Chinese history. I'm one of her biggest fans. I deeply feel sorrow and regret that she passed away so early, but she will forever live in the hearts of all her fans. 鄧麗君是中國歷史上最卓越的歌

手。我是她的超級粉絲。我深感遺憾和悲傷，她離世得太早，但她將永遠活在所有粉絲的心中。

33. to rack up 積攢，積累
例：In the past 20 years, Reese racked up a lot of money for her retirement. 在過去的 20 年裡，瑞茜為她的退休積攢了很多錢。

34. to make a big widening of 加大
例：Their marriage ended because the current situation significantly made a big widening of their differences in views on the world; unfortunately, this couple ultimately went in different directions. 他們的婚姻結束是因為當前的局勢加大了他們在世界觀上的分歧；不幸的是，這對夫妻最終走上了不同的道路。

35. spurious 假的，偽造的
例：
a) This businessman attempted to enter the country with a spurious passport; unfortunately, he was detained for further investigation. 這位商人試圖用假護照進入該國，不幸的是，他被拘留以供進一步調查。

b) The critic highlighted the spurious similarities between the two novels, arguing that one had plagiarized the other. 評論家指出了兩部小說之間偽造的相似之處，認為其中一部抄襲了另一部。

36. to shore up 加固，支持
例：To prevent flooding, all the people living along the coast are proactively participating in shoring up the riverbanks to face upcoming challenges. 為了防止洪水，所有沿海居民都在積極參與加固河堤，以應對未來的挑戰。

37. to compound sth 加劇，使加重，使惡化
例：The variants of the virus compounded the global spread and the difficulties in dealing with it. 病毒的變種加劇了全球傳播以及應對它的困難。
再比如：In my view, the entire world is compounding inflation by continually raising interest rates. That's insane. 在我看來，全

球通過提高利率，正在加劇通貨膨脹。

38. to fuel panic 加劇恐慌
例：An inexplicable rush to purchase can fuel panic, especially during a pandemic. 在疫情期間，一種莫名其妙的購買熱潮可能會加劇恐慌。

39. to speed up the tempo of 加快了 ...速度
例：Immigration Canada seems to be stepping up the application process, given the overwhelming backlog of cases. 由於案件積壓過多，加拿大移民局似乎正在加快申請流程。

40. fab 絕妙的，難以置信的
例：The skating championship performance is fab, which mesmerized me deeply.滑冰錦標賽真的絕妙，讓我著迷。

41. to tot up 加起來
例：I felt perplexed by the bill I paid, so I had to tot up each cost one by one. 我對帳單感到困惑，所以不得不把一項項地加起來。

42. to beef up 加強
例：The board beefed up the management to improve its flexibility and fairness in handling day-to-day issues. 董事會加強了管理，以提升其在處理日常事務時的靈活性和公平性。

43. to precipitate 加重、 加速（一般指不好的事）
例：Any stimulation could precipitate her depression, so her family members were deeply concerned about her condition, fearing that she might attempt suicide at any time or place. 任何刺激都可能加重她的抑鬱症，因此她的家人非常擔心她的狀況，害怕她隨時隨地都有可能自殺。

再比如：His disregard for the doctor's advice precipitated the rapid progression of his cancer 他無視醫生的建議，導致癌症病情加重。

44. to be sprinkled with 夾雜著
例：His speech is sprinkled with notes of sadness and

hopelessness 他的講話中夾雜著一絲悲傷與絕望。

45. impregnable 堅不可摧的，牢不可破的；不受影響的

例：Apple products, which continue to lead the industry, remain impregnable, no competitor has managed to surpass them. Their status is truly insurmountable. 蘋果產品依然在業內遙遙領先，堅不可摧，無人能夠超越。它的地位的確是不可逾越的。

46. to cling to 堅定

例: He is highly determined and insists on clinging to his own opinion so long as he believes it to be correct. 他非常堅定，只要認為是對的，他就會堅持自己的看法。

47. to spatter out 濺出來

例：The nurse pushed the needle into my left arm, and unfortunately, the blood spattered out instantly, causing intense pain. 護士將針頭插入我的左臂，不幸的是，血液瞬間濺了出來，導致劇烈的疼痛。

48. to bolster 堅定，激勵，增強

例：I was finally rewarded, which greatly bolstered my determination to see it through to the end. 我終於得到了回報，這極大地堅定了我堅持到底的決心。

49. unwavering 堅定不移的，不動搖的

例：My boss provided unwavering support for me to complete this task, and together, we achieved outstanding success. 我的老闆給予我堅定不移的支持，幫助我完成了這項任務，我們最終取得了傑出的成就。

50. staunchly 堅定地

例：I appreciate anyone who can staunchly stand by their beliefs or decisions 我欣賞任何能夠堅定信念或決策的人

51. to juggle 兼顧、魚和熊掌想兼得

例：From my perspective, juggling part-time work and part-time study is incredibly challenging. It baffles me how I can manage both, especially since I have to read 1,000 pages of textbooks daily. It's hard to imagine finding the time to work simultaneously. 在我看來，同時兼顧工作和學習是非常具有挑戰性的。尤其是我每天都需要閱讀 1000 頁的教材，這讓我感到困惑，真難以想像如何在同時進行這兩項工作。

52. terse 簡潔的
例：My new boss gave a terse speech, which saved a lot of time for the staff. 我的新老闆發表了簡潔的演講，這為員工節省了很多時間。

53. uphill 艱巨的, 艱難的
例：Completing an impossible task seems like an incredibly uphill battle.完成一項不可能的任務似乎是一場極其艱巨的戰鬥。

54. an arduous slog 艱巨的任務
例：Sending humans to Mars is an arduous slog, demanding immense time, effort, and resources. 把人類送上火星是一項艱巨而漫長的任務，需耗費巨大的時間、精力和資源。

55. Sisyphean 艱巨而徒勞的
例:Exploring the interior of the Sun is a Sisyphean task given our current technological capabilities. 以我們目前的技術水準，探索太陽內部無異于一項艱巨而徒勞的任務（西西弗式的任務）。

56. adamant 堅決的，固執的
例：He is adamant in rejecting this unequal treatment. 他堅決拒絕這種不平等的對待。

57. vitriolic 尖刻的
例：During the press conference, some journalists posed vitriolic questions, putting the speaker in an awkward position.在新聞發佈會上，一些記者提出了尖刻的問題，使發言人頗為尷尬。

58. vitriol 尖刻的言辭
例：The vitriol embedded in his speech hurt the public.他言語中隱藏的尖刻言辭傷害了公眾。

59. succinctly 簡明扼要地

例：When it's his turn to discuss the matter, he wraps it up succinctly, earning praise from his colleagues. 輪到他發言時，他簡明扼要地總結了要點，贏得了同事們的讚賞。

60. to allay 減輕

例：It is said that the disclosure of aliens living on the moon is being restricted to allay human fears on Earth, as global turmoil could erupt once the truth is known 據說，關於外星人居住在月球的消息被限制披露，是為了減輕地球上人類的恐懼，因為一旦真相公之于眾，全球可能會陷入混亂。

61. palliative 減輕痛苦的

例：Cancer patients hope to receive palliative care to ease their pain and improve their quality of life. 癌症病人希望得到減輕痛苦的治療。

62. gritty 堅韌不拔的

例：With her gritty persistence, she led the team and ultimately completed the development of a new medicine that effectively treats cancer 憑藉她堅韌不拔的毅力，她帶領團隊最終完成了一種能有效治療癌症的新藥的研發。

63. flinty 堅韌不拔的

例：He is a flinty individual, capable of overcoming any difficulty or adversity 他是一個堅韌不拔的人，可以克服任何困難和逆境。

64. tenacious 堅韌不拔的，頑強的

例：I truly admire her tenacious nature, which has deeply moved me emotionally. 我非常欽佩她堅韌不拔的性格，這深深地打動了我。

65. scathing 尖銳的，嚴厲的

例：Patrick was scathing in his remarks about the unfair treatment he received. 派翠克對自己受到的不公平待遇進行了尖銳的批評。

66. to dwindle 減少

例：The investment has dwindled as a result of the economic downturn. 由於經濟衰退，投資已大幅減少。

67. to curtail 減少，限制
例：Due to inflation and the depreciation of the national currency, the country was forced to curtail foreign exchange spending and step up efforts to boost exports in order to ease pressure on its foreign reserves. 由於該國通貨膨脹導致本幣貶值，外匯儲備承壓，他們不得不減少外匯支出，並努力擴大出口以獲取更多外匯收入。

68. to stomp on 踐踏
例：His performance stomped on the morality and credibility of that level, leaving a lasting negative impact. 他的表現踐踏了那個層次的道德和信譽，留下了持久的負面影響。

再比如：I admire her gritty determination in pursuing her studies in this field, and in the end, she achieved tremendous success. 我欽佩她在這個領域追求學術的堅韌精神，最終，她取得了巨大的成就。

69. to ride roughshod over 踐踏, 橫行霸道
例：The aggressors ignored international law and were reprimanded for riding roughshod over peace. 侵略者無視國際法，並因粗暴踐踏和平而受到譴責。

70. someone could scarcely believe 簡直不敢相信
例：I could scarcely believe that he made this decision because it was so absurd and humiliating. 我簡直不敢相信他做出這個決定，因為這太荒謬且令人羞辱。

71. to gin up 將…提升
例：A large amount of investment can gin up revenue and GDP by a significant percentage. 大量的投資可以大幅提升收入和 GDP。

72. to shed the cost 降低成本
例：This manufacturer tried to shed costs by using cheap materials, but it ended up losing both quality and credibility. To me, the trade-off simply wasn't worth it. 這家製造商試圖通過使用廉價材料來降低成本，但最終卻失去了品質和信譽。對我來說，這樣的權衡根本不值得。

73. to place a bet on 將賭注押在…上

例：I lost a lot of money in the stock market, and now I'm placing my final bet on this company in hopes of recovering my losses. 我在股市上虧了很多錢，現在我決定押上最後一注，寄希望於這家公司能幫我挽回損失。

74. fiddly 講究的, 繁瑣的

例：He had some fiddly habits and ways of speaking, yet his colleagues still admired him. 他有一些講究的行為和說話方式，但他的同事們仍然很欣賞他。

75. to hold someone in thrall 陶醉其中

例：His graceful gestures and artistic aura held the audience in thrall. 他優雅的動作和藝術氣質瞬間令觀陶醉其中。

76. stilted 僵硬的，呆板的

例：After the cosmetic surgery, her smile looks stilted, especially when she speaks and smiles at the same time. 整容後，她的笑容看起來僵硬，尤其是在她一邊說話一邊笑的時候。

77. to whisk 攪拌

例：Whisk the eggs first before frying. 在煎之前，你最好先把雞蛋攪勻。

78. dodgy 狡猾的，不可靠的

例：He gave the impression to others that he was a dodgy person. 他給別人留下了一種狡猾的印象。

79. devious 狡猾的，陰險的

例：He appears quite honest, but in truth, he's so devious that it astonishes many of his friends. 他看起來很誠實，但實際上非常狡猾，令許多朋友大吃一驚。

80. to swap 交流

例：People are actively swapping their stories on web chats, creating an emotional and touching atmosphere. 人們在網路聊天中積極地交流自己的故事，營造出一種感人至深的氛圍。

81. to thrash out 絞盡腦汁去做

例：Nowadays, scientists around the world are thrashing out the most effective medicines for the treatment of cancer and AIDS; unfortunately, to this day, there have been no significant breakthroughs.如今，世界各地的科學家們都在絞盡腦汁兒研發最有效的癌症和愛滋病治療藥物；遺憾的是，直到今天，仍未取得任何重大突破。

82. angst 焦慮，擔憂

例：I have been suffering from angst for a long time. I understand its seriousness, but I can't rid myself of it. 我一直在為焦慮所困擾，儘管我意識到其嚴重性，但卻無法擺脫。

83. to fray 焦慮

例：Delilah seems to be quite confident; however, the numerous errors in her question-and-answer responses during the test unexpectedly fray her composure.德萊拉看起來很自信，但在考試中的問答環節，她頻繁的錯誤意外地讓她的焦慮戰勝了鎮定。

84. to fork over 交錢

例：This driver violated the drunk-driving policy and was penalized by the police. He showed clear reluctance; otherwise, he would have been taken into custody. In the end, he preferred to fork over the money instead of being sent to prison.這名司機違反了酒駕政策，並被警方處罰。他表現出了明顯的抵觸情緒；否則，他會被拘留。最終，他寧願交錢受罰，而不是被送進監獄。

85. to hobnob 交談

例：They hadn't seen each other for quite a long time, so they got together and hobnobbed about their experiences over the past years.他們已經很久沒見面了，於是他們聚在一起，聊起了過去幾年的經歷。

86. fluke 僥倖

例：Joel rarely dedicated much time to his studies; however, unexpectedly, he passed the final exam, which was truly a fluke. 喬爾很少花時間專心學習，但出乎意料的是，他通過了期末考試，這簡直是一個僥倖的結果。

87. twitchy 焦躁不安的

例：Today is her debut on stage, performing in front of a sizable crowd, and she always feels a bit twitchy with anticipation before her big performance. 今天是她首次登臺演出，面對一大群觀眾，她總是會因期待而感到焦躁不安。

88. fretful 焦躁的

例：From my observation, single women over 35 tend to become more fretful and sensitive compared to married women. 根據我的觀察，35 歲以上的單身女性通常比已婚女性更容易焦躁和敏感。

89. high-grossing 叫座率高，高票房率

例:"Spider-Man" has become one of the highest-grossing movies of the year. 《蜘蛛俠》已成為今年票房收入最高的電影之一。

90. to cut loose 解雇

例：He was still cut loose, despite having worked at this company for almost 25 years. 儘管他在這家公司工作了將近 25 年，但他仍然被解雇了。

91. to sack 解雇

例：Due to his lackluster attitude towards his work, he was sacked. 由於他對工作的敷衍態度，他被解雇了。

92. to get hitched 結婚

例：The phenomenon of short-lived marriages after people get hitched has become increasingly prevalent among the younger generation. We must remain acutely aware of the far-reaching negative impacts this trend can have on our social and economic development. 越來越多的年輕人在結婚後婚姻持續時間較短，這一現象變得越來越普遍。我們必須高度警惕這一趨勢對社會和經濟發展的深遠負面影響。

93. skimpy 拮据的，不足的

例：Higher inflation and a reduction in my income have left my pocket tight, forcing me to survive on skimpy meals, cutting down from three a day to just one. 通貨膨脹加上收入減少讓我手頭拮据，只能靠少得可憐的一頓飯來維持生活，

從原本的一天三頓降到只吃一頓。

94. to iron out 解決，消除

例：The team leader tried to iron out any problems looming over the future of its development. 團隊領導試圖解決任何影響未來發展的潛在問題。

再比如：I tried to learn how to skillfully play the games to iron out the generation gap between my sons and me. 我努力學習如何熟練地玩遊戲，以消除我和兒子之間的代溝。

95. to eke out 竭力維持

例：In developing countries, people are trying to eke out a living by taking on two or three jobs and working longer hours each day. 在發展中國家，人們通過做兩三份工作並每天工作更長時間來竭力維持生計。

再比如：They tried to eke out their marriage before officially announcing their divorce. 他們在正式宣佈離婚之前，試圖勉力維持婚姻。

96. to construe 解釋

例：It is a very tough and absurd task to construe a concept that is both weird and murky. 要解釋一個既怪異又模糊的概念是一項非常艱難且荒謬的任務。

97. to shed light on 揭示，闡明

例：He sheds light on the awkwardness of the current situation by presenting ample evidence. 他通過提供充足的證據，揭示了當前情況的尷尬。

98. to wind up 結束

例：Due to the time limit, let's wind up our conversation and visit the site in person. 由於時間有限，我們就結束談話，親自去現場看看吧。

99. to wind down 結束(慢慢的）

例:He couldn't afford the higher rental fee during the pandemic, so he had to wind down his business within a week. 大流行病期間他負擔不起更高的租金，所以他不得不在一周內結束他的生意。

100. to snog 接吻擁抱

例：In pursuit of a Western lifestyle, many young people, including high school boys and girls, engage in public displays of affection, such as kissing. However, I don't think this aligns with traditional Chinese values. From a moral standpoint, I believe such behavior should not be encouraged. Even in the Western world, this phenomenon is not as widespread as some might think. Clearly, they have been misled. 為了追求西方生活方式，許多年輕人，甚至包括中學生，都會在公共場合接吻擁抱。然而，我認為這種行為不符合中國傳統的價值觀。從道德角度來看，不應提倡這種行為。即便在西方世界，這種現象也不是隨處可見的。顯然，我們的年輕人受到了誤導。

101. to husband 節約

例：Due to the emergency, the reserved food seems to be in short supply, so we must husband it carefully. 由於緊急情況，儲備的食物似乎不足，我們必須小心地節約使用它。

102. to swaddle 緊裹著

例：She was sitting on the couch, swaddled in a blue blanket, when her husband entered the room. She looked like she had caught a chill. 她坐在沙發上，用一條藍色的毯子緊裹著自己，當她丈夫走進房間時，她看起來像是著涼了。

103. afoot 進行中

例：The surgery was afoot, and his family members waited anxiously outside the door for the results. 手術正在進行中，他的家人焦急地在門外等待結果。

再比如：Changes are afoot in the world — and so is a shift in its pattern. 世界在變，格局也在變。

104. foray 進軍，涉足

例：Huawei's foray into the global market may spark widespread concern. 華為產品進軍全球市場可能會引發廣泛關注。

再比如：Many high-tech companies have morphed into

foraying into robot production.
許多高科技公司已逐步轉型
，開始涉足機器人製造領域
。

105. to be discreet in 謹慎
例：When getting along with your colleagues, you have to be discreet in how you speak to them, especially with the ladies. 與同事相處時，說話要謹慎，尤其是對女性同事。

106. to be chary of 謹慎，小心
例：Celebrities must be chary of their behavior and reputation, as any misstep could disappoint their fans. 名人必須謹慎對待自己的行為和聲譽，因為一旦出錯就可能讓粉絲失望。

107. prudent 謹慎的
例：As an employee, you must know how to be prudent in managing your relationship with your boss. 作為一名員工，你必須懂得如何謹慎地處理與上司的關係。

108. to proscribe 禁止
例：Stephen Hawking warned humanity and proscribed any communication with aliens, arguing that such contact could lead to catastrophic consequences—even the possible annihilation of mankind. 斯蒂芬·霍金警告人類，明令禁止與外星人進行任何交流，他認為這種接觸可能會導致災難性的後果，甚至人類的滅絕。

109. to clutch 緊抓住
例：She was watching a scary movie and, overwhelmed with fear, clutched the armrests of her seat. 她在看一部恐怖電影。她嚇得緊緊抓住座位的扶手。

再比如：He was on the brink of bankruptcy; however, a large sum of investment from a mysterious source might just be his clutching at straws. 他面臨破產的邊緣；然而，一筆來自神秘來源的大額投資或許只是他試圖抓住最後一根稻草。

110. infallible 絕對正確的
例：We are not saints, and no one is infallible. .我們不是聖人，孰能無過！

111. to rattle 驚慌失措

例：When hearing about the Ebola virus, people instantly rattle off concerns because it is difficult to prevent. 一聽到埃博拉病毒，人們就會驚慌失措，因為這種病毒很難預防。

再比如 Xavier was laid off recently, and the lack of income has rattled his entire family. 賽維爾最近被裁員了，失去了收入，整個家庭都變得驚慌失措。

112. pithy 精煉的，簡潔的

例：Hailey made a pithy speech during the meeting and received high praise from her boss and colleagues.
在會議上，海莉做了一個精練的演講，得到了老闆和同事的高度讚賞。

113. shrewd 精明的

例：This kid takes after his dad and is quite shrewd; he will likely be adept at doing business in the future. 這孩子跟他爸爸一樣精明。他會很善於做生意。

114. staggering 驚人的

例：During the pandemic, the pharmaceutical industry raked in staggering profits.
在疫情期間，製藥業獲得了驚人的利潤。

再比如：Climate change has led to staggering consequences, including global warming and a series of subsequent disasters.
氣候變化導致了驚人的後果，包括全球變暖以及一連串隨之而來的災難。

115. uncannily 驚人地，異乎尋常地

例：These two girls look uncannily alike, making it hard to tell them apart. I guess they must be twins. 這兩個女孩長得驚人地相似，很難分辨誰是誰。我猜她們一定是雙胞胎。

116. eyebrow-raising 驚人之舉的

例：He lifted nearly 1000kg over his head, leaving almost everyone at the scene stunned by his eyebrow-raising strength. 他舉起了將近 1000 公斤，幾乎讓在場的所有人都被他驚人之舉的力量震驚了。

117. schizophrenia. 精神分裂症

例：Hitler exhibited signs of schizophrenia,yes, he was a mad war criminal. 希特勒表現出精神分裂症的跡象。他是一個瘋狂的戰爭罪犯。

118. sprightly 精神矍鑠

例：Even at 90, she still looks sprightly, like a young lady. 即使

已經九十歲了，她看起來依然精神矍鑠，像個年輕女孩一樣。

119. to be wary of 警惕、留神 ...

例：We should teach our children to be wary of strangers. 我們應該教育孩子警惕陌生人。

再比如：You should be wary of the virus infection, which suggests that you still wear a mask. 你應該對病毒感染保持警惕，這意味著你仍然需要戴口罩。

120. to pout 撅嘴

例:She felt deeply aggrieved, pouting as tears started to well up in her eyes. Her elder son tried to comfort her. 她覺得很委屈，就撅著嘴哭了起來。 她的長子試圖安慰她。

121. to be proficient in 精通

例：Emily is proficient in several languages, including Spanish, English, French, Chinese, Japanese, and more. 艾米莉精通多種語言，包括西班牙語、英語、法語、中文、日語等。

122. to be versed in 精通

例：Leonardo is versed in many languages, including Spanish, Portuguese, Chinese, Russian, English, French, Japanese, German, and more. 萊昂納多精通多種語言，包括西班牙語、葡萄牙語、中文、俄語、英語、法語、日語、德語等。

123. to vie to 競相

例：Thanks to its superior quality, customers vie to buy it. 由於品質上乘，顧客們競相購買。

124. cherry-picking 精心挑選的

例：We exported all the cherry-picked fruits to other countries. 我們將所有精心挑選的水果出口到其他國家。

125. seasoned 經驗豐富的

例：As far as I know, almost all companies prefer seasoned employees to fill their openings. 據我所知，幾乎所有公司都更傾向于讓經驗豐富的員工來填補職位空缺。

126. hound 糾纏

例：This girl didn't love that guy, but she was often hounded by him. 這個女孩並不愛那個男孩，但她經常受到他的糾纏。

再比如：I was hounded by their complaints, leaving me confused all the time. 我被他們的抱怨纏擾，讓我一直感到困惑。

127. hand-wringing 絕望的

例：He decided to divorce her because he was absolutely hand-wringing, feeling overwhelmed and conflicted. 他決定和她離婚，因為他感到極度絕望，情緒複雜且矛盾。

128. to badger sb 糾纏某人,煩擾

例：My little dog is usually very mild and pleasant; however, yesterday she began to badger me repeatedly. I immediately realized something was wrong and that she needed my help.我的小狗通常非常溫順和友好；然而，昨天她開始一再地糾纏我。我立刻意識到她出問題了，需要我的說明。

再比如：Don't badger me with those trivial things. 別用那些瑣事糾纏我。

129. to clutch at straws 救命稻草

例：He was on the brink of bankruptcy; however, a large sum of investment from a mysterious source seemed to be his last desperate attempt. 他面臨破產的邊緣；然而，一筆來自神秘來源的大額投資似乎是他最後的絕望一搏。

130. be akin to 就像個…相當於

例：You are too naive; you are akin to a child. 你太天真了；你就像個孩子。

131. hulking 巨大笨重的

例：A robotic arm effortlessly lifts a hulking compressor weighing no less than 500,000 tons. It's a truly breathtaking sight. 一隻機器人手臂輕鬆地舉起一台巨大笨重的壓縮機，重量至少達到 50 萬噸。真是令人歎為觀止的場面。

132. whopping 巨大的

例：Through Bitcoin, he earned a whopping profit of up to $1 billion last year. 通過比特幣，他去年賺取了高達 10 億美元的巨額利潤。

133. immense 巨大的

例：Stepping foot on Mars by humans symbolized the tremendous advancement in technology and its strategically immense significance. 人類踏上火星象徵著科技的巨大進步，具有戰略意義，影響深遠。

134. prodigious 巨大的，驚人的

例：This man devoted his talent to the medical field and ultimately invented the most effective medication for treating cancer. He achieved a prodigious accomplishment and truly deserves to be regarded as a hero. 這位男子將自己的才華奉獻給了醫療領域，最終發明了最有效的抗癌藥物。他取得了巨大的成就，理應被視為一位英雄。

135. to condescend 居高臨下

例：I coached someone in learning how to drive and reached out to him multiple times afterward, but got no response. Eventually, I gently reminded him to check the messages I had sent. As expected, he came up with a series of excuses, but what truly upset me was that he thought I was condescending to him. I felt both aggrieved and astonished by such a distorted conclusion—especially after all the effort I had put into helping him, only to have my intentions so completely misunderstood. 我教過一個人學開車，曾多次聯繫他但都沒成功。於

是，我出於好意提醒他查看我發給他的消息。沒想到，他提出了很多藉口，而讓我真正生氣的是，他竟然覺得我好心提醒是在居高臨下對他。我感到很委屈，也很驚訝，因為我花了這麼多心思幫助他，結果他卻如此誤解了我的好意。

136. to muster 聚集
例：In China, it's typical for numerous seniors to muster in a park or square, engaging in singing and dancing activities that attract many onlookers who come to enjoy the lively spectacle.在中國，許多老年人常常聚集在公園內或廣場上，一起唱歌跳舞，吸引了許多人前來欣賞這一場熱鬧的景象。

137. to cluster 聚集, 群聚
例：All the experts clustered in Antarctic.所有專家都聚集在南極.

138. primly 拘謹的
例：Jaxson stood primly at the corner of the room, staring at the people inside. 傑克森拘謹地站在房間的角落裡，盯著裡面的人。

139. internment 拘留
例：Five flight crew members were placed under internment due to suspicions of drug smuggling. 五名機組成員因涉嫌販毒而被拘留。

140. to loom large 舉足輕重
例：Currently, the promotion of the three-child policy looms large in our country's long-term strategic planning. 目前，三胎政策的推廣在我國的長期戰略規劃中佔據著舉足輕重的地位。

141. to see little point in 覺得做 ...沒有意義
例：More and more young people see little point in pursuing further studies, as the prevailing mindset of relying on a wealthy and well-connected father—rather than personal effort—has completely upended their worldview. 越來越多的年輕人覺得繼續深造意義不大，因為如今流行的觀念是"拼爹"，而不是靠自己的努力，這種心態已經徹底顛覆了他們對世界的看法。

142. to elucidate (正式）解釋、 說明，闡明，

例：The insurance policy broker tries to elucidate all the terms of the contract to his client before finalizing the agreement. 這位元保險經紀人在簽署正式協定前，試圖向客戶解釋合同的所有條款。

K

1 to lodge 卡住

例：He accidentally tumbled over the cliff and became lodged among the trunks of trees, which ultimately saved his life. 他不小心從懸崖跌落，被卡在幾棵樹幹之間，這才最終撿回一條命。

2. to be off to a good start 開了一個好頭

例：His donation to the poor is off to a good start, encouraging the wealthy to follow suit. 他對貧困人群的捐助開了個好頭，激勵了其他富人紛紛效仿。

3. trailblaze 開拓

例：A trailblazing spirit is essential for the success of anything we pursue. 開拓精神對於我們想要取得的任何成功都是必不可少的。

4. to usher in 開創、迎來

例：Despite the economic downturn, we're still striving to usher in a new market to overcome the current difficult situation. 儘管經濟低迷，我們仍在努力開創新市場，以擺脫當前的困境。

再比如：Everyone has been locked down for almost three years since 2020 due to the rampant spread of the pandemic. Now, people eagerly look forward to ushering in a new era and the recovery of their normal lives. 自 2020 年以來，受疫情肆虐的影響，人們被封鎖了將近三年。如今，大家都熱切期盼迎來一個新時代，恢復正常的生活。

5. to frown upon 看不慣，不滿,不贊成

例：Due to the generation gap, seniors sometimes frown upon young people's behavior, such as playing video games all day or staying up late at night. 由於代溝的存在，長輩有時會對年輕人的一些行為看不慣，比如整天打遊戲或熬夜等。

6. to chop 砍掉（部門）

例：Due to the tight budget over the past few months, the government has had no choice but to chop a number of ambiguous departments and lay off employees as well. 由於過去幾個月預算緊張，政府不得不大刀闊斧地砍掉一些職責模糊的部門，同時還將裁員。

7. fervid 慷慨激昂的

例：His fervid presence has been indelibly imprinted in my mind. 他那慷慨激昂的氣息深深地烙印在我的腦海中。

8. to picket 抗議

例：A large number of Afghan people were picketing in front of the US embassy. 很多阿富汗人在駐美大使館前抗議。

9. hang-ups 困擾，麻煩

例：Her layoff has caused significant concern for her entire family, especially as she struggles with hang-ups that make it harder for her to pursue a better job. 她的被裁讓全家人都十分擔憂，尤其是因為她心裡有許多困擾與心理障礙，這讓她更難邁出找更好工作的那一步。

10. to flunk 考試不及格

例：Eveleigh flunked her math exam and felt very disappointed. 伊芙蕾的數學考試不及格，她感到非常失望。

11. to chasten 考驗，懲罰

例：God chastens you through the difficulties in your life, but in reality, you can benefit from them. 上帝通過你生活中的種種困難來考驗你，實際上，你可以從中獲益。

12. snarky 刻薄的，尖刻的

例：No matter how angry you are, it's crucial to refrain from making snarky remarks toward the other person, unless your intention is to irreparably damage the relationship. 無論你多麼生氣，都必須避免對對方說刻薄的話，除非你的目的是徹底破壞這段關係。

13. despicable 可鄙的，卑鄙的

例：Any behavior that involves speaking ill of someone behind their back is truly despicable. 任何在背後說別人壞話的行為都是非常可鄙的。

14. viable 可行的

例：The realization of our manned spacecraft mission to Mars is undoubtedly viable, as long as we are fully prepared. 只要我們做好充分準備，實現載人火星探測任務無疑是可行的。

15. to stint on 克扣

例:The government grants a large sum of money to the region affected by the disaster. Unfortunately, the local officials tried to stint on it and enrich themselves. 政府向遭受災難的地區撥款了大量資金，不幸的是，當地官員卻試圖克扣這些資金，自己謀取私利。

16. plastic 可塑性

例：Children are highly plastic and have great potential to be nurtured in areas like language learning, cognition, and more. 孩子們具有很強的可塑性，在語言學習、認知等方面具有巨大的潛力。

17. malleability 可塑性

例：The new generation of students displayed great malleability as they absorbed new information and adapted their understanding of the world. 新一代學生表現出了極強的可塑性，他們吸收新資訊並調整自己對世界的理解。

18. fungible 可替換的

例：This enterprise is looking for fungible raw materials to ensure the supply chain runs smoothly without interruption. Otherwise, it could seriously impact their production sustainability. 該企業正在尋找可替換的原材料，以確保供應鏈順暢運行，不受干擾。否則，這可能會嚴

重影響他們的生產可持續
性。

19. to hanker for 渴望
例： Despite his extensive
collection of luxury car models,
he continues to hanker for the
latest releases in the automotive
world. 儘管他擁有大量豪華
車模型，但他仍然渴望著汽
車界的最新發佈。

20. to aspire to 渴望得到
例： Undoubtedly, everyone
aspires to live better, wealthier,
and more comfortably, but we
often forget that we must work
hard to achieve it. 毫無疑問，
每個人都渴望過上更好、更
富裕、更舒適的生活，但我
們常常忘記，我們必須努力
工作才能實現這一目標。

21. risible 可笑的
例： The way she spoke to me
seemed risible, almost as if she
were joking. 她和我說話的方
式顯得很可笑，仿佛在開玩
笑一樣。

22. fishy 可疑的
例： His research seems pretty
fishy when it comes to the

veracity of its data. 就資料的真
實性而言，他的研究看起來
相當可疑

23. studiously 刻意地
例:The gentleman studiously
maintained his silence, skillfully
evading any inevitable trouble
that might come his way. 那位紳
士刻意地保持沉默，巧妙地
避開了可能降臨的麻煩。

24. discretionary 可自由支配
的
例:Many individuals are eager to
become bosses because it grants
them full control over
discretionary finances and
employment decisions, which can
bring numerous benefits.許多人
渴望成為老闆，因為這使他
們能夠完全掌控可自由支配
的財務和雇傭決策，從而帶
來許多好處。

25. importune 懇求
例： He importuned his mother
to allow him to join the battlefield,
eventually sacrificing his life for
his country. 他懇求母親帶他
上戰場，最終為國家獻出了
生命。

26. jitter 恐慌

例：The spread of the layout involving so many current employees caused unexpected jitters. 涉及眾多現有員工的佈局傳播引發了意想不到的恐慌。

27. to cow 恐嚇，威脅

例：We will not allow ourselves to be cowed by any nuclear threat. 我們絕不會因任何核威脅而被恐嚇住。

28. to rein in 控制，遏制

例：They failed to rein in the situation, and the wave of protest fluctuated and lingered. Everyone expressed deep concern about the prospect of launching a nuclear war. 他們未能控制局勢，抗議浪潮時起時伏，持續不斷。每個人都對爆發核戰爭表示深切關注。

29. spat 口角

例：Spats between these two colleagues could ruin their friendly relationship. 這兩個同事之間的爭吵會破壞他們的友好關係。

30. to skimp on 摳門兒，吝嗇

例：This guy always skimps on wooing the ladies, no wonder he's still single. 這個人總是對追求女士摳門兒，難怪他還是單身。

31. gripping 扣人心弦的

例：The author's latest book boasts a gripping plot that has enthralled readers worldwide, earning a devoted and sizable following. 這位元元作家的最新作品情節扣人心弦的，令全球讀者著迷，贏得了龐大而忠實的讀者群。

32. riveting 扣人心弦的，引人入勝的

例：His riveting speech captivated everyone present, leaving a lasting impression that many described as unforgettable. 他扣人心弦的演講吸引了在場的每一個人，並給他們留下了深刻的印象，許多人稱其為難以忘懷。

再比如：The plots of his novel are riveting, which has attracted a large number of readers and fans. 他的小說情節引人入

勝，吸引了眾多讀者和粉絲。

33. saliva, drool, slobber 口水
例：The delicious stewed steak made saliva pool in his mouth uncontrollably. 美味的燉牛排使他不自覺地流口水。
還比如：Ryker began to drool as he smelled the delicious food 萊克聞到了美味的食物，開始流口水。而 slobber 更強調情不自禁地流出口水，主要用於動物流口水，如果用在人身上大有侮之意。

34. tough love 酷愛
例：His blend of tough love and unwavering dedication to Chinese opera ultimately propelled him to the forefront, making him one of the most renowned opera actors in China. 他將酷愛與對中國戲曲的執著投入結合起來，最終使他躋身中國最著名的戲曲演員之列。

35. to flounder with (for) 苦苦掙扎
例：Many people in Africa are floundering in the face of severe food shortages. 非洲有許多人正因持續的糧食短缺而苦苦掙扎

36. a rueful smile 苦笑
例：He suffered a total loss in the stock market, and a rueful smile crept across his face. 他在股市中血本無歸，臉上浮現出一抹苦笑。

37. to overblow 誇大
例：During the interview, this young man overblew his abilities to demonstrate his eagerness for the job, but it ultimately backfired. 在面試中，這位年輕人為展示自己對工作的熱情，過度誇大了自己的能力，結果適得其反。

38. to overstate 誇大
例：I make a conscious effort to distance myself from people who tend to overstate their experience, background. 我儘量遠離那些喜歡誇大自己經歷或背景的人。

39. bombastic 誇誇其談的
例：No matter how bombastic his rhetoric is, no one will ultimately care about what he says.無論他如何誇誇其談，

本質上沒人會在乎他說什麼。

40. hyperbole 誇張
例：We are coerced into doing extra work without any remuneration, which might sound like hyperbole. 我們被迫做額外的工作卻沒有任何報酬，這聽起來很誇張。

41. to polish off 快速完成
例：I never recommend that ordinary people polish off their dinner in just a couple of minutes, as it will gradually damage their digestive system—except for soldiers. 我從不建議普通人快速把晚餐在幾分鐘內吃完，因為這會逐漸損害他們的消化系統—，但對於士兵來說除外。

42. leniency 寬容、寬大，仁慈
例：The minister believes that granting any leniency towards criminal behavior is tantamount to condoning the crime itself. 部長認為，對犯罪行為給予任何寬容等同於縱容犯罪本身。

43. magnanimous 寬宏大量的
例：To get along with others, we must adopt a magnanimous approach to everything. 要與他人相處好，我們必須在處理一切事務時採取寬宏大度的態度。

44. orgy 狂潮
例：If experts suggest eating onions, the market will be flooded with all kinds of onions, triggering an orgy of consumption 如果專家建議吃洋蔥，市場上就會湧現各種洋蔥，掀起一場搶購的狂潮。

45. fanatical 狂熱的
例：I am a fanatical fan of Michael Jackson. 我是一位狂熱的邁克爾·傑克遜粉絲。

46. cultish 狂熱的
例：He is a cultish gamer, dedicating his whole life to gaming. 他是一個狂熱的遊戲玩家，將一生都獻給了遊戲。

47. frenetic 狂熱的
例：Investment in real estate is a frenetic pursuit. Sooner or later, the buyers will face the bitter

consequences. 房地產投資是一種狂熱的行為。遲早，買家將面對痛苦的後果。

48. to dog someone 困擾某人

例：She lost her baby, and the sadness dogged her for the rest of her life. 她失去了她的孩子，悲傷困擾著她一生。

再比如：How to deal with others and get along with them has been dogging him for a long time. 如何與人友好相處，這個問題困擾了他很長時間。

49. swagger and hubris 狂妄自大

例：One can only make progress by avoiding swagger and hubris. 只有避免炫耀和傲慢，才能取得進步。

50. rout 潰敗

例：During the war, any soldiers who tried to quit or desert during a rout could be executed on the spot 在戰爭期間，任何在潰敗時試圖逃跑或擅自離開戰場的士兵都可能被當場處決

51. to poke around 窺探

例：Some people prefer to poke around other person's privacy. That's really weird. 有些人喜歡窺探別人的隱私，真的很奇怪。

52. to poke into 窺探，打聽

例：Don't poke into other people's privacy. 不要窺探別人的隱私。

53. strapping 魁梧的

例：Nowadays, a considerable number of young men are infatuated with an effeminate image, rather than the strong and strapping appearance traditionally associated with masculinity. 如今，相當多的年輕男性癡迷於女性化的形象，而不是傳統上與陽剛之氣聯繫在一起的強壯魁梧的外表。

54. to bedevil 困擾

例：As a mother, she knew all too well that her son's ignorance and stubbornness bedeviled her; she felt both puzzled and hopeless. 作為母親，她深知兒子的無知和固執困擾著她；她感到迷茫和無助。

再比如：The complex situation bedeviled me from making a wise judgment, leaving me feeling thoroughly puzzled. 複雜的局勢讓我無法做出明智的判斷，我感到十分困惑。

55. to keep a lid on 控制
例：The government is trying to roll out a new policy to keep a lid on the impending economic turmoil. 政府正在推出一項新政策，以控制即將到來的經濟動盪。

L

1. to elongate 拉長
例：The twilight elongated her shadow along the wall. Her beauty magnified everyone's imagination and illusions. 暮光拉長了她的影子沿著牆壁延展。她的美麗放大了每個人的想像與幻覺。

2. to trail 落後於
例：After the war, Iraq still trailed behind America, despite its efforts to recover its economy. 戰爭結束後，儘管伊拉克努力恢復經濟，它仍然落後於美國。

3. dowdy 邋遢
例：She looks quite modern, but unfortunately, a bit dowdy. 她看起來相當現代，但遺憾的是，卻看起來有些邋遢。

4. scruffy 邋遢，骯髒的
例：He was young and handsome, but many years later, when I saw him again, he had become scruffy, weak, and aged. 他曾年輕英俊，但多年後，當我再次見到他時，他變得邋遢、虛弱，且老了。

5. provenance 來源，出處
例：I was puzzled by this slang, so I decided to delve into its provenance. 我讓這個俚語給搞糊塗了，所以，我決定尋根求源。

6. sleazy 爛的，低級庸俗的
例：With the refinement of individuals' tastes, people can

distinguish and judge which movies are considered sleazy or lacking in sophistication. 個體口味的提升使人們能夠區分和評判哪些電影被認為是爛片兒或缺乏精緻感。

7. indolent 懶惰的

例：Nowadays, more and more private enterprises are refusing to nurture indolent employees, who may be swiftly dismissed as soon as their laziness is detected. 如今，越來越多的私營企業不再養懶人，一旦發現他們表現懶惰，可能會被立即解雇。

8. to squander 浪費

例：It is unbelievable that some young people squander money recklessly without feeling any guilt. That's truly insane 一些年輕人毫無愧疚感地肆意浪費金錢，真讓人難以置信。簡直瘋了。

9. to dissipate 浪費，揮霍

例：Earning money is not easy; I don't understand why you dissipated it. 掙錢不容易，我不明白你為什麼要浪費它。

10. to guzzle 狼吞虎嚥

例：Avoid guzzling your food; instead, it's better to take your time and savor it slowly. 避免狼吞虎嚥，最好慢慢享受食物，細細品味。

11. to squiggle 潦草寫 ...

例：I felt quite annoyed when I tried to decipher some of the doctors' squiggled prescriptions. 當我試圖解讀一些醫生潦草寫的處方時，我感到非常煩惱。

12. to harp on 嘮叨，喋喋不休

例：My mom often harps on my studies every day, which literally distracts me from focusing on my homework. 我媽媽每天總是嘮叨我的學習，結果真的讓我分心，無法集中精力做作業。

再比如："Stop harping on!" I shouted at my wife in frustration. Suddenly, a sharp silence filled the room. All I could hear was the sound of water dripping from the tap. "別再嘮叨了！"我沮喪地對妻子喊道。突然，屋子裡陷入了死一般的寂靜。唯

一能聽到的聲音是水龍頭裡水滴落的聲音。

13. to keep a firm grip on 牢牢抓住 ...
例：Only those who can keep a firm grip on opportunities can ultimately achieve success. 只有那些能夠保持牢牢把握機會的人，才能最終取得成功。

14. veteran 老手，經驗豐富的人
例：He is a seasoned veteran in love, yet he remains single. 他是一個戀愛老手；然而，卻仍然是單身。

15. to nag 嘮叨
例：My mom nagged me every day, but from my perspective, it was a sign of her concern for me. 我媽媽每天嘮叨我，我認為這是她關心我的表現。

16. nagging 嘮叨的
例：His constant nagging stirred up the entire community, leaving everyone feeling upset. 他的不斷嘮叨激起了整個社區的反感，大家都感到不悅。

17. upbeat 樂觀的，積極向上的
例：Jace is full of an upbeat mood, spreading positive energy to everyone around him. 傑斯充滿了樂觀的情緒，將正能量傳遞給周圍的每一個人。

18. to stoke up and out of joint 火上澆油，樂極生悲
例：I kindly remind you not to get involved in this case; otherwise, you risk stoking tensions and throwing things out of joint. 我善意地提醒你不要捲入這個案子，否則, 你會火上澆油，讓事情變得一團糟。

19. to tighten one's belt 勒緊褲腰帶
例：During the war, people had no choice but to tighten their belts in order to survive the tough times. 戰爭期間，人們別無選擇，只能勒緊褲腰帶度過艱難時光。

20. to extort 勒索，敲詐
例：His ex-wife attempted to extort a sum of money from him, but she failed. .他的前妻試圖

勒索他一筆錢，但最終未能得逞。

21. to be chuffed to 樂於接受，有喜出望外的感受。

例：I'm absolutely chuffed to be appointed as the chief executive of the region, as it gives me the opportunity to fully leverage my abilities in expanding the domestic market. 我樂於接受被任命為該地區的首席執行官，因為這讓我有機會充分發揮自己的能力，拓展國內市場。

22. hard-headed 冷靜的

例：When faced with difficulties, you must maintain a hardheaded sense of judgment to find a better way to resolve them. 當你陷入困境時，必須保持冷靜而理性的判斷，才能找到更好的解決辦法。

23. to pillage 掠奪

例：Many people believe that the true goal of launching the war against Iraq was to pillage the petroleum resources in the Middle East. 許多人認為，發動伊拉克戰爭的真正目的就是為了掠奪中東的石油資源。

24. cooling-off period 冷靜期

例：Purchasing a unit in a condo fortunately comes with a cooling-off period, even after signing the sales contract, which offers the buyer more leeway. 購買公寓單元幸運地享有冷靜期，即使已經簽署了購房合同，這也為買家提供了更多的迴旋餘地。

25. callousness 冷酷無情

例：As his wife, she fell into despair due to his callousness, which ultimately led to their divorce. 作為他的妻子，她對他的冷酷無情感到絕望，最終導致他們離婚。

26. notionally 理論上

例：Notionally the battery can last 20 hours in the lab test. However， in the real world, it only can endure 10 hours. 理論上，這種電池在實驗室測試中可以持續使用 20 小時。然而，在現實世界中，它只能持續 10 個小時。

再比如：Notionally, electric cars save a lot of money and produce ostensibly lower pollution. However, they emit even more pollution than conventional fossil fuel vehicles. 電動汽車表面上污染更低，理論上可以節省很多錢，但實際上它排放的污染比傳統的化石液體還要多。

27. off-the-chart 離譜，超標
例：What he described was off-the-chart. 他所描述的情況簡直離譜。

28. preposterously 離譜地，
例：With the worsening inflation, prices for everything are surging preposterously. 隨著通貨膨脹的加劇，所有東西的價格飆升得離譜。

29. to strive to 力求，努力做
例：Nevaeh strives to satisfy everyone; however, some remain insatiable, always reaching for more after getting a little. 內瓦赫力求讓每個人都滿意，然而，有些人仍然是貪得無厭的，總是在得到一點後就想要更多。

30. to tap 利用
例：Each year, we find that a lot of money has been wasted, so the key issue is to improve our management and tap into it more effectively. 每年，我們發現大量資金被浪費，因此關鍵問題在於改進管理，巧妙地利用這些資源。

31. to harness 利用
例：We still face challenges in effectively and efficiently harnessing nuclear power in safe. 我們在安全高效利用核電方面仍面臨挑戰。

32. to be cluttered with 亂七八糟地堆滿了 ...
例：I visited my cousin and found her desk cluttered with all sorts of fast food. I'm really concerned about her daily life. 我去看了我的表妹，發現她的桌子上亂七八糟地堆滿了各種速食。我對她的日常生活感到相當擔憂。

33. to prey on 利用
例：His colleagues prey on his kindness and naivety, which leads him to become disappointed and lose trust in

everyone psychologically. 他的同事們利用他的善良和天真，這使他感到失望，並在心理上失去了對任何人的信任。

34. coalesce 聯合，合併
例：During the Ukraine war, many European countries coalesced to impose sanctions on Russia.在烏克蘭戰爭期間，許多歐洲國家聯合對俄羅斯實施制裁。

35. in a row 連續
例：The stock price dropped sharply for three days in a row, and day traders lost a tremendous amount of money. 股票價格連續三天急劇下跌，短線交易者損失了大量的錢。

36. to slither 跟蹌走
例：He drank too much, so he slithered out of the room and toward me. 他喝得太多，於是跟蹌地從房間裡走出來，朝我走來。

37. verbose 囉嗦的
例：Caleb gave a speech that was absurd and overly verbose. Almost everyone found it boring and frustrating. 凱萊布發表了一篇又荒謬又囉嗦的演講。幾乎所有人都感到非常無聊和沮喪。

38. begrudge 吝嗇
例：Chinese parents wouldn't begrudge investing in their children's education, often spending a lot of money to give them the best opportunities. However, they reap little in return, as their children leave to enjoy their lives abroad and contribute to other countries. Do you think this is fair to those parents? 中國父母通常不會吝嗇在孩子教育上的投資，往往花費大量金錢為孩子提供最好的機會。然而，他們得到的回報卻很少，因為孩子們離開了他們，去國外享受生活並為其他國家做出貢獻。你認為這對這些父母公平嗎？

39. to cast a shadow over 令…蒙上陰影
例：The emotional distance between fathers and their sons will cast a shadow over the kids' future. 父親和兒子之間的隔

離令孩子們的未來蒙上陰影。

40. to underwhelm 令⋯失望
例：The way they handled my complaint about their service genuinely left me underwhelmed. 他們處理我對服務投訴的方式真令我感到失望。

41. limber 靈活的，彈性的
例：Nowadays, the quality of products has improved tremendously, and prices have become more flexible for a wide range of consumers 如今，產品品質大幅提升，價格對各類消費者來說變得更加靈活。

42. piecemeal 一點一滴的
例：I encourage our students to fully make use of their piecemeal efforts to complete their experiments 我鼓勵我們的學生充分利用他們一點一滴的努力來完成實驗。

43. to buckle someone 令某人精神崩潰
例：Her conspiracy with her lover buckled me; I ultimately realized that I had loved the wrong person. It seems too late now, and I am deeply disappointed in myself, even loathing myself.她與情人的陰謀令我精神崩潰；我最終意識到自己愛錯了人。如今，似乎已經太晚，我對自己深感失望，甚至厭惡自己。

44. cringe worthy 令人感到尷尬的
例：She used the wrong word to express her feelings, which seemed pretty cringe-worthy to the entire audience.她用了不恰當的詞語來表達她的感受，這令所有觀眾相當尷尬。

45. to flabbergast 令人目瞪口呆
例：He pretended to be a rich man. However, as I drove through the intersection, I saw him begging for money at the corner of the street, which completely flabbergasted me 他假裝是個富人。然而，當我開車穿過十字路口時，看到他在街角乞討，這令我目瞪口呆。

46. mind-boggling 令人難以置信的

例：The sheer amount of homework kids are given every day is mind-boggling, so the government took action to put an end to this intolerable phenomenon. 孩子們每天的作業量令人難以置信，因此政府採取了措施制止這一無法容忍的現象。

47. grating 令人惱火的

例：My ticket was unreasonably canceled without any prior notice, which is truly grating. 我的票在沒有事先通知我的情況下被莫名其妙地取消了，這真是令人惱火。

48. jaw-dropping 令人瞠目結舌的

例：A celebrity who suddenly became a monk left his fans in jaw-dropping astonishment 一位名人突然出家，讓他的粉絲們瞠目結舌。

49. obnoxious 令人討厭的

例：I felt hurt and reluctant to have dinner with many people, some of whom used their chopsticks to stir the food in the dishes. Their behavior was very obnoxious to me. I don't think it's hygienic, and it looks pretty disgusting. 我感到很不舒服，不願與許多人一起吃飯，其中有些人用筷子在菜裡亂翻，這種行為令人討厭。我認為這樣不衛生，而且看起來很噁心。

50. offensive 令人討厭的，無禮的

例：You'd better change your attitude and not be too offensive; then you'll be more welcome and respected. 你最好改變一下性格，別令人討厭，這樣你會更受歡迎和尊重。

51. wringer 令人心煩意亂

例：Being busy all day has really put me through the wringer. 整天忙得我心煩意亂。

52. heart-rending 令人心碎的

例：This boy's parents passed away, and he became an orphan. His heart-rending story left everyone stunned. Now, he has achieved tremendous success and earned his doctorate. 這個男孩的父母去世了，他成了孤兒。他那令人心碎的故事

讓每個人都感到震驚。現在，他取得了巨大的成就，獲得了博士學位。

53. to rummage 亂翻
例：I felt outraged that the customs officers often rummaged my luggage each time I entered that country.我感到憤怒的是，每次我進入那個國家時，海關人員都經常亂翻我的行李。

54. mawkish 令人作嘔的
例：His mawkish statement and behavior incited a backlash from the public. 他那過於令人作嘔的言論和行為引發了公眾的強烈反應。

55. sporadic 零星的
例：The increasing frequency of sporadic earthquakes indicates that a catastrophe is drawing near. 日益增多的零星地震表明災難即將來臨。

56. writ 傳票、令狀（一般指法院發佈的）
例：The court finally issued a writ ordering the suspect to stay away from the victim. 法院最終發佈了傳票，要求嫌疑人與受害人保持距離。

57. to trickle out 原意是滴出，但常常被用作資訊流出。還有常用在表示絡繹不絕、流出，進進出出
例：The company immediately cut off the electricity to prevent any data from trickling out. 公司立即切斷了電源，以防止任何資料流出。

再比如：At the border between China and Russia, thousands of people trickle in and out every day to conduct business. 在中國和俄羅斯的邊境，每天都有成千上萬的人進進出出做生意。

還有：She was so emotional that the tears in her eyes were welling up and almost trickled out 她太激動了，淚水在眼眶裡打轉，幾乎要流了出來。

58. to reel off 流利背出
例：At the tender age of 3, he managed to reel off 300 poems continuously, leaving everyone in the audience completely astonished. 他年僅三歲，就

流利背出了 300 首詩，令在場的每個人都驚訝不已。

59. to leave mark on 留下 …印象
例：The achievement of higher education left its mark on him, and Jose successfully established his own business after graduating from university. 高等教育的成就給他留下了印象，喬斯大學畢業後，成功地創辦了自己的企業。

60. to be shrouded 籠罩在 …
例：People worldwide are shrouded in fear due to the pandemic. 全球人民都籠罩在疫情的恐懼中。

61. loophole 漏洞
例：This company frequently updates its app software to fix many loopholes. 這家公司經常更新其應用軟體，以修補許多漏洞。

M

1. second-guessing 馬後炮，事後諸葛
例：Many people perceive this so-called help as second-guessing, and now it's too late to make amends. 許多人會把這種所謂的幫助當作馬後炮。彌補為時已晚。

2. to burrow through 埋頭苦幹
例：They burrowed through the arduous task with determination and ultimately achieved tremendous success. 他們埋頭苦幹，終於取得了巨大的成就。

3. insouciance 漫不經心
例：He responded with complete insouciance to what I was saying, which left me both puzzled and disappointed by his attitude. 他對我跟他說的話漫不經心，我對他的態度感到困惑和失望。

4. nonchalantly 漫不經心地，若無其事地、滿不在乎地
例：He was casually sorting through his belongings when he suddenly came across a precious gift from his late friend—a poignant reminder of their time together in the old days. He stood

there, lost in memory. 他漫不經心地整理著自己的物品時，突然發現了一件已故朋友送的珍貴禮物——那是他們昔日相聚時的動人回憶。他就那樣站著，陷入了回憶之中。

再比如：He saw two young men brawling, but he sat there nonchalantly, sipping his coffee and sinking into his own thoughts. 他看到兩個年輕人在打架，但他仍若無其事地坐著，喝著咖啡，沉浸在自己的思緒中。

還有：She tried to ask him when he could marry her, but unfortunately, he responded nonchalantly, " I am not ready. "她想問他什麼時候可以娶她，可惜他滿不在乎地說，"我還沒準備好"

5. tacitly 默默地，心照不宣地
例：Caleb tacitly loves Avery. 凱萊布默默地愛著艾弗裡。

6. savage 蠻橫的
例：Due to his savage attitude, his application was canceled for violating our rules. 由於他蠻橫的態度，他的申請因違反我們的規定而被取消。

7. to trundle around 慢慢前行
例：It's my first time visiting my friend's new house, and since I didn't know its location, I had to drive slowly, with my car trundling around as I checked the house numbers one by one. 這是我第一次去朋友的新房，因為我不知道它的位置，所以我只得慢慢前行，一邊繞著街區一棟棟地查看門牌號。

8. to amble 慢吞吞移動
例:She was frightened when she saw a crocodile ambling across the street and immediately started to shriek. 她看到一條鱷魚慢吞吞地穿過街道，嚇了一跳。她開始尖叫起來。

9. sprawling 慢慢膨脹、蔓延的，擴張的
例：Recently, some scientists discovered that our cosmos is sprawling and its rotation is accelerating. 最近，一些科學家發現我們的宇宙正在慢慢膨脹，並且其旋轉速度正在加快。

10. to have one's hands full 忙得不可開交
例：She owned a small restaurant in this quaint town. At times, she was overwhelmed, especially during dinner rush. 她在這個小鎮開了一家小餐館。有時，她忙得不可開交，尤其是在晚餐高峰時段。

11. hectic 忙碌的，繁忙的，忙亂的
例：After a crazily hectic week, I finally got a chance to relax at home and cook dinner for myself. 經歷了一周的忙碌，我終於有機會在家放鬆一下，自己做晚餐。

12. to make a fetish of 盲目崇拜
例：Nowadays, many people tend to make a fetish of statements from so-called experts. In reality, not all expert opinions make sense—some are even misleading or deceptive. 如今，許多人傾向于對所謂專家的言論盲目崇拜。實際上，並非所有專家的意見都有道理，有些甚至是誤導性的，甚至是欺騙性的。

13. to ruffle feathers 冒犯某些人
例：Almost everyone prefers to hear kind words; otherwise, it's easy to ruffle feathers and create tension. 幾乎所有人都喜歡聽好話，否則很容易冒犯他人，造成緊張氣氛。

14. to take the plunge 冒險
例：One of my friends lost nearly all his money in the stock market. However, his addiction to gambling led him to take the plunge and risk his down payment for a condo. As expected, he faced the same outcome and lost all of his remaining funds once again. 我的一個朋友在股市中幾乎失去了所有的錢。然而，他對賭博的上癮促使他冒險拿出購房首付去下注。正如預料的那樣，他再次遭遇相同的結果，失去了所有剩餘的資金。

15. ailing 每况愈下的
例：The company has been trying to survive the ailing and awkward situation. 公司一直在努力度過這個每況愈下且尷尬的局面。

16. oomph 魅力

例：His powerful singing performance carried real oomph, catching the attention of many women. 他那獨特的歌唱魅力吸引了許多女性的目光。

17. charisma 魅力，領導力

例：His personal charisma played a crucial role in helping him win the election. 他個人的魅力在贏得選舉中起到了關鍵作用。

18. to squirm 沒面子，不舒服、羞愧

例：Sometimes, someone's overly straightforward expression can make others squirm. 有時候，有些人過於直白的表達會讓別人感到沒面子。

再比如：I got great scores on all my quizzes and tests throughout the term, but I awkwardly failed the final exam — which really made me squirm, especially when I had to face my classmates afterward. 我整個學期的小測驗和考試成績都很好，但卻在期末考試中尷尬地掛了科——尤其是在面對同學時，我簡直感到沒面子。

19. to fall on deaf ears 沒人理睬，對 ...置若罔聞

例：The public calls to reduce tax fell on deaf ears.
公眾要求減稅的呼聲沒人理睬。

20. to impound 沒收

例：He tried to smuggle a Rolex watch, but it was unfortunately impounded by customs. 他試圖走私一塊勞力士手錶，不幸被海關沒收了

21. to rumble on 沒完沒了的

例：My parents' days-long quarrels rumbled on and, sadly, irked me. 我父母幾天來沒完沒了的爭吵讓我很苦惱。

22. interminable 沒完沒了的，無休無止的

例：Adrian gave an interminable speech that no one wanted to keep listening to, so many people left early. 阿德里安的發言沒完沒了，沒人願意繼續聽，結果很多人提前離場了。

再比如：I sat on the train, reflecting on everything I had experienced over the past couple of months. The rhythmic roar of the train lulled me to sleep. When I finally woke up, it felt as if time had frozen — the journey seemed interminable, as though the train would never stop. 我坐在火車上，回憶著過去幾個月裡經歷的一切。火車有節奏的轟鳴聲讓我慢慢睡著了。過了很久我醒來時，感覺時間仿佛靜止了，旅程仿佛無休無止，火車似乎永遠不會停下。

23. delectable 美味的

例：He prefers enjoying a delectable seafood dinner with his family.
他更喜歡和家人一起吃美味的海鮮晚餐。

24. to be devoid of 沒有

例：The ropy building stood empty and devoid of furniture, a stark reminder of its abandonment. 那座破舊的建築物空空蕩蕩的，沒有傢俱，成了其荒廢的沉痛象徵。

25. to hone sth. 磨練

例：Military training for children can hone their willpower and spirit. 孩子的軍訓可以磨練他們的意志和精神。

26. to be given no heads-up about 沒有事先通知

例：One of my friends was suddenly laid off and was given no heads-up about any it rom his boss. 我的一個朋友突然被解雇，老闆沒有事先通知他。

27. to be not oblivious to 沒有忘記

例：During World War II, she lost her husband and all three of her children; to this day, she is not oblivious to the pain. 在二戰期間，她失去了丈夫和三個孩子；直到今天，她仍沒有忘記那份痛苦。

28. muggy 悶熱的

例：It feels really muggy today—I can't stand it. 今天看起來很悶熱，我受不了。

29. to lambast 猛烈抨擊

例：Her abusive behavior toward her mother was lambasted by the public. As a daughter, she became the focus of media attention. 她虐待母親的行為遭到了公眾的猛烈抨擊。作為女兒的她，成了媒體關注的焦點。

30. coveted 夢魅以求的
例：Finding true love is often difficult, and the hope of marrying someone you truly love,who loves you just as deeply in return, can feel like an elusive, coveted dream. 尋找真愛往往很困難，而嫁給一個你真心愛、也同樣深愛你的人，這種希望仿佛如同夢魅以求的的美夢。

31. to hurl 猛甩、猛扔
例：His boss was so furious that he hurled the report at her face, looking absolutely unhinged. 他的老闆怒不可遏，把報告猛甩到她臉上，看起來簡直瘋了。

32. to stash 囤積
例：Someone suggested that stashing gold might be the best way to counter currency devaluation. Is that really true? 有人認為囤積黃金可能是抵禦貨幣貶值的最有效方式。這是真的嗎？

33. labyrinthine 迷宮般的
例：I felt completely lost while wandering through the streets of Tianjin, which resembled a labyrinth.我在天津的街頭徘徊時感到完全迷失了方向，那些街道仿佛迷宮般。

再比如：The client found the architecture designed by this company to be labyrinthine—overly complicated and unreasonably demanding. 客戶覺得這家公司設計的建築迷宮，如此複雜和不合理。

34. to bridge the rift 彌合
例：After the war between the two countries, with the strengthening of their economies, they sought to bridge the rift in their relationship. 在兩國戰爭結束後，隨著經濟的增強，它們試圖彌合彼此之間的裂痕。

35. clandestine 秘密的
例：This company rolled out a clandestine product aimed at preventing glass from breaking.

這家公司推出了一款秘密的產品，旨在防止玻璃破裂。

36. inextricably 密切地,不可分開地

例: Cancer is inextricably linked to the food we eat, underscoring the importance of consuming healthy and organic foods to help prevent its development. 癌症與我們食用的食物密切相關，這強調了食用健康和有機食品有助於預防癌症的發生。

37. to disorientate 迷路

例：I noticed that many women tend to become disoriented and struggle to distinguish "left" from "right." 我注意到很多女性都容易迷路，不能清楚地分辨"左"和"右"。

38. egregious 彌天的，最惡劣的

例：He told an egregious lie to cover up his ugly conspiracy. 他撒了個彌天大謊來掩蓋他那醜惡的陰謀。

39. to enthrall 迷住

例：All varieties of snacks enthrall tourists around the world. 各種各樣的小吃迷住了世界各地的遊客。

40. to face a stern test 面臨著嚴峻的考驗

例：Humanity is facing a stern test from the threat of the pandemic. 人類正面臨著疫情威脅的嚴峻考驗。

41. to obliterate 抹去

例：Much like happiness, pain is incredibly hard to obliterate from people's memories.就像幸福一樣，痛苦也很難從人們的記憶中抹去。

42. to scrape 勉強做…

例：Despite my poor math skills, I managed to scrape through my statistics exam.
儘管我的數學很差，我還是勉強通過了統計學考試。

再比如：Despite still struggling in poverty, his parents scraped together enough money for his tuition fees. 他的父母雖然仍在貧困中掙扎，但還是勉強湊足了他的學費。

43. to make do with 勉強應付
例：He pretends to be very busy handling everything to make do with his boss's maximum demands. 他假裝非常忙碌，處理一切事務，以勉強應付他老闆的最大需求

44. impunity 免受懲罰
例：No laws in this world allow anyone to kill with impunity. 世界上沒有任何法律允許濫殺無辜而免受懲罰。

45. coyly 靦腆地
例：She met a boy who left a good impression on her. She smiled coyly at him, wanting to discuss something with him. 她遇到了一個給她留下好印象的男孩。 她靦腆地沖他笑了笑，想和他談談。

46. to flout 藐視
例：He flouted the court's orders and was sentenced to an additional three years in prison. 他藐視法院的命令，被判再加三年監禁。

47. to sip 抿了（一小口酒或其它液體之類的飲料）

例：This manager has some health issues, so he can't drink much; he only sips a little wine to show politeness to his clients. 這位經理有一些健康問題，所以他不能多喝酒，只能輕輕地抿一點酒，以表示對客戶的禮貌。

48. veritable 名副其實的
例：Audrey Hepburn is a well-known and veritable beauty in the acting world. 奧黛麗·赫本是一位名副其實的美女演員。

49. to be etched into 銘刻在…
例：Loyalty is etched deeply into her soul and spirit. 忠誠已經銘刻在她的靈魂和精神中。

50. insouciant 漠不關心的, 漫不經心的
例：I must say, I really dislike your insouciant attitude toward seniors. After all, they could be your grandparents or even your own parents—the very people who raised you. Everyone should remember: nothing in life should ever be taken for granted. 我實在不喜歡你對長輩那種漠不關心的態度。畢竟，他們可

能是你的祖父母，甚至是養育你長大的父母。每個人都應銘記於心：世上沒有什麼是理所當然的。

51. to mimic 模仿

例：Robots have started to mimic human behavior, raising serious concerns among people about the possibility of being replaced in the future. 機器人開始模仿人類行為，因此人們對未來可能被取代感到強烈擔憂。

52. to ape 模仿

例：Children aged six to eight tend to ape their parents' behavior, so it's important for parents to set a good example. 六到八歲的孩子喜歡模仿父母的行為，因此父母必須以身作則。

53. to emulate 模仿

例：As parents, we must set good examples for our children, since they tend to emulate our behavior and attitudes toward others. Otherwise, when they are blamed, we too will be humiliated. 作為父母，我們必須為孩子樹立良好榜樣，因為他們往往會模仿我們對他人的行為和態度。否則，當他們受到指責時，我們也會感到羞辱。

54. to impersonate 模仿

例：He has a unique talent for impersonating the voices and mannerisms of various celebrities, which always adds a touch of humor and joy. 他有一種特殊的天賦，能模仿各種名人的聲音和舉止，總能帶來一些幽默與歡樂。

再比如：His remarkable ability to impersonate a wide range of characters has consistently earned him numerous opportunities from directors. 他出色的模仿各類角色的能力，始終為他贏得了眾多導演的青睞與機會。

55. to discredit 抹黑

例：Her competitors are attempting to discredit her by collecting evidence, and now she is determined to fight back. 她的競爭對手正在通過收集證據來抹黑她，而她現在也決心反擊。

56. fuzzy 模糊不清的, 毛茸茸的

例：I find the prescriptions doctors scribble down are so fuzzy, I wonder who could possibly read them. 我發現醫生寫的處方非常模糊不清，我真不知道誰能讀得懂。

再比如：I have no idea what you're talking about because we're on the phone, and your voice became fuzzy. 我完全聽不懂你在說什麼，因為我們在電話裡，你的聲音變得很模糊不清。

還比如：I touched the towel and felt fuzzy. 我摸了摸毛巾，覺得毛茸茸的。

57. to grope around 摸索（多指暗中摸索）

例：The power suddenly went out, so my grandma groped around in the darkness, trying to find a candle. 突然停電了，我奶奶在黑暗中摸索著，試圖找到一根蠟燭。

58. chummy 密切

例：Please always keep in mind that, as an employee working in a company, you should avoid being too chummy with your colleagues and bosses; otherwise, you risk being bullied, having your personal information disclosed, or even getting fired. 請始終記住，作為公司員工，你應該避免與同事和老闆的關係過於密切，否則你可能面臨被欺負、個人資訊被洩露，甚至被解雇的風險。

N

1. to stake 拿..... 冒險

例：Jerry wouldn't want to stake his life on it. 傑瑞不願拿自己的生命冒險。

2. to stump up 拿出

例：Many young people in China are unable to get married because they can't stump up enough dowry, and their incomes are too meager. 中國的許多年輕人無法結婚，因為他們拿

不出足夠的嫁妝，而且收入也太微薄。

再比如：Everyone in this office stumped up $2 for a lottery ticket, and luckily, they unexpectedly won $20 million. 這個辦公室的每個人都拿出 2 美元買了一張彩票，幸運的是，他們意外地贏得了 2000 萬美元。

3. to scowl at sb 怒視某人
例：His father scowled at her, bitterness evident on his face. She had once been his cherished gem, but now her behavior left him feeling desperate. Finally, he forced out the words: "Get out of my sight." 他的父親對她怒目而視，臉上滿是憤怒。她曾經是他手心裡的珍珠，但現在，她的行為讓他感到絕望。最終，他艱難地擠出幾個字：「滾出我的視線。」

4. unpalatable 難吃的
例：This fast food is literally unpalatable; it's too salty. 這種速食真的很難吃，太鹹了。

5. sticky 難堪的，棘手的
例：When my mom and my wife started quarreling, I felt caught in a sticky situation between them. I often tried to avoid getting involved and quickly found excuses to run away. 當我媽媽和我妻子開始爭吵時，我感到自己夾在她們之間，處境十分難堪。我常試圖避免捲入其中，並迅速找藉口逃避。

6. conundrum 難題
例：How to fly at superlight speed remains a conundrum that has puzzled scientists around the world. 如何以超光速飛行仍然是一個難題，令全世界的科學家困惑不已。

再比如：How to build a usable quantum computer is still a conundrum for scientists. 如何打造一台可用的量子電腦，仍然是令科學家們頭疼的難題。

7. impenetrable 難以理解的
例：I'm perplexed by his impenetrable explanation and justification for his behavior. 他對自己行為的解釋和辯解過於難以理解，讓我感到十分困惑。

8. haunting 難以忘懷的，縈繞心頭的

例：Even though we've been apart for many years, her haunting smile still lingers in my mind.儘管我們分別多年，她那令人難以忘懷的微笑依然在我腦海中揮之不去。

9. inconceivable 難以想像的，不可思議的

例：In ancient China, a man could marry multiple women, sometimes even several at once. However, in today's China, such a phenomenon is inconceivable. 在古代中國，一個男人可以娶幾個甚至更多的女人，但在今天的中國，這種現像是難以想像的。

10. implausible 難以置信的

例：He exhibited an implausible behavior that left everyone at the scene stunned. 他做出了一個令人難以置信的舉動，讓在場的人都目瞪口呆。

11. to stick 難住（這個詞的中文意思很多，具體可以參閱詞典）

例："You really stuck me with this question. Let me figure out how to deal with it.你這問題真把我難住了，讓我想想怎麼應對。

12. to fall out with 鬧掰了

例：He quarreled and fell out with his colleague, even though they had worked together for nearly 30 years. 儘管他們已經共事將近三十年，他還是和同事吵了一架，鬧掰了。

13. tetchily 惱火地

例：I was just joking with him, but unfortunately, he reacted tetchily.我只是跟他開了個玩笑，沒想到他的反應很惱火。

14. farcical 鬧劇的

例：His joke went too far and became farcical. .他的玩笑開得太過火了，變成了鬧劇。

15. to reel 內卷，踉蹌；倒退；感到震驚，心煩意亂

例：The status quo among universities around the world is reeling under the pressure of fierce competition. 世界各地大學之間的現狀正因激烈的競爭而內卷。

16. velvet glove 內柔外剛
例：Due to his somewhat frail appearance, many people underestimated him. However, in reality, he was the velvet-glove type—gentle on the surface but firm in essence. 由於他外表顯得有些脆弱，許多人誤解了他。然而，實際上，他是一個"內柔外剛"型的人。

17. intrinsic 內在的
例：She naturally emanates an intrinsic charm that undeniably draws the attention of many young entrepreneurs. 她散發出的內在氣質，無疑吸引了那麼多年輕的創業者。

18. ropy 粘稠的 ,破舊的
例：You can cook the congee a bit longer to make it more ropy. 你可以多煮一會兒粥，這樣會更黏稠。

19. to boil over into 釀成，演變成
例：The regional conflicts eventually boiled over into a full-scale war, utterly destroying the civilians' normal lives. Houses and apartments were reduced to ashes, and tragically, people were left homeless and plunged into starvation. 該地區接連不斷的衝突最終釀成全面戰爭，徹底摧毀了平民的正常生活。房屋和公寓被夷為平地、燒得精光。可憐的人們無家可歸，陷入了饑餓之中。

20. to exact a toll 釀成代價
例：Her negligence exacted a heavy toll, causing the company to lose $100 billion. 她的疏忽釀成了沉重的代價，使公司損失了一千億美元。

21. to forge 捏造
例: I was slandered by someone who forged "facts." I would prefer the escalation of your investigation to prove my innocence. 我被某人誹謗，他們捏造了"事實"。我更希望你們的調查能夠進一步展開，以證明我的清白。

再比如：This professor was involved in fudging the essay writings, which is a scandal for this prestigious university. 這位教授參與了篡改論文寫作的行為，這對於這所著名大學來說是一個醜聞。

22. to fudge 捏造，敷衍

例：One of our partners fudged a speech to cover up his conspiracy. 我們的一個合作夥伴捏造了演講內容，以掩蓋他的陰謀。

23. to tussle 扭打

例：He got injured while tussling with the people who bullied him. 他在和那些欺負他的人扭打時受了傷。

24. nexus 紐帶

例：Singapore is a nexus for exchanging culture and high technology with the outside world. 新加坡成為與外界交流文化和高科技的紐帶。

25. to warp 扭曲

例：I realized that he completely warped my point and misled people into thinking that I intentionally wanted to spoil their good relationship. 我知道他完全扭曲了我的觀點，誤導人們認為我故意想破壞他們的良好關係。

26. travesty 扭曲，侮辱

例：a}The unfair trial was a travesty of justice, as the innocent defendant was wrongfully convicted based on fabricated evidence. 這場不公正的審判是對正義的扭曲，因為無辜的被告根據偽造的證據被錯誤定罪了。

b) The decision to cancel the highly anticipated concert at the last minute was a travesty for the disappointed fans who had been eagerly waiting for months. 在最後一刻取消備受期待的音樂會的決定對於已經熱切等待數月的失望歌迷來說是一種侮辱。

27. to twist sth into 把…扭曲成…

例：The pandemic twisted the global situation into one that is less efficient and less free. 疫情將全球形勢扭曲成一種效率較低、自由較少的狀態。　。

28. to buck the trend 扭轉而上

例：The currency conversion rate from the US dollar to the Canadian dollar seems stronger. The Canadian dollar had been relatively weak, but with the economic recovery and the surging employment rate in Canada, it has bucked the trend.

美元兌加元的匯率似乎較
強，加元曾相對較弱，但隨
著加拿大經濟復蘇和就業率
上升，加元逆勢而上。

29. to turn the ride 扭轉局面

例：The recently invented effective medicine for Omicron has turned the tide in the fight against the spread of Covid-19. 最近為奧密克戎研發的有效藥物已經扭轉了抗擊新冠病毒傳播的局勢。

30. livid 怒不可遏的

例：He became livid upon discovering that his son had been bullied at school. 他得知兒子在學校被欺負後怒不可遏。

31.effeminate 娘炮、女人氣的，娘娘腔的，

例：We need to educate young boys to avoid becoming effeminate and instead encourage them to grow into genuine men 我們必須教育小男孩避免成為娘炮，而是鼓勵他們成長為真正的男人 。

P

1. pomp 排場，盛況

例：I loathe the pomp of wedding ceremonies. Instead, simplicity makes me feel more at ease 我討厭婚禮擺排場。相反，簡單會讓我感到舒適。

2. to flush out 排除

例：To accomplish this task, we must flush out a lot of barriers along the way. 要完成這項任務，我們必須排除路上的許多障礙。

3. to parry over 排除

例：The inspectors parried through a lot of information mixed with key clues in order to uncover the evidence. 為了找到證據，檢查員排除了許多混雜著關鍵線索的資訊。

4. loiter 徘徊

例：He lost his job and felt deeply sad and disappointed. On a sunny day, he loitered through the streets, trying to find some solace in the beautiful weather. 他失去了工作，感到非常悲

傷和失望。在一個陽光明媚的日子裡，他徘徊在街頭，試圖從美麗的天氣中尋求一絲慰藉

5. to ostracize 排擠

例：The boss often ostracized the lovely lady, so she decided to quit 老闆經常排擠這位可愛的女士，於是她決定辭職。

6. to shunt 排擠

例：I was hired by that company, but I felt shunted aside and spent the whole day there with nothing to do. It was literally boring. 我被那家公司錄用了，但我覺得自己被排擠了，整天呆在那裡無所事事。真的很無聊。

7. sycophancy 拍馬屁

例：I loathe someone's sycophancy, especially when you became rich.我討厭別人拍馬屁，尤其是當你變得富有的時候。

8. to curry favour with 拍馬屁，巴結

例：He tried to curry favor with his boss, but unfortunately, he was laid off in the end. 他試圖拍他老闆的馬屁。不幸的是，但最終還是被裁了。

9. adulatory 拍馬屁的，諂媚的

例：I loathe people who are excessively adulatory toward their leaders "我厭惡 那些整天拍領導馬屁的人 。

再比如：He tends to use adulatory words when speaking to his boss. 他喜歡給老闆拍馬屁。

10. chubby 胖乎乎的

例：This chubby little boy was so adorable that almost everyone loved him during our trip. 這個胖乎乎的小男孩非常可愛，旅途中幾乎所有人都喜歡他。

11. to hobble 蹣跚

例：In my memory, he was handsome and full of energy. But when I saw him again, I could hardly believe he had become so weak and hobbled.
在我的記憶中，他曾經英俊又充滿活力。但當我再次見到他時，我簡直不敢相信他已經變得如此虛弱，步履蹣跚。

12. Ponzi scheme 龐氏騙局

例：My brother realized he had fallen into a Ponzi scheme and now faces the possibility of losing his entire investment.我哥哥發現自己陷入了一個龐氏騙局，現在可能面臨血本無歸的風險。

13. to scoot about 跑來跑去

例：The kids are dancing to celebrate their birthdays, with dogs and chickens scooting about, filling the place with happiness. 孩子們跳舞慶祝他們的生日，狗和雞跑來跑去,充滿了幸福的氛圍。

14. froth 泡沫

例：When you notice froth on the surface of your urine, you should be highly alert to potential kidney issues. 當你發現你的尿液表面有泡沫時，你應高度警惕你的腎臟問題。

15. to jettison 拋棄，擺脫

例：Bennett decided to jettison the distractions and interruptions from the outside world to focus entirely on his invention 班內特決定拋棄外界的干擾和打擾，專心致力於他的發明

16. to fizzle out 泡湯了，失敗

例：My wife suddenly fell ill, so our trip to Europe fizzled out. .我妻子突然病了，所以我們的歐洲之行泡湯了。

再比如:The municipal governor tried to beef up the revival of local real estate development. Unfortunately, his efforts fizzled out 市長曾試圖重振當地房地產的發展，不幸的是，他的努力以失敗告終。

17. to lob 拋向

例：He was so excited that he lobbed the admission notice into the air upon learning that the top-tier universities had accepted him 他興奮得將錄取通知拋向空中，得知自己被頂尖大學錄取時，激動不已。

18. to groom 培養

例：Parents should groom their kids to learn essential skills early, such as cooking, washing clothes, and repairing small electrical gadgets, so they are better prepared to face challenges in the future. 父母應儘早培養孩子學習一些基本技能，如做飯、洗衣服和修

理小型電器等，以便他們能更好地應對未來生活中的挑戰。

19. to belch out 噴發
例：It is magnificent to witness a volcano belching out dramatic lava in person. 親眼目睹火山噴發出熾熱岩漿的景象，真是壯觀無比。

20. flak 抨擊
例：The local government received a lot of flak for advocating higher taxes, which affected millions of businesses and consumers. 地方政府因主張提高稅收而遭到大量抨擊，這一舉措影響了數百萬家企業和消費者。

21. to flutter 砰砰亂跳
例：Their hearts will flutter when they meet their loved ones, whether they're boys or girls. 無論是男孩還是女孩，在見到自己所愛的人時，心中都會砰砰亂跳。

22. to plop 撲通一聲扔到…落下
例：My wife was carrying a bunch of books that looked so heavy she could barely stand, so she plopped them down on the ground. 我妻子抱著一大堆書，沉得她幾乎站不住腳，只好撲通一聲把它們放到了地上。

23. pet 偏愛的
例：Basketball is a pet sport activity for his brother. 籃球是他哥哥偏愛的運動項目。

24. lopsided 片面的
例：I never encourage my son to read this author's books because they're inundated with lopsided opinions. 我從不鼓勵我兒子讀這位作家的書，因為書裡充斥著片面的觀點。

25. chunky 偏胖的，臃腫的
例：I need to find a better way to lose weight because I feel really anxious about my chunky body. 我得找個更好的方法減肥，因為我對自己胖胖的身體感到很焦慮。

26. far-flung 偏遠的
例：My grandpa prefers to live in a far-flung region because he enjoys the fresh air and organic food. 我爺爺喜歡住在偏遠地

區，因為他享受新鮮空氣和有機食品。

27. quackery 騙子的行為 例：I think any promotion that boasts or exaggerates the functions, features, or benefits of medications is likely to be quackery. 我認為任何吹噓或誇大藥物的功能、特點或好處的宣傳大多都是騙子的行為。

28. plagiarize 剽竊　另外還有一個非正式用詞 crib
例：The academic committee discovered that he had plagiarized extensively from other authors in his essay, so they decided to revoke his doctorate degree. 學術委員會發現他在自己的論文中剽竊了許多其他作者的文章，所以決定取消授予他的博士學位。

29. virtuous 品德好的
例：A virtuous person is welcomed wherever they go. But the same can't be said for everyone no matter how talented or capable you are, without virtue, you won't earn respect or be entrusted with important responsibilities. 一個品德好的人，無論走到哪裡都會受到歡迎。但並非人人如此——無論你有多麼聰明或有能力，如果缺乏品德，就得不到尊重，也不會被賦予重任。

30. penury 貧困
例：His brother fell into a state of severe penury, struggling with dire financial circumstances, all due to the loss of his savings in the stock market. 他哥哥陷入了極度貧困的境地，身陷困頓的經濟狀況，這一切都源於他在股市中失去了所有的積蓄。

31. underwhelming 平淡無奇，有點平庸，未留下深刻印象
例：These rhetorics, however, are somewhat underwhelming. 然而，這些言辭有些平淡無奇。

32. bland 平淡無味的
例：I watched a documentary recently and found its content to be bland, filled with boring material rather than any insightful takeaways. 我最近看了一部紀錄片，發現它的內容平淡

無味，充斥著無聊的東西，而沒有任何啟發性的收穫。

再比如： You should eat more bland staples if you want to live longer. Consuming too much red meat may increase the risk of cancer. Instead, organic fish and chicken are better for your health. 如果你想活得更長久，最好多吃一些平淡無味的主食。攝入過多紅肉可能增加患癌症的風險。相比之下，有機魚和雞肉對健康更有益。

33. crumbling 破破爛爛的、搖搖欲墜的、破滅

例：Due to the poor quality of the materials used in the construction, its appearance may seem impressive at first. Unfortunately, after a few years, it will start crumbling.由於建築材料品質差，外觀一開始可能顯得很亮眼。然而，不幸的是，幾年後，它將變得破破爛爛。

再比如：The expectations and hopes of overseas Chinese for the government to accept dual nationality are crumbling. 海外華人對政府能夠接受雙重國籍的期望和希望正在破滅。

34. anodyne 平和的

例：He was livid, even though the advice his coworkers gave him was entirely anodyne. 他非常憤怒，儘管同事們給他的建議完全是平和的。

35. emollient 平和舒緩的、溫和的

例: I admire his character for its emollient attitude towards others, finding joy in interactions that soothe and comfort.我欣賞他的性格，因為他對待他人的態度是平和舒緩的，享受與他人交往的愉悅。

再比如：From the beginning, he appeared aggressive, but now he has become more emollient, realizing that his aggression would ultimately ruin the negotiation of this ongoing project, which could be detrimental to both parties. 從一開始他就顯得咄咄逼人，但現在他變得平和舒緩了，因為他知道他的激烈態度最終會破壞這個正在進行的項目

的談判，這可能對雙方都沒有好處。

36. mean 平均的 （一提到平均的,大多數人一定會想到 average, 可殊不知 mean 也可以表達平均的意思， 比如：mean price, mean temperature, etc...平均價格，平均溫度等 …

例：In winter, the mean temperature in Beijing is -15°C. 冬季，北京的平均氣溫為零下 15 攝氏度。

37. lackluster 平淡無奇、無生氣的
例：The average spending by consumers is lackluster. 消費者的平均消費水準平淡無奇。

38. to go bust 破產
例：He lost all his investments in the stock market and had no alternatives but to go bust. 他在股市中失去了所有的投資，只能無奈破產，沒有其他選擇。

39. to ravage 破壞
例：Heavy pollution has ravaged the environment.

嚴重的污染破壞了環境。

40. decrepit 破舊不堪的
例：Due to the inferiority of the materials, the building became decrepit in just a few years. 由於材料低劣，只過了幾年這座建築就很快破舊不堪了。

41. derelict 破舊的
例：The six-person family lived in the derelict building for almost 20 years. Fortunately, they bought a new house and moved in last week. They are celebrating the beautiful living place.一家六口在這棟破舊的樓裡住了將近 20 年。 幸運的是，他們上周買了一套新房子搬進來了。 他們正在慶祝美麗的生活場所。

42. clunkers 破爛兒,破舊的汽車電器等
例：We should allocate more funds to support people who depend on selling clunkers for their livelihood — including old cars, furniture, appliances, and other second-hand items. 我們應該撥出更多資金，支持那些靠出售破爛兒謀生的人，

包括舊汽車、舊傢俱、舊家電以及其他二手物品。

43. to dash (希望或願望）破滅
例：My willingness to marry her was dashed. 我想和她結婚的願望破滅了。

44. to thump to the ground 撲通摔倒在地上
例：While walking with my mom, she suddenly thumped to the ground. I immediately helped her up, and fortunately, she wasn't hurt.我和媽媽一起散步時，她突然重重摔倒在地。我立刻扶她起來，所幸她沒有受傷。

45. to scupper 破滅，搞砸
例：Her sudden illness scuppered her dream of becoming a new leader in this company. 她突然生病，使她成為這家公司新領導的夢想破滅了。

46. nannyish 婆婆媽媽的，過於謹慎的
例：He used to be a decisive person, but he's suddenly become nannyish, and many people are struggling to adapt to his new style. 他以前是個很果斷的人，但現在突然變得婆婆媽媽，很多人都難以適應他這種新的風格。

47. run-of-the-mill 普通的
例：I prefer to be a run-of-the-mill citizen rather than a famous star. 我寧願做一個普通的市民，也不願成為一顆耀眼的明星。

48. to get lumbered with 迫使扛起
例：So many people in this company left for vacation, and now the rest get lumbered with overloaded tasks, which has them crazily busy. 這家公司有這麼多人去度假，而目前剩下的人還得被迫扛起超負荷的工作，忙得發瘋。

49. oblige sb to do sth 迫使某人做某事
例：Looking for a better job forced me to take various exams, which left me exhausted. 尋找更好的工作迫使我參加了各種考試，結果讓我筋疲力盡。

50. mouldering 破碎的，崩塌的

例：The old Summer Palace became mouldering debris after being looted by invaders. 圓明園在被侵略者掠奪後，變成了破碎的廢墟。

51. to dissect 剖析

例：I remember that my Chinese teacher in high school preferred to dissect an article to extract the author's ideas, emotions, and writing style, allowing us to learn something more valuable from it. Now, I can understand how important that was for us. 我記得高中時我的語文老師喜歡剖析一篇文章，挖掘作者的思想、情感和寫作風格，讓我們從中學到更有價值的東西。現在，我能理解這對我們有多重要。

52. rife 普遍的、比比皆是

例：Running a red light in Canada seems to be quite rife, even though drivers can face higher penalties for it. 在加拿大，儘管司機可能會面臨更高的罰款，闖紅燈似乎相當普遍。

再比如：Scams involving internet celebrities are rife nowadays. 如今，涉及網路紅人的詐騙案件比比皆是。

53. to cull 撲殺

例：Due to the spread of avian flu, a large number of chickens have been culled. 由於禽流感的傳播，大量雞隻已被撲殺。

Q

1. to undulate 起伏蕩漾例：The volcano erupted violently, spewing molten lava that flowed in undulating patterns across the hills, casting a fiery red glow in every direction. I found myself uncomfortably close, unable to escape the searing, awe-inspiring heat. 火山猛烈爆發，噴出熔融的熔岩，沿著山丘以起伏蕩漾的姿態流動，四周散發著熾熱的紅光。我發現自己離得異

常近，無法逃避那灼熱且令人震撼的溫度。

2. It is odd to 奇怪 ...

例：It seems odd to provide too much detail unless they were already familiar with it and felt uncomfortable.除非他們事先已經瞭解，否則解釋過多細節似乎顯得有些奇怪。

3. to heckle 起哄

例：I saw some people heckling him while a group of hooligans was attacking the disabled person. 我看到一群流氓在襲擊那個殘疾人的時候有人在起哄。

4. idiosyncratic 奇葩的

例：The chaos in the market seems to make everything idiosyncratic, irregular, and absurd.市場上的混亂似乎讓一切變得奇葩、不規則和荒謬。

5. outlandish 奇葩的，古怪的

例：From my point of view, young women, both physiologically and psychologically, should get married before the age of 30; otherwise, their temperaments and behaviors may become somewhat outlandish. 在我看來，年輕女性在生理和心理上都應在 30 歲之前結婚，否則她們的性格和行為可能會變得有些奇葩。

6. chicanery 欺騙

例：Her explanation is fraught with a lot of chicaneries and lies. 她的解釋充滿了欺騙和謊言。

7. to bilk 欺騙

例：Some people may appear quite honest, but in reality, they can skillfully bilk you. 有些人看起來很誠實，但實際上卻能巧妙地騙你。

再比如：I often received phone calls from unknown numbers, and I suspected the callers were trying to bilk me out of money. Fortunately, they didn't get a single penny from me. 我經常接到一些陌生號碼打來的電話，我懷疑這些人是想欺騙我的錢。幸運的是，他們一分錢也沒騙到。

8. to nobble(採用不正當手段)欺騙,賄賂

例：Despite gracefully bowing out of the bidding, her kindness prevailed, she made no attempt to nobble her competitors. Instead, she ingeniously secured victory through an alternative approach. 儘管她優雅地退出了競標，但她的善良占了上風她並沒有試圖賄賂競爭對手。相反，她巧妙地通過另一種方式贏得了勝利。

再比如： He attempted to nobble the police in hopes of persuading them to waive the penalty, but unfortunately, it didn't work.他試圖賄賂員警，希望他們能免除罰款，但可惜沒有成功。

9. skulduggery 欺騙，造假

例：Everyone should stay far away from people who engage in skulduggery. 每個人都應該遠離那些喜歡搞欺騙的人。

10. to tick up 起色，上升

例：After the pandemic recovery, the economy has ticked up, driven by a surge in people's aspiration to purchase essential properties. 疫情恢復之後，經濟有起色了，這主要是由於人們對購買基本資產的渴望激增所推動的。

11. air of 氣質

例：You were born with an air of an artist.你天生就有藝術家的氣質。

12. protean 千變萬化的

例：Gongfu is composed of various approaches and is a protean art form as well. 功夫由各種招數組成，也是一門千變萬化的藝術。

13. to lurk 潛伏，潛藏

例：The novel coronavirus is very cunning, it can lurk anywhere and on the surface of anything.新型冠狀病毒非常狡猾，它可以潛伏在任何地方和任何東西的表面。

再比如：During the pandemic, the greatest concern was people who lurked the virus without showing any symptoms. 在疫情期間，最令人擔憂的是那些潛伏著病毒卻沒有任何症狀的人。

14. to implicate 牽扯

例：If you decide to play the stock market and end up losing money, please make sure you do not implicate me in any way. 如果你決定進入股市並最終虧損，請確保不要以任何方式牽連我。

15. pious 虔誠的，(有很強的宗教色彩）

例：His younger brother is a pious Buddhist who believes in reincarnation. 他的小弟弟是一個虔誠的佛教徒，相信輪回。

16. latency 潛伏期

例：The latency of this virus can last up to nine months.
這種病毒的潛伏期可以持續長達九個月。

17. to beholden to sb 欠某人人情

例：He wouldn't accept any help from his friends because he dislikes being beholden to them. 他不願意接受朋友的任何幫助，因為他不喜歡欠他們的人情。

18. far-fetched 牽強的，離譜的

例：The content of his speech seems too far-fetched; I don't find it believable or realistic. 他演講的內容似乎太牽強了，我覺得既不可信也不現實。

19. latent 潛在的

例：She focused on his latent capability to handle the issues very quickly and efficiently, so she decided to hire him. 她看中了他潛在的快速有效地處理問題的能力，所以決定雇用他。

20. underlying 潛在的，表面下的，根本的

例：His success was the result of some underlying conditions unknown to outsiders. 他的成功源于一些外人所不瞭解的潛在因素。

21. to rail against 譴責

例：Almost every day, gun shootings in Toronto leave people stunned. The government has railed against the violence and is working on more effective ways to control firearms. 幾乎每天，多倫多的槍擊事件都會

讓人震驚。政府對此表示強烈譴責，並正在尋求更有效的方法來控制槍支。

22. to deplore 譴責，強烈反對

例：We must deplore any behavior that involves abusing or even brutally killing one's parents. 我們必須譴責任何虐待甚至殘忍殺害父母的行為。

再比如：His parents deplore his intention to marry a girl from a remote rural area. 他的父母強烈反對他想娶一個來自偏遠地區農村女孩。

23. to castigate 譴責

例：The whole world castigates the superpower for its relentless exploitation of smaller and weaker nations to monopolize their oil and mineral resources. 全世界都在譴責這個超級大國無情地剝削弱小國家，以壟斷它們的石油和礦產資源。

再比如：Any invasion of another country must be castigated by peace- and justice-loving people around the world. 任何對他國的入侵都必須受到全世界熱愛和平與正義人民的譴責。

24. harbinger 前兆

例：The heavy snowfall this winter is a harbinger of intense rainfall in the coming summer. 今年冬天的強降雪是即將到來的夏季強降雨的前兆。

再比如：The tense relationship between the couple was a harbinger of divorce. 這對夫妻之間緊張的關係是他們將要離婚的前兆。

25. potent 強大的

例：She had a potent, insurmountable brain, and her intelligence was something I greatly admired. 她有一個強大的、不可逾越的大腦，而且非常聰慧，我非常欽佩。

26. to snap up 搶購

例：This watch is a limited edition, so many people are lining up to snap it up. 這種手錶是限量版的，所以很多人都排著隊搶購。

再比如：The latest model of the iPhone series is so prevalent that within just a few hours of its debut, they were all snapped up. 最新款蘋果手機系列非常流行，發佈僅幾個小時內就被搶購一空。

27. a dearth of 缺乏
例：So many African children have died due to a lack of food and water. 許多非洲兒童因為缺乏食物和水而死亡。

28. have/has hogged the limelight 搶盡了風頭，備受矚目
例：This movie has hogged the limelight at this year's Oscars, thanks to its exceptional cinematography, compelling drama, brilliant editing, and outstanding director. 這部電影憑藉其卓越的攝影、引人入勝的劇情、精彩的剪輯和傑出的導演，在今年的奧斯卡頒獎典禮上搶盡了風頭。

29. to resuscitate 搶救，復蘇
例：My dad suddenly lost consciousness right in front of the emergency room. Unfortunately, despite the doctors' best efforts to resuscitate him, he passed away. 我父親在急診室前突然失去了知覺。不幸的是，儘管所有的醫生都盡力搶救他，可他還是去世了。

30. scant 缺乏的，不足的
例：I've been annoyed by my scant confidence, especially when I get nervous speaking in front of a large audience. 我一直為缺乏自信而感到煩惱，尤其是在眾多人面前講話時感到緊張。

31. to volley against 強烈抨擊
例：President Biden volleyed against the assassination attempt on Trump. 拜登總統對特朗普的刺殺未遂進行了強烈抨擊。

32. to be fiercely critical of 強烈批評
例：The board chairman is fiercely critical of their abuse of funds for marketing promotions. 董事會主席對他們濫用資金進行市場推廣表示強烈批評。

33. censure 強烈譴責

例：The EU censured Russia's invasion of Ukraine. 歐盟強烈譴責俄羅斯入侵烏克蘭。

34. intransigent 強硬的

例：As the owner of the company, he was so intransigent that there was no room for negotiation, especially on the price, so we had to find a better way to purchase from other suppliers. 作為這家公司老闆，他非常強硬，價格方面更是沒有任何談判餘地，因此我們不得不想辦法從其他供應商那裡採購。

35. nemesis 強硬的對手或死對頭

例：He won the first title in the Olympic Game by defeating his nemesis. 他擊敗了強硬的對手而獲得奧運會第一個冠軍。

36. to pre-empt 搶佔、搶先

例：This company devised a perfect strategy to pre-empt the market by lowering the price of its products. 這家公司制定了一個完美的策略，通過降低產品價格搶佔市場。

再比如：During the road test, you must try to preempt braking when you observe any potential hazards. Otherwise, the examiner will brake for you, which could result in a failure. 在路考中，當你觀察到潛在的危險時，你必須儘量搶先刹車。否則，考官會替你刹車，這可能導致你未通過考試。

37. to snub 瞧不起

例：Not all wealthy people snub the poor; it depends on the individual's personality. 並不是所有富人都瞧不起窮人；這取決於個人的性格。

38. to prise open 撬開

例：She lost her door key and couldn't get in. With no other option, she had to prise open the door. 她丟了門鑰匙，無法進門。別無選擇，她只好撬開門。

39. a knack 竅門兒，訣竅

例：Nicolas has been figuring out a knack for a better solution for his home renovation. 尼古拉斯一直在找個竅門兒，更好地解決他的家庭裝修問題。

40. to finesse 巧妙處理
例：It is an art to finesse the relationships among people, especially among you, your colleagues, and your boss, while working in a company.在公司工作時，巧妙處理好人際關係是一門藝術，尤其是你、同事和老闆之間的關係。

41. to excise 切除
例：Excising a tumor from the human body is not a unique way to treat cancer; now, we invented many new ways, like immunotherapy, which will be the latest treatment.從人體切除腫瘤並不是治療癌症的唯一方法；現在，我們發明了很多新的方法，比如免疫療法，這將是最新的治療方法。

42. to choke off the supply of 切斷供應鏈
例：Since the pandemic began, the supply of chips for industries has been choked off. 自從疫情爆發以來，工業用晶片的供應鏈被切斷。

43. to toggle 切換
例：In terms of convenience, this equipment has two buttons that toggle seamlessly from one to the other at any time. 就便利性而言，這款設備有兩個按鈕，可以隨時無縫切換。

44. to snaffle 竊取
例：Some of the satellites are spy satellites that can snaffle vast amounts of information without alerting anyone. 其中一些衛星是間諜衛星，可以在不引起任何人注意的情況下竊取大量資訊。

45. to poach 竊取，挖走(人才)
例：He poached the architectural design from his colleagues to apply to his own scheme. It's shameful.他竊取了同事的建築設計，應用到自己的方案中。這真是令人可恥。

再比如：This computer giant tried to poach talent from another company but ultimately failed to reach an agreement on salary. 這家電腦巨頭試圖從另一家公司挖走人才，但最終未能就薪資達成協議。

46. infringe someone's right to sth 侵犯了某人的 ...權利

例：The netizens believe that the rules infringe on my copyright. 網友們認為這些規定侵犯了我的版權。

47. crony 摯交的、親密的、裙帶的

例：It is easy to find an ordinary friend, but it is difficult to find a true crony in one's life. 找一個普通朋友很容易，但在一生中找到一個摯交卻很難。

再比如：The policy in our company focuses on preventing any crony relationships, which could seriously impact long-term development and strategy. 我們公司政策的重點是防止任何裙帶關係，因為裙帶關係可能嚴重影響公司的長期發展和戰略。

48. to call in sick 請病假

例：Sophia asked her parents to call in sick for her, as she can't go to school. She has to stay in bed for a couple of days because of her fever. 索菲亞讓她的父母替她請病假，因為她不能去學校。由於發燒，她需要在床上待幾天。

49. to weed out 清除

例：This company is on the brink of bankruptcy. The local government tried to weed out its bad debts to save it, but in the end, all efforts failed. 這家公司瀕臨破產，地方政府試圖清除壞賬以挽救公司，但最終所有努力都失敗了。

50. breezily 輕輕地

例：The summer wind breezily blew across her face, and she looked so beautiful in the dappled sunlight. 夏日的微風輕輕拂過她的臉龐，她在陽光斑駁的陰影中顯得格外美麗。

51. to slight 輕視

例：Nowadays, very few merchandisers remember that they should not slight any of their customers, as they may become potential clients. 如今，很少有商家能記得不該輕視任何客戶，因為他們可能會成為潛在客戶。

52. spick and span 清爽的

例：This company launched a new cosmetic cream for ultra-sensitive skin, which went viral after its release. Many consumers gave it high praise, as they applied it to their faces and felt spick and span. 這家公司推出了一款針對超敏感肌膚的全新化妝霜，在發佈後迅速走紅。許多消費者給予了高度評價，因為他們將其塗抹在臉上，感到清爽潔淨。

53. light-hearted 輕鬆的

例：Very few people can earn light-hearted money; most of us must rely on our hard work and dedication. 很少有人能輕鬆賺到錢；我們大多數人必須依靠辛勤的努力和奉獻。

54. sober 清醒的

例：After drinking too much, he was involved in a serious car accident. Fortunately, he survived. The police brought him to the station, where he sobered up overnight. 他喝多了，捲入了一場嚴重的車禍。 幸運的是，他還活著。 員警把他帶到警察局； 他一夜之間清醒了過來。

再比如：Please keep in mind that you must remain sober when facing trouble; never let your emotions dictate how you deal with it. 請記住，在遇到麻煩時，你必須保持清醒，千萬不要感情用事。

55. to defang 去除，中和

例：Washing vegetables with baking soda or white vinegar is believed to defang pesticides, allowing you to enjoy much healthier and cleaner produce. 人們認為用小蘇打或白醋清洗蔬菜可以去除農藥殘留，使你能夠享用更健康、更乾淨的蔬菜。

56. to bend 屈從

例：When you withdraw your own money from the bank, you may often be asked why and how you plan to spend it. This completely infringes on your rights, sounds absurd, and we should not bow to such a ridiculous policy. 當你從銀行取出自己的錢時，銀行可能常常問你為什麼以及打算如何花這些錢。這完全侵犯了你的權利，聽起來荒謬，我們不應屈從於這種荒唐的政策。

57. to capitulate 屈服，認輸

例：No one would want to capitulate, knowing that their benefits would be affected. 沒有人願意屈服，因為他們的利益將會受到影響。

58. to supplant 取代

例：We face a difficult challenge, as AI or robots are set to supplant many current jobs. 我們面臨一個艱難的挑戰，因為人工智慧或機器人將取代許多現有的工作。

59. to usurp 取代，篡位，奪取

例：All men must remember that a "ladybro" should never usurp the place of their wife in their life. 所有男人都必須記住，"閨蜜"永遠不能取代妻子在他們生活中的地位。

60. to notch up 取得，贏得，獲得

例：With her team's great support, she notched up a significant success and ultimately broke the record in this field. 在團隊的巨大支持下，她取得了顯著的成功，並最終刷新了這個領域的紀錄。

61. to outlaw 取締、禁止

例：I can hardly believe that Western governments are also exerting efforts to outlaw prostitution and whoring. 我簡直不敢相信西方政府也在努力取締賣淫和嫖娼。

62. flaw 缺陷

例：Considering the flaws in this strategy, we must redesign it to better adapt to frequent changes. 考慮到這個策略的缺陷，我們必須重新設計它，以便更好地適應頻繁的變化。

63. to hinge on 取決於

例：How much you can get paid will hinge on your capability. 你能拿多少薪水取決於你的能力。

64. to spur on 推動，驅使

例：Cheaper and faster personal computers have been spurred on by advancements in smaller chip technology. 更小的晶片技術推動了更便宜、更快的個人電腦的發展。

65. congenial 趣味相投的，志同道合的

例：Usually, people prefer to get along with congenial friends, and the same applies to marriage. 通常，人們更喜歡與趣味相投的朋友相處； 婚姻也是如此。

66. in droves 群體

例：The Covid virus variants spread rapidly, and people across the world got infected in droves. 新冠病毒變種傳播迅速； 全世界的人都容易被群體感染。

67. to revoke 取消，剝奪

例：Due to his misuse of doping during the competition, his championship title was eventually revoked. 由於在比賽中濫用興奮劑，他的冠軍頭銜最終被取消了。

68. to poke fun at 取笑，嘲弄

例：This crosstalk pokes fun at disabled people, which has enraged the public. 這段相聲取笑殘障人士，激起了公眾的憤怒。

69. to jump on 趨之若鶩

例：Many people are jumping on the electric vehicle bandwagon, but they tend to overlook potential issues such as limited driving range, long charging times, and the need for frequent recharges. 許多人對電動汽車趨之若鶩，但他們忽視了一些潛在的問題，如駕駛距離短，等待時間長，頻繁充電等。

70. to deign to 屈尊做…、降低身份去做…

例：He is too snobbish to deign to purchase affordable cars. 他太傲氣了不願意屈尊買便宜的車。

71. full-blown 全面的

例：The current global situation has become dire, and a full-blown nuclear war may be in the offing. 當前的全球局勢已經變得十分嚴峻，一場全面的核戰爭可能即將爆發。

72. full-fledge 全面的

例：Ethan submitted a full-fledged marketing strategy plan outlining the business expansion over the next two years in the

Asia-Pacific region. 伊森提交了一份全面的行銷戰略計畫，內容涉及未來兩年在亞太地區的業務擴展的計畫。

73. to overhaul 全面改革

例：The education system needs a complete overhaul to keep pace with the demands of social development. 教育體制需要全面改革以適應社會發展的需求。

74. to remonstrate sb. 勸某人…

例：My younger brother lacks social experience, so I remonstrated with him about the importance of improving his interpersonal skills. 我弟弟缺乏社會經驗，所以我勸他要重視提高與人打交道的能力。

75. a set-up 圈套

例：He rolled out a rhetorical description of this product, and I think it's a setup. 他對這個產品進行了一番花言巧語的描述，我認為這是一個圈套。

76. purview 許可權

例：It is beyond my purview, even though I am the manager of this store. However, I will do my best to help you resolve the issue. 儘管我是這家店的經理，這超出了我的許可權。不過，我會盡力幫你解決問題。

77. expedient 權宜之計的

例：Our decision is an expedient response to the current situation; we'll have ample time to figure out a better way to address it. 我們的決定是對現狀的權宜之計； 我們將有足夠的時間找出更好的方法來處理它。

再比如：Frequently changing policies as an expedient measure for economic recovery is aimless and unwise. 頻繁改變政策是經濟復蘇的權宜之計，那是漫無目的和不明智的。

78. drawback 缺點， 不足之處

例：The room's main drawback is its small size. With six people living in it, I don't think it will be suitable for us. .這個房間的主要缺點是太小了。我們有六個人住在裡面，所以我覺得它不適合我們。

79. to pinpoint 確定

例：It is difficult to pinpoint the exact cause of the coronavirus' responsibility for the deaths of around 100 million people worldwide. 很難確定是什麼原因導致了新冠病毒在全球造成大約一億人的死亡。

80. .to speak above a whisper 輕聲細語

例：He prefers to speak above a whisper to avoid bothering others. 他喜歡輕聲細語地說話，以避免打擾他人。

R

1. to circumvent 繞過

例：When the reporter asked him a sensitive question, he tried to circumvent giving a direct answer. 當記者提出一個敏感問題時，他試圖繞過直截了當的回答。

2. screed 冗長的文章

例：His lengthy screed on the marketing plan lacked substance, and the board couldn't approve it. 他那篇關於市場計畫冗長的文章內容空洞，董事會無法通過。

3. to stagger 讓震…驚不已

例：His sheer creativity staggers his colleagues and spreads like wildfire overnight 他的創意讓同事們震驚不已，並在一夜之間迅速走紅。

4. to be underwhelmed by 讓 ...失望

例：As her driving instructor, I was underwhelmed by her decision to abandon the road test after her first failure. 作為她的駕駛教練，她的第一次失敗後決定放棄讓我感到失望。

5. to be redolent of 讓…想起

例：The woman saw a girl whose appearance was suddenly redolent of her daughter, who had tragically lost her life in a serious car accident. The striking resemblance flooded her with memories, filling her with bittersweet sorrow. 那位女士看

到一個女孩，突然間她的模樣讓她想起了已經在一場嚴重車禍中失去生命的女兒。那驚人的相似讓她的回憶湧上心頭，心中充滿了苦澀的悲傷。

6. to keep sth at bay 讓⋯壓制
例：The children were quite naughty and often tried her patience, but their adorable smiles kept the young mother's anger at bay—her love for them was simply too deep. 孩子們雖然很淘氣，常常讓她心煩，但他們天真可愛的笑容總能壓住這位年輕媽媽的怒火——因為她對他們的愛實在太深了。

7. to toss out 扔掉
例：People who casually toss out garbage everywhere are, at the very least, revealing something problematic about their values. 那些隨意亂扔垃圾的人，至少說明他們的價值觀可能出了問題。

8. to intrigue 讓⋯著迷
例：The discovery of life on Mars and the possibility of aliens from other planets has intrigued me for almost 20 years. 火星上發現生命以及其他星球外星人的可能存在讓我著迷了近二十年。

9. to mesmerize 讓⋯著迷
例：The performance tonight is stunning, and it unexpectedly mesmerized me 今晚的表演真是美麗動人，意想不到，讓我著迷。

10. to budge 讓步
例：Considering the benefit for our children, we won't budge on unreasonable conditions. 考慮到孩子們的利益，我們不會為不合理的條件讓步。

11. to keep sb on his/her toe 讓某人保持警覺
例：The 'lie flat' phenomenon is bound to keep governments on their toes "躺平"現象勢必會讓各級政府保持警惕。

12. to catch someone off guard 讓某人措手不及
例: Her sudden change of plan caught all the employees off guard.她突然改變計畫，讓所有員工措手不及。

13. to leave sb gobsmacked 讓某人大吃一驚

例：When I met him in person, his appearance left me gobsmacked; he looked stronger and older than I had imagined based on our phone conversation. 當我親自見到他時，他的外表讓我大吃一驚；他看起來比我在電話交談中想像的更強壯、更老成。

14. to enmesh sb in heavy debt 讓某人負債累累

例："jiebei and huabei" enmeshed so many young people in heavy debt."借唄和花唄"讓無數年輕人負債累累。

15. to revile 辱罵

例：So many trolls reviled him, but he grew stronger as a result. 儘管許多網路噴子辱罵他，他卻變得更堅強。

16. to devour 如饑似渴地

例：This novel captivated her; she was intoxicated by it, devouring its pages and trying to sense the characters' inner worlds. 這本小說吸引了她，她沉浸其中，如饑似渴地閱讀著並試圖感知人物的內心世界。

17. to leave sb in limbo 讓某人陷入困境

例：The suspension of his salary has left him in limbo. Now, he can't even afford his daily food. 他的工資被暫停，導致他陷入了困境。現在，他甚至連日常的食物都買不起。

18. suavely 柔和地

例：She suavely persuaded her son to face his challenges, guiding him toward a meaningful accomplishment in life. 她柔和地勸說兒子面對困境，帶領他實現人生中的重大成就。

19. mellow 柔和的(這個詞有很多的解釋，典型的一詞多義）

例：I prefer mellow colors, as they have the ability to soothe both my mind and body, creating an indescribable warmth that envelops me. 我偏愛柔和的色調，因為它們能安撫我的身心，帶來一種無法言喻的溫暖包圍著我。

20. to dishearten 讓人心灰意冷、讓人心寒

例：So many times, failure never disheartened him; instead, it made me stronger.許多次的失敗並沒有讓他灰心。相反，使我更堅強。

21. to roil 擾亂

例：Fake currencies can roil any country's economic stability. As a result, policymakers around the world are intensifying efforts to eliminate them. 假幣可能擾亂任何國家的經濟穩定，因此全球的決策者正加緊努力消除這一問題。

22. litany 冗長而枯燥的陳述.

例：Zion deleted the entire litany from his speech and tried to simplify it. 錫安刪除了他演講中的所有冗長而枯燥陳述，並試圖讓其更簡練。

23. to irk 惹惱

例：My lawyer sent a legal letter to that company, but there was no response. Their arrogance and negligence irked all of us. My lawyer has now promised to take further action by filing an official lawsuit against the company. 我的律師向那家公司發出了律師函，但他們沒有任何回應。他們的傲慢與疏忽惹惱了我們所有人。我的律師已承諾將採取下一步行動，正式對該公司提起訴訟。

24. fanfare 熱鬧非凡，大張旗鼓

例：The celebration was filled with fanfare, joyful dancing, the beat of drums, and melodic music. 慶典現場充滿了盛大的儀式感、歡樂的舞姿、激昂的鼓點和悠揚的音樂。

25. to rankle 惹怒，激怒

例：They quarreled, and he truly rankled her by angrily smashing everything in the house. After that, his wife called the police — an action that ultimately led to their divorce. 他們吵了一架，他怒氣衝衝地砸壞了家裡的所有東西，徹底惹怒她。之後，他妻子報警了，而這最終導致了他們的離婚。

26. to lionise 熱捧為 ...

例：Ezekiel colleagues lionized Ezekiel as a "brave driver" who pushed his car speed up to 300km/h on the highway. That's insane.西結·埃塞基爾的同事們熱捧他為一名"勇敢的司機"，他在高速公路上把車速開到高達 300 公里/小時，這簡直就是瘋了。

27. ardour 熱情
例：His ardour for designing gaming programs deeply impressed me. 他對遊戲程式設計的熱情讓我印象深刻。

28. civic-minded 熱心公益事業的
例：So many celebrities are civic-minded individuals, always eager to give back to society. 許多名人都是熱心公益事業的，願意回饋社會。

29. to burst at seams 人滿為患，擁擠不堪
例：After the lockdown, people began shopping again, and nearly all the malls were bursting at the seams. 封鎖解除後，人們開始購物，幾乎所有的商場都人滿為患。

30. to swallow small insults in 忍氣吞聲
例：Many employees swallow small insults to avoid being sacked, which has become quite common in companies these days. 許多員工忍氣吞聲，以避免被解雇，這在如今的公司中似乎已經變得相當普遍。

31. to throw in the towel 認輸
例：She failed the exam twice, but she refused to throw in the towel. After putting in tremendous effort, she finally passed. 她兩次考試失敗，但拒絕認輸。憑藉堅定的意志和不懈的努力，她最終通過了考試。

32. anthropogenic 人為的
例：The surge in commodity prices seems to be driven by anthropogenic factors, prompting the government to initiate an investigation. 飛漲的商品價格似乎受到了人為操控的影響，為此，政府已介入展開調查。

33. to be buoyed by 讓某人感到…的鼓舞
例：All the students are buoyed by the internship opportunities provided by the company. 公司提供的實習機會讓所有學生都感到振奮。

34. capricious 任性
例:I don't think he's available for this job due to his capricious nature.我認為由於他的任性， 無法勝任這項工作。

35. wayward 任性的
例：Logan is too wayward to get along with others.洛根太任性了， 無法與別人相處。

36. petulant 任性的
例：We must avoid being impulsive and petulant when handling key issues with our clients, especially the most valuable ones. 在與客戶處理關鍵問題，尤其是與最有價值的客戶相處時，我們必須儘量避免衝動和任性。

37. ersatz 人造的，替代的
例：It is reported that some countries have invented ersatz blood, which could be used on the battlefield or in medical surgeries. However, I haven't heard any further information about it since then.據報導，世界上一些國家已經發明了人造血，可能會應用於戰場或外科手術等領域。然而，自那以後我就再也沒聽說過它的進一步消息。

38. to muse on 認真思考
例：Our experts must carefully muse on what they say, regardless of the content they prefer, because at times, their words have confused people and caused a loss of confidence and trust. 我們的專家無論偏好什麼內容，都必須認真思考自己所說的話，因為他們有時會讓人感到困惑，甚至失去對他們的信心和信任。

39. to put in stints at 任職
例：As far as I know, this guy put in stints at a seven-star restaurant. I have no idea why he quit so suddenly. Word has it he left to immigrate to another country 據我所知，這哥們兒曾在一家七星級餐廳任過職，我不知道他為什麼突然辭職，據說是為了移民到另一個國家。

40. to vituperate 辱罵、謾罵
例：He went through a lot of struggles, including being vituperated by people who deliberately gave him a hard time. 他經歷了許多磨難，有

些人故意為難他，還對他辱罵。

41. to take wing 日益凸顯，成為現實
例：The trend of AI robots replacing human roles is taking wing. 人工智慧機器人取代人類角色的趨勢日益凸顯。

42. long-winded 冗長的，囉嗦的
例：I loathe long-winded expressions when presenting my thesis, and some professors can't tolerate them either. 在進行論文答辯時，我非常討厭冗長的表達，一些教授也無法忍受。

43. ponderous 冗長的,死板的
例：Ezra wrote a ponderous article detailing his years of experience, which left readers bored and drowsy 以斯拉寫了一篇冗長的文章，描述了他的多年經驗，讀起來讓人感到無聊和昏昏欲睡。

44. to be piqued at 惹怒
例：Jose's parents were piqued at his decision to abandon his university studies. 何塞放棄大學深造的決定惹怒了他的父母。

45. to dim 讓…失去光澤，變得暗淡
例：The consecutive failures in launching rockets to the moon dimmed the company's future prospects and strategy. 向月球發射火箭的連續失敗讓這家公司的前途和戰略暗淡無光。

46. to embroil 讓捲入，讓混亂
例：The day-long quarrels embroiled the entire family in a mire of sorrow and emotional turmoil. 一整天的爭吵讓全家捲入了悲傷與情緒的漩渦之中。

47. to put someone beyond the pale 讓某人難以接受
例：She suddenly proposed breaking up with me, which put me beyond the pale 她突然提出要和我分手，這讓我難以接受。

48. to leave sb in a lurch 讓某人備受煎熬

例：His extramarital affair with another woman left his wife in the lurch.他與其他女人的婚外情讓他的妻子備受煎熬。

49. to stigmatize 讓某人蒙受恥辱

例：The decision made by the company's board stigmatized me, leaving me no choice but to resign. 公司董事會所作的決定讓我蒙受恥辱，我最終決定辭職。

50. leave (the whole family or company) stuck in a rut 讓全家或公司陷入困境

例：His brother was a pillar of the family; unfortunately, his sudden death left the entire family stuck in a rut. 他哥哥曾是整個家庭的頂樑柱，不幸的是，他的突然離世讓全家陷入了困境。

S

1. to maul 撕咬

例：I saw a person accidentally slip into the river, and within moments, he was mauled to pieces by crocodiles 我看到一個人不小心滑進河裡，然後他立刻被鱷魚撕成碎片。

2. to be an aversion to 是 ...厭惡的

例：The bad guys inject poisonous substances into the food, which is an aversion to consumers. 壞人在食物中注入有毒物質，這是消費者所厭惡的。

3. to slop 灑在 ...

例：Parents must teach their children to avoid slopping food on the table while eating. Wasting food is a crime. 父母必須告誡孩子們在吃飯時避免將食物弄灑在桌子上。浪費食物是罪行。

4. to peddle 散佈（謠言）

例：A lot of rumors peddled online have made people confused.許多在網上散佈的謠言讓人們感到困惑。

5. to sow panic 散佈恐慌
例：You exaggerated the impact of the virus; to some extent, you're sowing panic. 你誇大了病毒的影響；在某種程度上，你是在散播恐慌。

6. to emanate 散發
例：This picturesque scene emanated the rich culture of the 18th century, enticing numerous artists to emulate its style. 這幅風景圖散發著 18 世紀濃厚的文化氛圍，吸引了眾多藝術家模仿其風格。

7. to hail sb 頌揚，稱讚
例：Lu Xun is hailed as one of the greatest writers in the history of Chinese literature. 魯迅被頌揚為中國文學歷史上最偉大的作家之一。

8. to forfeit 喪失
例：If you give it up, that indicates that you forfeit your right to protect yourself. 如果你放棄了，就意味著你失去了保護自己的權利。

9. to banish 掃除，清除
例：I always advised my son to banish all the barriers and difficulties on his path to success. 我一直告誡我的兒子，要掃除通往成功道路上的所有障礙和困難。

10. to perturb 騷擾，擾亂，令人心神不定
例：Her ex-boyfriend often perturbed her and caused her great sadness. 她的前男友經常騷擾她，令她感到非常難過。

11. to harry 騷擾，折磨
例：While staying in that small town, I was harried by the locals, who humiliated me by pouring dirty sewage water on me. 在那個小鎮待著的時候，當地人騷擾我，他們通過把髒污水潑到我身上來羞辱我。

12. to take special pains to 煞費苦心地
例：Skylar literally takes special pains to figure out a better solution for her clients; unfortunately, she was still misunderstood. 斯凱拉確實付出了特別的努力去為她的客戶找到更好的解決方案，然而，她仍然被誤解。

13. simpleton 傻瓜，笨蛋

例：He appears to be a simpleton, easily vulnerable to deception. 他看起來像個傻瓜，容易上當受騙。

14. raucous 沙啞的，喧鬧的，刺耳的，粗聲的

例：This veteran expert's voice was raucous, likely because he had talked too much. 這位資深專家的聲音有些沙啞，可能是因為他說得太多了。

再比如：There are so many raucous people and vehicles around the house I rent that I can't fall asleep until 3 am 我租的房子周圍有很多吵鬧的人和車輛，導致我直到淩晨三點才能入睡。

15. to be deft at 擅長

例：He is deft at mischief, but it annoys his fans. 他很擅長搗亂，但這讓他的粉絲感到惱火。

16. to be brilliant at 擅長

例：He is brilliant at music; he composes songs for famous singers.他擅長音樂; 他為著名歌手作曲。

17. to be adept at 擅長 ...

例：Ava is more adept at directing movies than at being an actress. 艾娃更擅長執導電影，而不是當演員。

18. to scrub 刪除

例：The improper statement involving discrimination made by the director has been scrubbed. 這位導演發佈的涉及歧視的不當言論已被刪除。

19. to prune away 刪除

例：His article was too redundant, so we had to prune away some content to make it more concise. 他的文章太冗長了，所以我們不得不刪除一些內容，使其更簡潔。
再比如：I don't want to plant an apple tree because it requires me to constantly prune away branches each season, and I'm too busy to take care of it. 我不想種蘋果樹，因為每個季節都得修剪掉多餘的枝條，而我太忙，沒時間打理。

20. alimony 贍養費

例：After the divorce, he has to pay his ex-wife alimony every month. 離婚後，他必須每個月支付贍養費給前妻。

近有商店, 我的老闆跑卻捨近求遠到另一個地方去買。

21. uptick 上漲
例：During the bidding, the price of this antique saw a crazy uptick. 在拍賣過程中，這件古董的價格瘋狂上漲。

再比如：This year's uptick in production didn't affect its market surge and expansion. 今年產量的上升並未影響其市場的激增和擴張。

22. ritzy 奢華的，時髦的
例：Dubai is renowned for hosting some of the ritziest hotels and restaurants in the world. 迪拜以擁有世界上一些最奢華的 酒店和餐廳而聞名。

23. on the lower rungs 社會地層的
例：He cried out loudly for the people on the lower rungs of society. 他為社會底層的人們大聲呼喊。

24. to traipse 捨近求遠 ...
例：My boss traipses to another place to buy it, even though there's a store nearby. 儘管附

25. to shape 塑造，影響等等（意思實在太多，可謂典型的一詞多義）
例：His insurmountable talent and sharp insight shaped his unique and personal worldview. 他無與倫比的才華和敏銳的洞察力塑造了他獨特的個人世界觀。

26. to dabble 涉足、涉獵
例：He dabbled in a lot of fields apart from his core business. 除了他的核心業務，他涉足了很多領域。

再比如：He dabbled in many hobbies, but almost nothing could capture his interest or hold it for long. 他涉獵了許多愛好，但幾乎沒有什麼能長時間引起他的興趣。

27. stochastic 隨機的
例：The lottery generated a winning number through a stochastic process controlled by a computer program. 彩票通過電腦程式控制的隨機過程生成了中獎號碼。

28. esoteric 深奧的

例：Some statements and theories put forward by so-called experts were highly esoteric, making it difficult for ordinary people to understand. This bewildered them, which, to some extent, compounded the situation and made it worse. That's why so many people dislike 'experts. 一些所謂專家提出的理論和觀點非常深奧，普通人難以理解。這讓人感到困惑，在某種程度上使局勢更加複雜和惡化。這就是為什麼這麼多人不喜歡'專家'。

29. recondite 深奧的

例：Some people prefer his poems but I don't like them because they are recondite.有些人喜歡他的詩，但我不喜歡，因為太深奧了。

30. perky 神采奕奕

例：He still looks perky even though he is 85 years old.儘管他已經 85 歲高齡，但他看起來仍然神采奕奕。

31. to vet 審查

例：This movie has been vetted due to its harmful content, such as sexual themes, coarse language, and violent scenes that may negatively impact young people. 這部電影已被審查，因為它包含有害內容，如性暗示、粗俗語言和暴力場景，可能會對年輕人產生不良影響。

32. to be deranged 神經錯亂的，發瘋的

例：Kinsley looks pretty amable, but unfortunately, after severe quarreling with her husband, she became completely deranged. 金斯利看起來相當和藹可親，但不幸的是，在和丈夫激烈爭吵之後，她徹底神經錯亂了。

33. to set nerves jangling 神經緊張

例：He has a panic disorder, and just speaking in front of a large crowd instantly sets his nerves jangling 他患有驚恐症，每當在眾人面前演講時，他的神經便會立刻緊張起來。

34. freewheeling 隨心所欲的

例：You can maintain your freewheeling lifestyle at home, but not in public, as strangers are unlikely to tolerate or accept it. 你可以在家裡保持你隨心所欲的生活方式，而不是在公共場合，因為陌生人是無法容忍和接受的。

35. to dent 損害，影響
例：His decision dented our tactical and strategic plan for implementing the marketing development. 他的決損害了我們實施市場開發的戰術和戰略計畫。

再比如：The withdrawal of the investment by the other board members dented my motivation and confidence in continuing to run this business. 其他董事成員撤回的投資，損害了我繼續經營這家公司的動力和信心。

36. inscrutable 神秘莫測的，難以理解的
例：NASA captured a stunning video through its telescope, showing a UFO, roughly the size of Earth, seemingly charging itself near the Sun before quickly fleeing. This case remains inscrutable. 美國國家航空航天局通過望遠鏡捕捉到一段令人震驚的視頻，一個像地球一樣大小的 UFO 似乎在太陽附近充電，然後以很快的速度離開，該事件仍然神秘莫測，無法解釋。

37. to ruminate 深思，反芻
例：We must ruminate on how to improve our strategy for expanding our market value in the EU. 我們必須深思如何改善我們的策略，以擴大在歐盟的市場價值。

再比如：It is said that Muslim people only eat meat from ruminating animals. 據說穆斯林只吃反芻動物的肉。

38. infiltrate 滲透
例：His cancer has spread throughout his body and has already infiltrated his brain 他的癌症已經擴散到全身，並已經滲透到大腦。

39. sanity 神智
例：His behavior and manner of communication raised doubts about whether his sanity was normal. 他的行為和溝通方式讓人懷疑他的神智是否正常。

40. to take root 生根發芽

例：Without proper cleanup, the wild grass will take root and grow uncontrollably, potentially damaging your house. 如果不好好清理，野草就會生根發芽，不受控制地瘋狂生長，甚至毀壞你的房子。

41. to seeth with 生悶氣

例：He sat there, silently enduring his boss's abuse, seething with anger.他坐在那裡，默默忍受著老闆的辱罵，生著悶氣。

42. for fear that... 生怕，只怕，就怕 ...

例：He seeks to yoke together all the 'golden words' attributed to famous figures, using them to assert his authority and influence others to believe in him. 我暫時得找個地方躲起來，生怕他發現我。

43. to yoke together 生拼硬湊在一起

例：He seeks to yoke together all the 'golden words' attributed to famous figures, employing them to assert his authority and sway others to believe in him.他試圖將所有被名人說過的'金句'聯繫在一起，用它們來鞏固自己的權威並影響他人相信自己。

44. to take umbrage 生氣

例：I guess he will take umbrage if he is not invited to the party.如果他沒有被邀請參加聚會，我想他會生氣的。

45. to huff 生氣地說

例：His boss huffed, 'You're fired.他的老闆很生氣地說：'你被解雇了。'

46. be browbeaten into 受到恐下

例：All parents must convey to their children that no one should be browbeaten into tolerating bullies 所有的父母都必須告訴孩子;沒有人會因為恐嚇會容忍霸淩。

47. fete 盛宴

例：Tonight, a large audience enjoyed this musical fête, which featured some of the most renowned violinists and pianists from around the world. 今晚，眾多觀眾欣賞了這場音樂盛宴，其中不乏來自世界各地

最著名的小提琴家和鋼琴家。

48. to make them redundant 使…變得多餘

例：The extra procedure added to this application program will render it redundant. 給這個應用程式加入額外流程將使其變得多餘。

49. to take the wind out of the sails. 使…蒼白無力

例：My boss's ugly scandal has taken the wind out of the sails of his explanation and clarification. 我老闆的醜事使他的解釋和澄清變得蒼白無力。

50. to appall 使 …大為震驚

例：Some rumors revealing that aliens are preparing to attack humanity appalled almost everyone on Earth. 一些關於外星人準備攻擊人類的謠言讓地球上的幾乎使所有人都感到大為震驚。

51. to handicap 損害，對 …不利

例：Her disloyalty and dishonesty handicapped her capability. 她的不忠和不誠實損害了她的能力。

52. to fester 使 …惡化

例：The quarrel with his wife festered their close relationship, ultimately，escalating into physical confrontations between them. 與妻子的爭吵使他們的關係惡化，最終導致他們彼此互毆。

53. to be inimical to 損害，有害

例:Smoking and drinking are inimical to people's health and can shorten their longevity. 吸煙和飲酒有害健康，還可能縮短壽命。

54. to entrench 使 …惡化，使 …根深蒂固，加劇等

例：During the pandemic, the consecutive floods entrenched the deterioration of the global situation. 在疫情期間，接連不斷的洪災使全球局勢的惡化。

55. to infuriate sb 使 …發怒，激怒

例：While dating a boy or a girl, you'd better intentionally infuriate him or her once, just to observe their reaction—it's one way to test whether they truly love you. 在和男生或女生約會時，你最好故意激怒他/她一次，看看他們的反應——這是檢驗對方是否真心愛你的一種方式。

56. to flummox 使 ...困惑

例：The labyrinthine architectural design of the new chip flummoxed the producers, who had expected to churn it out in large quantities. 新晶片錯綜複雜的架構設計使生產商感到困惑，而他們原本還指望能大批量生產。

57. to vex 使...傷腦筋

例：The kids' obsession with online gaming vexed many parents, who have been trying to find better solutions to help their children break free from this troubling trend, as more and more youngsters are losing their eyesight and becoming increasingly distracted from their studies. 孩子沉迷于網路遊戲使很多父母傷透了腦筋，他們一直在尋找更好的辦法，幫助孩子擺脫這一令人擔憂的趨勢，因為越來越多的孩子視力受損，學習也越來越難以集中精神。

58. to round up 四捨五入

round 這個詞的意思太多了，這裡我們只想探討的是它的"四捨五入"的含義。至於其它用法，大家可以另行查字典瞭解。

例：The decimal point of that figure is too long, so we have to round it up. 那個數字的小數點太長，所以我們必須進行四捨五入。

59. to rive 撕裂

例：Two villages, riven by a vast mountain, present contrasting scenes on either side. 兩個村莊被大山撕裂開，呈現出兩種不同的景象。

60. to go sprawling 四腳朝天

例：He was so tired to sleep profoundly and went sprawling. 他太累了，睡得很沉，四腳朝天。

61. to plunge sb into 使⋯陷入 ...

例：The laid-off plunged her into a difficult situation in her life.

下崗使她陷入了生活的困境。

62. to put sb through the wringer. 使⋯陷入困境
例：The surging of the mortgage interest rate put so many house owners through the wringer. 抵押貸款利率的飆升使許多房主陷入困境。

63. to bring ...to a standstill 使⋯陷入停頓，或陷入僵局
例：Owing to the shortage of provision for spare parts, it will bring our market to a standstill. 由於備件供應不足，使我們的市場陷於停頓。

64. to predispose 使⋯易患，使 ...容易感染
例：His weakness predisposes him to contracting influenza. 他的虛弱使他容易患上流感。

65. to leave in tatters 使⋯一落千丈，聲名狼藉
例：She appears to be a decent person; unfortunately, her unbelievably harsh behavior has left her image and reputation in tatters. 她看起來是個體面的人；不幸的是，她那令人難以置信的嚴厲行為讓她的形象和聲譽一落千丈。

66. to oscillate 使⋯震盪
例：The poor financial plan caused the stock markets to oscillate, potentially leading to an escalation of economic instability. 糟糕的財務計畫使股市震盪，可能引發經濟不穩定的加劇。

67. to maim 使 ...致殘
例：He was permanently maimed after his survival from the severe earthquake. 他在大地震中倖存下來後，終身致殘。

68. flop 失敗
例：The implementation of the marketing strategy proves to be a flop. 這個行銷策略的實施是失敗的。

69. to go bung 失敗
例：His business went bung due to his mismanagement and poor financial situation. 由於他的管理不善和糟糕的財務狀況，他的生意失敗了。

70. to bend someone to one's will 使別人屈從自己的意志

例：If you want a perennial friendship or love with someone, you'd better avoid constantly bending the other party to your will. 如果你想與某人建立長久的友誼或愛情，最好避免總是使對方屈從于你的意願。

71. it is time to roll up one's sleeves 是到了大幹一場的時候了

例：It is time to roll up my sleeves to sit down and face to face talk about how to earn big dollars. 是大幹一場的時候了，坐下來面對面地談談如何賺大錢了。

72. counter-productive 適得其反的

例：Never force your kids to focus on studying. Parents should guide them patiently and systematically; otherwise, the result may be counterproductive. 永遠不要強迫孩子專注于學習。家長應該耐心且有系統地引導他們，否則結果可能適得其反。

73. to desiccate 使乾燥

例：Since this type of food is prone to molding, you should consider desiccating it to preserve it longer 鑒於這種食物容易發黴，應該考慮使其乾燥，以延長保質期。

74. to exacerbate 使加劇，使惡化

例：His aggressive attitude exacerbated their relationship, and eventually, they parted ways. 他咄咄逼人的態度加劇了他們之間關係的惡化，最終兩人分道揚鑣。

75. by rote 死記硬背

例：Our educators must motivate students to understand what they are learning, rather than just memorize it by rote 我們的教育者必須激勵學生去理解他們所學的內容，而非僅僅通過死記硬背來學習。

76. to rip up 撕毀

例：The buyer blatantly ripped up the sales agreement and refused to release the payment on the due date. His outrageous behavior shows he has completely lost his credibility 這

個買家公然撕毀了銷售合同，並在付款日拒絕付款。他這種離譜的行為說明他已經徹底失去了信用。

再比如：During the negotiation, he was so enraged that he ripped up the sales contract. His rude behavior left everyone stunned. 在談判過程中，他勃然大怒，撕毀了銷售合同。他粗魯的行為使大家大為震驚。

77. heft 實力
例：They have the heft to bounce back, even though they lost this game. 儘管輸了這場比賽，他們仍有實力扳回一局。

78. hip 時髦的
例：You look pretty hip, and your clothes are quite fashionable, especially your rare limited edition Jordans 你看起來很時髦，衣服也非常時尚，特別是你穿的那雙限量版喬丹鞋。

79. snappy 時髦的
例：She wore a snappier red skirt as she stepped onto the stage, capturing the attention of the entire audience. 她穿上了一條更時髦的紅色裙子走上舞臺，吸引了全場觀眾的目光。

80. snazzy 時髦的，時尚的
例：She picked out a plethora of clothes, each one exuding a snazzier appeal. The garments she chose were not only stylish but also possessed a distinct flair, adding an extra touch of elegance and eye-catching charm. 她挑選了許多衣服，每一件都散發著更加時髦的魅力。她選擇的衣服不僅時尚，而且具有獨特的風格，增添了一份優雅與引人注目的魅力。

81. plausible 似乎有道理的
例：His explanation seems plausible, but unfortunately, it runs counter to the truth and the facts. 他的解釋似乎有道理，但不幸的是，它與事實和真相相悖。

82. to slosh around 四處遊蕩
例：The suddenly laid-off deeply impacted his life, so his spirit, like a ghost, sloshed around, and he lost the direction of his future and

hope.突然的下崗深深影響了他的生活，他的精神像幽靈一樣四處遊蕩，他失去了未來的方向和希望。

83. to make sb more stretched 使某人變得更加緊張

例：Increasing taxes will make people's lives more stretched. 提高稅收將使人們的生活更加緊張。

84. to make somebody neuralgic about 使某人感到頭痛

例：All parents prefer their kids to be more active; however, if it is excessive, it will make them feel neurotic about their kids' naughtiness. 所有的父母都希望他們的孩子更活躍，但如果過度的話，就會讓他們對孩子的調皮感到頭痛。

85. brazen 肆無忌憚的，無恥的

例：His speech was fraught with brazenly discriminatory content, which provoked public outrage. 他的演講充斥著肆無忌憚的、厚顏無恥的歧視性內容，激起了公眾的憤怒。

86. to badger sb 死纏著某人 ...

例：One of my relatives badgered me to lend money to him.我有個親戚死纏著我借錢給他。

87. to cast someone into poverty 使某人陷入困境

例：He lost his job, and having no income cast him into a difficult situation. 他丟了工作;沒有收入使他陷入困境。

88. to put sb in a pickle 使某人陷入困境

例：The failure of my investment put me in a pickle. 我這次投資失敗，使我陷入困境。

89. to lose one's cachet 失去聲望

例：His disloyalty made him lose his cachet, and it will be extremely difficult for him to regain it. 他的不忠使他失去了聲望，而要重新贏回它將異常艱難。

90. to put it 說

例：In a public speech, US President Donald Trump put it

bluntly: "You're fired.在一次公開演講中，美國總統唐納德·特朗普直截了當地說："你被解雇了。"

91. ipso facto （來自拉丁語）事實

例：The sentence for him is appropriate, and his crime is ipso facto apparent, meaning he ought to be penalized. 對他的判決是恰當的，他的罪行事實清楚，因此他應該受到懲罰。

92. to dip one's toes in 試水

例：Some developing countries are tentatively dipping their toes into opening up to the outside world in an effort to revamp their economies. 一些發展中國家正試探性地向外界開放，以圖振興經濟。

93. brick-and-mortar store 實體店

如今,很多人都通過互聯網買東西，優點是更便宜送貨快捷，容易退貨。缺點是你購買前無法觸摸要買東西的質感。為此，傳統的實體店依然有存在的必要。在西方，很多人到名牌實體店去體驗要買物品的手感和用料的品質，然後，再到該店品牌的網站以更便宜的價格買入。

例：My sister wanted to buy a pair of shoes. She browsed online and found plenty of styles at cheaper prices. However, she still preferred to go to a brick-and-mortar shoe store to try them on before making her final selection. 我妹妹想買一雙鞋。她在網上流覽了一番，發現有很多款式而且價格更便宜。然而，她還是更傾向於去實體鞋店試穿之後再做最終決定。

94. soggy 濕透的

例：As she walked in the rain, she became completely soggy from head to toe. 她走在雨中，渾身從頭到腳都濕透了。

95. to be sodden with 濕透了

例：She ran to the school to pick up her kid, but on the way back home, it started pouring, and they ended up completely sodden. 她跑去學校接孩子，回家的路上突然下起了大雨，他們被淋得渾身濕透。

96. to put sb at odds 使某人為難

例：Frankly speaking, your borrowing money from me literally put me at odds. 坦率地說，你向我借錢真的使我很為難。

97. grub 食物

例：My uncle rushed in, said he needed some grub, and that he had to dash off to pick someone up at the airport. 我叔叔沖進來，說他想吃點東西，然後得趕緊去機場接人。

98. to sap 使削弱

例：His repeated failures in the test sapped his confidence and wore down his persistence. 他在考試中的屢次失敗削弱了他的信心，也逐漸耗盡了他的堅持。

再比如：The global chip shortage will unpredictably sap already feeble car sales. 全球晶片短缺將不可預測地削弱本已疲軟的汽車銷售。

99. to renege on 食言，違背

例：Our company has sufficient financial strength to make timely payments. We will never renege on our agreements. 我們公司有足夠的能力按時付款，絕不會食言。

100. to backfire 事與願違

例：She wanted to pamper or curry favor with her boss but unfortunately backfired.她想討好她的老闆，但不幸的是事與願違。

101. to beguile 使著迷

例：The dancer's spectacular performance beguiled countless young people with its charm and grace.這位舞者精彩絕倫的表演以其魅力與優雅使無數年輕人著迷。

102. to crank up one's power 使足了勁兒

例：To achieve tremendous results, each team member cranked up their power, dedicating themselves fully to this promising cancer treatment project. 為了取得非凡成果，每位團隊成員都使足了勁兒，投入到這個前景廣闊的癌症治療項目中。

103. at the mercy of 受…擺佈

例：She and her friends co-founded a company specializing in B2B services. Unfortunately, she has decided to resign because she does not wish to be at the mercy of the company's board. 她和她的朋友們共同創辦了一家專注於 B2B 服務的公司。不幸的是，她決定辭職，因為她不再想任由公司董事會擺佈。

104. to coin 首次使用。（除了硬幣的意思外）

例："Fen Si," a term coined by the Chinese, refers to the fan in English. "粉絲"這個由中國人首次用的詞，指的是英語中的"fan"。

105. pliant 順從的、唯唯諾諾的

例:She doesn't want to be a pliant wife; she aspires to freedom, so she decides to divorce her husband.她不想做一個順從的妻子，她渴望自由，所以她決定和丈夫離婚。

再比如：I never advocate pliant behavior to curry favor with anyone. 我從不提倡唯唯諾諾的行為來討好任何人。

106. to take a knock 受到衝擊

例：Our original lifestyle will take a knock with the further development of AI. 隨著人工智慧的進一步發展，我們原本的生活方式將受到衝擊。

107. to take a battering 受到衝擊，重創，打擊

例：The global economy has taken a battering from the vicious spread of the virus. 全球經濟已經受到病毒迅速蔓延的嚴重衝擊。

108. to be shattered by 受到極大的打擊，

例：Jaxon was shattered by his girlfriend's betrayal. 女友的背叛讓傑克遜受到極大的打擊。

109. to be pilloried 受到強烈抨擊

例：The actress was pilloried by the public for her lackluster performance in the film. 這位女演員因在電影中表演平淡無奇而受到公眾的強烈抨擊。

110. to find favour 受到青睞

例:High-quality products with the most favorable prices can find favor. 高品質、價格最優惠的產品能夠獲得青睞。

111. to be plagued 受到災害，困擾等

例：Many people are deeply concerned that we may be plagued by a third World War due to the escalating conflicts among superpowers. 許多人深感擔憂，認為由於超級大國間衝突的升級，第三次世界大戰會讓我們受到災難。

112. to be hamstrung by 受到阻礙

例：The implementation is hamstrung by misguided guidance, so we need to correct it. 實施受到了錯誤指導的阻礙，所以我們需要糾正它。

113. sleight 手法，技巧

例：Magic performances mainly depend on the performer's sleight of hand. 魔術表演主要依賴於表演者的巧妙手法。

114. to recoup 收回

例：Some companies poured a lot of money into investments across various industries during the pandemic, but now they feel disappointed as it has become difficult to recoup their costs. 一些公司在疫情期間將大量資金投入到各個行業中，但現在他們感到非常失望，因為很難收回成本。

再比如：This young man invested nearly 1 million dollars into setting up an online business, expecting to recoup his investment within three years. 這位年輕人投入近 100 萬美元建立了一家線上業務，並預計在三年內收回投資

115. to undermine the reputation of 損害 ...的名譽或聲譽

例：His rudeness clearly undermined the reputation of our school, so we must step in and investigate the matter. 他的粗魯行為顯然損害了我們學校的聲譽，因此我們必須介入並調查此事。

116. to stall 折在、 拖住
例：Some vehicles are stalled on the highway due to severe accidents. 由於嚴重的事故，一些車輛折在高速公路上 。
再比如：The bank clerk was highly alert. Remaining calm, he stalled the robber and pressed the button to alert the police. 銀行職員非常警覺。他保持冷靜，拖住了搶劫犯的行動，並按下按鈕報警。

117. to home in on 鎖定
例：The fantastic stuff equipped on the missile can quickly accurately home in on a target.這個裝在導彈上的神奇玩意兒可以快速準確地鎖定目標。

118. to be under siege 受困
例：So many people were under siege by the flood, an event that had never occurred in history. 許多人在洪水的圍困下，這種情況在歷史上從未發生過。

再比如：He supports the whole family, but unfortunately, he was laid off, and now his family is under siege.他養活整個家庭，但不幸的是，他被裁員了，現在他的家庭受困。

119. to empower 授權
例：Without being empowered, this guy dared to practice medicine. That's crazy. 在沒有獲得授權的情況下，這個人竟敢行醫，太瘋狂了。

120. yawning income 收入可觀
例：He recently found a better job and will earn a yawning income. 他最近找到了更好的工作，將獲得一筆可觀收入。

121. to be aggrieved 受委屈
例：I apologize for having you aggrieved. I'm sorry for the mistake I made that caused you to lose your job and reputation.對不起，讓你受了委屈； 我向你道歉，因為我犯了一個錯誤，導致你丟掉了工作和名譽。

122. to delineate 鎖定
例：In the thick of war, delineating the exact position of the opposing force before taking aim is crucial for targeting the enemy, regardless of which faction you're in. 在戰爭的激烈時刻，準確劃定敵方位置後

再鎖定至關重要的，無論你屬於哪個陣營。

123. to hold vigils for 守夜
例：I saw so many young people holding candles to vigil for the hero who saved three children. It was very touching to witness. 我看到那麼多的年輕人手捧蠟燭為這位拯救了三個孩子的英雄守夜。現場非常感人。

再比如：Each year, people hold candlelight vigils to honor the souls lost in the 911 tragedy. 每年，人們都會舉行燭光守夜，緬懷在 9·11 災難中逝去的靈魂。

124. to be less vulnerable to 不太容易，不那麼脆弱。
例：Wilson is strong enough that he's less vulnerable to catching a cold. 威爾遜身體夠強壯，不太容易感冒。

125. to ordain 授予
例：He was finally ordained a Ph.D. by the prestigious university, yet a deep gloom shadowed his face. Apart from the title, he had lost nearly everything, and he constantly questioned whether the path he had chosen was ever worth it. 他終於被這所名校授予了博士學位，然而他臉上卻籠罩著濃濃的陰霾。除了這個頭銜，他幾乎失去了一切，也一直在質疑自己當初選擇這條路到底值不值得。

126. to shackle 束縛
例：I prefer freedom over shackling myself to routine. I can't tolerate the monotony of a typical 9-to-5 job, doing the same thing day after day. I loathe having to watch other people's ever-changing moods just to get by. 我嚮往自由，而不是把自己束縛住。我無法忍受那種朝九晚五、日復一日重複同樣事情的單調生活。我厭惡看他人臉色行事，只為混口飯吃。

再比如：Traditional concepts may shackle our imagination, stifle innovation, and constrain creativity. 傳統觀念可能會束縛我們的想像力，壓制創新，限制創造力。

127. to tease out 梳理
例：You guys have been arguing for quite a while without

reaching any resolution. How about we sit down together, tease out what really happened, and calmly work out a better solution to the problem? 你們已經爭執了好一陣子，卻毫無結果。不如我們坐下來，梳理事情的來龍去脈，冷靜地想出一個更好的解決辦法？

128. smug 舒適的，整潔的
例：Of course, almost everyone wants a job where they can feel smug about their success and comfort but not everyone is lucky enough to enjoy such a privilege in their career. 當然，幾乎每個人都想擁有一份能讓自己感到舒適和愜意的工作，但並不是所有人都能在職業生涯中享受到這種待遇。

129. to atone for 贖罪
例：There's an old saying: killers must atone with their lives, and debtors must atone with their money. 有句古話，殺人償命，欠債還錢。

130. to juggle with sb. 耍某人
例：Don't juggle with me; I've already sensed something off, something wrong with this strategy. 別耍我，我已經察覺到哪兒不對勁兒，這個策略有問題。

131. to pay lip service to 耍嘴皮子，嘴上說得好聽；口頭上承認
例：Many wealthy people pay lip service to contributing to the construction of this primary school; unfortunately, they never follow through with any action. 許多富人耍嘴皮子說要為這所小學的建設做出貢獻，然而他們從未付諸任何實際行動。

132. to slap with sth to sb 甩 ... 給某人
例: A cop stopped me and told me I was speeding. I argued with him for a while, he eventually lost his patience, finally slapping a ticket on me 一個員警攔住了我，說我超速了。我和他爭論了一會兒，他顯然失去了耐心，最後，他甩給了我一張罰單。

133. to ebb 衰敗
例：After the pandemic, the global economy began to ebb, exacerbating inflation and

geopolitical tensions, which led to a deterioration in employment and an increase in heavy debt. 在疫情過後，全球經濟開始衰敗，惡化了通貨膨脹和地緣政治緊張局勢，導致就業形勢惡化並加重了債務負擔。

134. enervation 衰弱

例:The enervation of the global economy is set to usher in a depression, marking a sharp contrast to the era of prosperous globalization. 全球經濟的衰弱即將引發一場經濟蕭條，與繁榮的全球化時代形成鮮明對比。

135. a double-edged sword 雙刃劍

例：A knife is a double-edged sword. It can be used to cut ingredients for making a delicious meal, or it can be employed to harm someone. .刀是一把雙刃劍。它可以用來切食材,製作美味的食物，也可以用來傷害他人。

136. double-whammy 雙重打擊

例：His divorce and the loss of his wife delivered a double whammy to his spirit. 他的離婚和失去妻子對他的精神造成了雙重打擊。

T

1. quixotic 不切實際的，堂吉歌德式的

He is a quixotic guy, full of craziness, determined to realize his dream. 他是一個充滿瘋狂不切實際的人，決心實現自己的夢想 。

2. to catapult 彈射，突然快速移動

例：To survive, the pilots must catapult themselves out of the plane when it is completely out of control. 為了生存，當飛機完全失控時，飛行員必須把自己彈射出去。

3. to tell of 談到，講述

例：He always feels delighted when telling of his sons, who have achieved outstanding academic awards in their careers. 他總是很高興講到他的兒子

們，他們在職業生涯中獲得了卓越的學術獎項。

4. cupidity 貪婪
例：He consistently professed disinterest in that lavish timepiece, yet I could discern both cupidity and longing in his eyes.他一貫聲稱對那只奢華的手錶毫無興趣，但我能從他眼中看出貪婪和渴望。

5. rapacious 貪婪的
例：People should not be too rapacious, or they risk self-destruction. 人們不能太貪婪，否則他們可能自取滅亡。

6. voracious 如饑似渴的
例：I am a voracious collector of car models, especially Ferraris and Mercedes. 我是一個如饑似渴的汽車模型收藏家，收集的車模尤其有法拉利，梅賽德斯等。

7. to hide its strengths and bide its time 韜光養晦等待時機
例：Any developing country should hide its strengths and bide its time to make its economy more robust.任何發展中國家都應該隱瞞自己的優勢，韜光養晦等待時機以使其經濟更加強健。

8. to cozy up to 討好
例：I don't want to cozy up to anyone, that's my bottom line.我不想討好任何人，這是我的底線。

另外，也可以使用 fawn on sb.

9. to blandish 討好，奉承
例：The more you blandish someone, the more you will be looked down upon or even be bullied. 你越是討好別人，你就越會被人看不起，甚至被人欺負。

10. a gold rush 淘金熱
例: In the past 20 years, with the further development of its technology, China has become the center of a global business gold rush. 在過去的 20 年裡，隨著中國技術的進一步發展，中國成為了全球商業淘金熱的中心。

11. to hash out 討論來討論去，沒完沒了的討論

例：They have been hashing out this issue for almost 10 years, but nothing has happened, and there is still no solution.他們已經就這個問題討論來討論去折騰了近 10 年，但什麼都沒有發生，依然沒有解決方案

12. to diminish 淘汰

例：Anyone must follow the trend of development in time. Otherwise, they may be diminished.任何人都必須及時跟上發展的趨勢，否則就有可能被淘汰。

13. gushing 滔滔不絕的，過分熱情的，誇大其詞的

例：The hollow and gushing speech he delivered made everyone feel uncomfortable 他那空洞而滔滔不絕的演講使大家都感到不舒服。

例：I don't trust that guy because his rhetoric was always gushing.我不信任那個傢伙，因為他的言辭總是過於誇大其詞。

14. heinous 滔天的，極其罪惡的

例：This suspect committed a heinous crime, upending everyone's worldviews. 這個嫌疑犯犯下了顛覆大家三觀的滔天罪行。

15. pesky 討厭的

例：Some reporters put him in many awkward situations; he murmured that they were downright pesky.一些記者讓他陷入了許多尷尬的境地，他嘟囔著說這些人實在是討厭透頂。

16. to disown 脫離關係

例:Her elder son failed to uphold filial piety, so she decided to disown him 她的大兒子未能盡孝，所以她決定與他脫離關係。

17. maverick 特立獨行

例：Mary's personality is too much of a maverick to easily get along with others in the company; even the boss has to yield to her. 瑪麗的性格太特立獨行了，在公司裡很難與他人相處，甚至連老闆都得讓她幾分。

18. to broach 提出
例：He felt pretty awkward when a reporter broached that sensitive question. 當記者提出那個敏感問題時，他感到很尷尬。

19. to come up with 提出，想出
例：Hunter came up with a better suggestion—that you all work together and share with one another 亨特提出了一個更好的建議——你們可以合作並彼此分享。

20. to lodge a complaint 投訴
例：If riders lodged a lot of complaints, the driver should be fired. 如果乘客投訴太多，司機應該被解雇。

21. to put up 提供
例：Never impulsively put up a guarantee for anyone, as you may risk taking responsibility for their defaults. 千萬不要衝動地為任何人提供擔保，否則你可能會承擔他們違約的責任。

22. to underpin 提供（證據）
例：If you want to allege someone for improper behavior, you need to underpin your claim with solid evidence to win the case 如果你想指控某人行為不當，你需要提供確鑿證據來支撐你的說法，才能贏得這場官司。

23. to offer solace to 提供安慰
例:In my experience, offering solace to people who have lost a loved one, failed an important exam, or are caught in the throes of heartbreak and fury often proves futile, as their pain and anger are at their peak.根據我的經驗，安慰那些失去親人、考試失敗，或因感情受挫而陷入憤怒與悲傷的人，往往是徒勞的，因為他們正處氣頭兒上。

24. to burnish 提升
例：Higher education and some working experience can burnish your capability in your career. 高等教育和一定的工作經驗可以提升你在職業生涯中的能力。

25. to epitomize 體現

例：Compared to Rolex, Tudor watches also epitomize elegance, durability, and lasting quality—yet they come at a much more affordable price, often only a third or even less. 與勞力士相比，帝舵腕表同樣體現了優雅、耐用和持久的品質，卻以更加親民的價格出售，往往只需勞力士三分之一甚至更低的價格。

26. salubrious 天氣清爽

例：Oh, the weather today is remarkably salubrious. Fancy going on a picnic? 哇，今天天氣清爽。你想去野餐嗎？

27. to be cut out to 天生不是做…的料

例：You are just not cut out to be a ballet dancer.你天生就不是當芭蕾舞演員的料。

28. spoon-feeds 填鴨式

例：We must abandon the spoon-fed education system to fully tap into each student's potential. 我們必須摒棄填鴨式的教育機制，充分挖掘每個學生的潛力。

29. to instigate 挑撥

例：He tried to instigate the breakdown of our relationship, but his efforts flopped in the end. 他試圖挑撥我們之間的關係，但最終他的圖謀以失敗告終。

30. choosy 挑剔的

choosy 從某種程度上說就是 picky 的同義詞，但兩者還是有些區別。choosy 更注重挑剔的是否符合自己的品味，比如口味，欲望以及要求。而 picky 是一定要對的東西。

例：Blake is quite choosy when it comes to his clothes. 布萊克在穿衣方面相當挑剔。

再比如：Avery is too choosy about what he will write even though no matter what he can write, he still can get a lot of money.艾弗裡對寫什麼太挑剔了，儘管不管寫什麼他都能賺很多錢。

31. to winnow 挑選，篩選

例：He spent the entire night working on a project to meet the deadline. In the end, he completed several plans and submitted them to his boss, who carefully winnowed out the most cost-effective one. 他為了趕上截止日期，整整熬了一夜做項目。最後，他完成了幾個方案並提交給老闆，老闆仔細挑選出了那個最節省成本的。

32. to tweak 調整

例：I suggest you tweak some of the expressions before submitting them to the board. 我建議你在提交給董事會之前稍微調整一下其中的一些表達。

再比如：This movie hasn't been approved yet, but the censor suggested that the producer tweak a bit of its content to ensure a successful final debut. 這部電影尚未獲得批准，但審查員建議製作人稍微調整一些內容，以確保順利首映。

還有：I found that Apple covertly tweaked the quality and design of their products, which seems to have raised some buzz in the market. 我發現蘋果公司偷偷調整了其產品的品質和設計，這在市場上引起了關注。

33. to rejig 調整

例：Sales this month have been less than ideal, prompting the company to rejig its marketing strategy to better adapt to the changing landscape. 本月銷售狀況不盡如人意，因此公司決定重新調整行銷策略，以更好地適應變化的環境。

34. monolithic 鐵板一塊、整體的

例：Their relationship is not monolithic; ostensibly, it may seem so, but in reality, it is not. 他們的關係並不是鐵板一塊的，表面上看似如此，但實際上並非如此。

35. the point of no return 停不下來了，無法挽回了等

例：Never slam on the brakes once you've entered the "point of no return," even if the yellow light suddenly comes on; otherwise, you risk being hit from behind, as the car following you won't be able to stop in time. 一旦進入"停不下來的点"，即使黃燈突然亮起，也不要猛踩刹車，

否則你會因後面的車無法及時停車而被追尾。

36. to be at loggerheads with 同…意見不合

例：All the staff in this office are at loggerheads with each other, which could seriously affect production efficiency. 這個辦公室所有的員工彼此意見不合，這可能會嚴重影響生產效率。

37. to doff 脫帽，脫衣

例：In terms of courtesy, please doff your hat before making an official speech in public; unfortunately, some people still don't understand why. 從禮儀角度來說，在公共場合發表正式演講前，請脫帽；不幸的是，一些人仍然不明白其中的原因。

38. to abhor 痛恨

例：I abhor people who speak ill of you behind your back while praising you to your face. It is truly hypocritical. 我痛恨那些背後說你壞話，卻在你面前稱讚你的人。這真是太虛偽了。

39. to tally 統計，計算，合計

例：We must work together, sorting and tallying all kinds of data. 我們必須共同努力，整理和統計各種資料。

40. to bewail 痛哭

例：She bewailed the disappointment of true love. 她為失去真愛而痛哭。

41. eponymous 同名的

例：The director adapted an eponymous novel into a movie; unfortunately, he turned it into an unrealistic and distorted version. 導演將一部同名小說改編成電影；不幸的是，他把它改編成了一個不真實且失真的版本。

42. namesake 同名同姓

例:China has one of the largest populations in the world, so it's common for many people to have namesakes. 中國是世界上人口最多的國家之一，所以很多人同名同姓是很常見的。

43. to booze 痛飲開懷

例：All colleagues rarely meet each other often due to their business, finally they met and happily booze. 由於工作繁忙，同事們很少有機會見面，最終他們聚在一起，痛飲開懷。

44. to slack off 偷懶
例：Don't slack off while doing your work; stay focused and responsible. 工作時不要偷懶，要保持專注並負責任。

45. to divulge 透露，洩露，洩露
例：Everleigh made a killing, but she's reluctant to divulge how she got rich in such a short time. 埃弗裡賺了一大筆錢，但她不願透露自己是如何在短時間內致富的。

46. to pour... into 投入
例：This company is pouring a significant amount of money into the R&D of electric vehicles. 這家公司正在向電動汽車的研發投入大量資金。

47. to pitch in 投入
例：Only the largest companies can ultimately resolve the energy shortage facing humanity by pitching in and collaborating on the development of new energy sources. 只有最大的公司才能最終解決人類面臨的能源短缺問題——通過共同投入，合作開發新能源。

48. furtive 偷偷摸摸的
例：The case was cracked when a police officer on the station platform noticed the felony killer's furtive behavior, which immediately aroused suspicion. 當一名月臺上的員警注意到這名重罪殺手偷偷摸摸的行為並立刻起了疑心時，這樁案件終於被偵破了。

49. covertly 偷偷摸摸地
例：If a girl covertly glances at you often, it might indicate that she has developed some feelings for you. 如果一個女孩經常偷偷地瞥你，那可能意味著她對你產生了些許感情。

50. surreptitiously 偷偷摸摸地
例：I found that many gas stations surreptitiously add 'something' to the gasoline, causing each tank to run fewer kilometers. 我發現許多加油站偷偷地在汽油中添加"某種物

質"，導致每次加滿油後的行駛里程減少。

51. by stealth 偷偷摸摸地

例: He left the office by stealth without notifying anyone, leaving them astonished by his creepy behavior. 他偷偷摸摸地離開了辦公室，沒有通知任何人，令大家對他怪異的行為感到震驚。

52. to sneak 偷偷摸摸地做

例：I encountered a bizarre thing. A theft stole something from my house and snuck them back 我遇到了一件非常奇怪的事情。一個小偷把從我家偷的東西又偷偷地送了回來。

53. vertiginous 頭暈目眩的

例：Standing beside a valley, I felt vertiginous, almost as if I were about to drop into it. 站在山谷旁，我感到頭暈目眩，差點掉進去。

54. giddy 頭暈眼花

例：My girlfriend drove too fast on the highway, and I felt giddy 女友在高速公路上開車太快了，我感到頭昏眼花。

再比如：This is my first time visiting a bar. The noise of the music and the dazzling, colorful lights made me feel a bit giddy. 這是我第一次去酒吧。音樂的噪音和耀眼的五光十色的燈光讓我有些頭暈。

55. delinquency 拖欠

例:The contract clearly stipulates that any delinquency in rent will lead to the immediate termination of your rental housing 合同明確規定，任何租金拖欠將導致立即終止您的租賃合同。

56. to jut out 突出，伸出

例：I saw a new mansion jutting out from half of the mountain, and I'm wondering who built it. 我看到一座新豪宅從半山腰突出，我在想是誰建造的。

57. salient 突出的，顯著的

例：Giving cash to the public is the most salient way to stimulate the domestic economy. 向公眾發放現金是刺激國內經濟突出的方式。

再比如：The measurements he took and the ingredients he used to control the insect invasion and spoilage of the crops are salient. 他採取的措施和用於控制昆蟲入侵並破壞農作物的成分非常顯著。

58. to disgorge 吐出來
例：Since you deceived me out of my money, you must disgorge it 既然你騙了我的錢，你就得吐出來。

59. to crop up 突發
例：His asthma has cropped up after 25 years of living in North America. Unpredictably, He had no family history of asthma, and he have no idea when or why he developed it 在北美生活了 25 年後，他的哮喘突然發作了。出乎意料的是，他家族中沒有哮喘病史，他也不知道自己什麼時候以及為什麼得了哮喘。

再比如: Some studies show that sudden death can crop up in young people who take a shower immediately after intense exercise.一些研究表明，年輕人在劇烈運動後立即洗澡可能會突然發生猝死。

還有：The young generation must be educated on how to deal with issues that crop up, so they can stay calm, adapt, and resolve them effectively. 年輕一代必須接受教育，學會如何應對突發問題，從而能夠保持冷靜、靈活應變並有效解決。

60. leaps and bounds 突飛猛進
我們常說某某事物的發展突飛猛進，或某項技術有了突飛猛進的發展等 ...
例：In the past 20 years, China's technological development has advanced by leaps and bounds.在過去二十年裡，中國的科技發展突飛猛進。

61. to slather on 塗抹
例：In summer, many people have to slather on sunscreen to protect their skin from getting burned — and men are no exception. 在夏天，許多人不得不厚厚地塗上防曬霜來防止皮膚被曬傷，男性也不例外。

62. frumpy 土氣，傻裡傻氣的

例：After spending 30 years in the countryside, her first venture into the city left her amazed by its dazzling atmosphere though she couldn't help but feel a bit frumpy amidst the chic urban crowd.在鄉下生活了三十年之後，她第一次踏入城市，被那光鮮亮麗的環境驚豔到了儘管在時髦的都市人群中，她不由得感到自己有些土氣。

63. to flip-flop 突然變卦，嘰嘰歪歪的

例：Ezekiel suddenly flip-flopped on his promise, leaving everyone both astonished and frustrated. 以西結 突然變卦了他的承諾，這讓所有人都感到震驚和沮喪。

再比如：Though he was one of my best friends, he always treated me in a flip-floppy way, which made me uneasy about his reluctance. 作為我最好的朋友之一，他對待我總是嘰嘰歪歪的，所以我對他的不情願感到不舒服。

64. to branch out 拓展

例：Investing in your education will help branch out your future opportunities. 投資於你的教育將有助於拓展你的未來發展。

65. to precipitate 突然加速

例：Continuing to drink alcohol will precipitate the deterioration of liver disease. 持續飲酒會突然加速肝病的惡化。

66. to snap 突然情緒崩潰

例：She suddenly snapped and burst into tears, leaving everyone at the scene astonished. 她突然情緒崩潰並哭了出來，令在場的所有人都感到震驚。

67. to alight on 突然想到 …

例：I've alighted on a new method that assists Chinese English learners in enhancing their writing skills.我突然想到了一個新方法，可以幫助中國的英語學習者提高寫作技巧。

68. pooled purchase 團購

例：Nowadays, Chinese buyers prefer pooled purchases, which have become more popular than ever before because they allow buyers to get much cheaper prices. 如今，中國買家更喜歡團購，這種方式比以往更加流行，因為買家可以以更便宜的價格購買商品。

69. to roll out 推出
例： The government recently rolled out a new benefit to help many low-income families overcome the pandemic.政府最近推出了一項新福利，幫助許多低收入家庭度過疫情難關

70. to impel 推動
例：AI technology has impelled the development of more efficient medicines for the treatment of AIDS, moving us closer to its ultimate termination. 人工智慧技術推動了更高效的愛滋病治療藥物的發展，使我們更接近最終根除愛滋病的目標。

71. decadent 頹廢的
例：Giving up on learning leads to a decadent life. 放棄學習會導致墮落的生活。

72. to press ahead with 推進
例：Without my boss's tremendous support, this project couldn't have progressed successfully. 如果沒有老闆的巨大支持，這個項目無法順利推進。

73. to regress 退縮
例：Anyone who regresses in the face of challenges will be a loser. 任何在面臨挑戰時退縮的人都將是敗者.

74. to wince 退縮
例：This graduate tried many ways and many times to set up his own business, but regretfully ended up failing. However, he never gave up and never winced. Ultimately, he became successful by exerting all his efforts.這位畢業生嘗試了很多方法，很多次去創辦自己的事業，但遺憾的是最終失敗了。然而，他從未放棄，也從未退縮。最終，他通過全力以赴取得了成功。

75. to prevaricate 推諉，搪塞；支吾其辭，閃爍其辭
例：Parents must collaborate on their children's education, which

will fail if they prevaricate with each other instead of addressing the issues head-on. 父母必須在孩子的教育上密切合作，如果他們互相推諉，而不是直接解決問題，教育將會失敗。

76. to flog 兜售，削弱

例：She tried to flog me a special insurance package, enthusiastically touting its many benefits for my future retirement. 她試圖向我兜售 一款特別的保險計畫，熱情地宣傳它對我未來退休生活的諸多好處。

再比如：The currency devaluation undermines the ability to import goods from other countries; however, it benefits exports by making them more competitive abroad. 貨幣貶值削弱了從其他國家進口商品的能力；然而，它通過提高出口商品在海外的競爭力，從而促進了出口。

77. to gobble up 吞噬

例：The black hole's gravity has the ability to gobble up stars of all sizes and densities.黑洞的引力有能力吞噬各種大小和密度的恒星。

78. to splutter 吞吞吐吐，支支吾吾

例：He reluctantly tried to argue with his wife, but the words caught in his throat. In the end, he spluttered out an admission that he had a lover outside. Naturally, the inevitable result was their divorce. 他不情願地試圖與妻子爭論，但話卡在了喉嚨裡。最終，他吞吞吐吐地承認自己在外面有情人。自然，結果就是他們離婚了。

79. hiatus 脫節

例：The hiatus between the senior technicians and new ones are very striking and seriously affects the continuity of the further development of product renovation.老技術人員與新技術人員之間的脫節非常明顯，嚴重影響了產品創新進一步發展的連續性。

80. to bog down 拖垮，陷入困境

例：The global financial crisis bogged down the economy,

leading to widespread layoffs and salary cuts.全球金融危機拖垮了經濟，導致了大規模的裁員和薪資削減。

81. to drag on 拖延
例：The case was too complex, thus it has dragged on for a couple of years. 這個案子太複雜了，所以拖延了好幾年。

再比如：In Canada, the so-called basic income guaranteeing the people with low income, $2000 per person each month, has dragged on for five years of discussion in the parliament. 在加拿大，保障低收入者每人每月 2000 加幣的所謂基本收入，在議會的討論中拖了 5 年。

還比如：A survey found that many construction companies intentionally dragged things on to get more money. 據一項調查結果顯示，很多建築企業為了得到更多的資金，故意拖延工期。

W

1. to dredge up 挖出
例：After a guy exposed some scandals about his team leader, netizens began dredging up the leader's background. 一個人曝光了他領導的一些醜聞後，網友們開始翻舊賬，挖出這位領導的背景。

2. to scoop out 挖掉
例：You still shouldn't eat any overripe fruit, even if you've scooped out the rotten parts it may cause cancer, especially liver cancer. 即使把腐爛的部分挖掉，也不要吃腐爛的水果，這可能會致癌，尤其是肝癌。

3. to tap into 挖掘，充分利用
例：Our parents and teachers must do their utmost to tap into children's potential. 我們的父母和老師必須盡最大努力挖掘孩子們的潛力。

4. inexorably 無情地，無法阻擋地

例：I was inexorably devastated in academics when I failed to pass the exam. 考試沒通過讓我在學業上無情地遭受了打擊。

5. to outsource 外包

例： Some of the manufacturers outsourced their processing in terms of lowering their costs. 為了降低成本，一些製造商把加工過程外包出去。

6. obdurate 頑固的，冷酷無情的

例：When it came to balancing the relationship between his mother and his wife, he acted with obdurate stubbornness, which left his mother disappointed. 在如何平衡母親與妻子的關係這一問題上，他表現得十分頑固，讓母親感到失望。

7. to skew 歪曲，曲解

例：I was misunderstood because some of my opinions were unreasonably skewed. 我被誤解了，因為我的一些觀點被無理地歪曲了。

8. stalwart 頑固分子，忠誠者

例：Game-playing stalwarts indirectly ruin their lives and futures, especially for young people who are intoxicated by gaming. 沉迷遊戲的頑固分子們間接地毀掉了他們的生活和未來，尤其是那些被遊戲迷住的年輕人。

9. to spare 挽救，饒恕，赦免

一提起 spare 很多人立刻就想到 spare time 多餘的時間，spare key 備用鑰匙等。它本身的意思非常多，除了做形容詞，還可以作動詞。

例：Henry did his best to spare his uncle from blame of others. 亨利盡力保護他的叔叔免受外界的責難。

另外還有一種用法就是 spare a thought for someone. 為別人著想。

再比如：I urge you not to waste money. You have to understand that I am sparing a thought for you. 我勸你不要浪費錢。你要明白我這是為你著想。

10. to toy with 玩弄
例：It is hazardous to toy with the other person's emotions, and it is also immoral.玩弄他人的感情是危險的； 這也是不道德的。

11. impish 頑皮的
例：This boy is quite impish, but he is also very smart and kind. 這個男孩相當頑皮，但他又非常聰明和善良。

12. dogged 頑強的
例：My boss has a dogged personality, and I respect him from the bottom of my heart. 我的老闆有著頑強的個性，我由衷地尊敬他。

13. entirely 完全地（和它相近的還有 totally, absolutely, thoroughly, fully, completely etc.）
例：So many people saw a UFO hovering silently above before it suddenly disappeared entirely. 許多人看到一艘 UFO 在空中靜靜地懸停，隨後突然完全消失。

14. heartthrob 萬人迷
例：This young star astonishingly became the heartthrob overnight in our country. 這位年輕明星令人驚訝地在一夜之間成為我們國家的萬人迷。

15. foolproof 萬無一失的
例：Never disregard anything that takes you by surprise, because nothing in this world is entirely foolproof. 永遠不要忽視任何突然出現在你意料之外的事情，因為在這個世界上沒有什麼是萬無一失的。

16. to feel daunted 望而卻步，畏懼
例：Although she earned $3000 per month, she felt daunted by the steep price tag of any luxury items. 雖然她每個月的收入是 3000 美元，但面對昂貴的奢侈品價格，她還是感到望而卻步。

17. to put gold on one's face 往某人臉上貼金
例：Her mom shouted at her dad, "Stop putting gold on your face. Have you been looking after our kids?" She was clearly very angry about his shameless confidence.她媽媽對她爸爸大喊道："別再往臉上抹金了，

孩子們你照顧過嗎？"顯然，
她對他那種無恥的自信感到
非常生氣。

18. buoyant 旺盛的
例：Young people's energy is
more buoyant than that of
seniors. 年輕人的精力比老年
人更旺盛。

19. to chart new paths for
為…的未來開闢新的道路
例：Leaders should chart new
paths for the further development
of the enterprises in cities and
towns. 領導們要為城鎮企業
進一步發展開闢新的道路。

20. to fret over　為…煩惱
例：In the Western world, many
low-income families constantly
fret over financial scarcity,
leading to deep concerns about
their livelihoods 在西方社會，
許多低收入家庭常常為經濟
拮据而焦慮，對生計問題產
生了深切擔憂。

21. lament about 為…感到惋
惜
例：She lamented about the fact
that she couldn't pass her final

exams.她為沒有通過期末考
試而感到惋惜。

你也可以說：　She lamented
the fact that she couldn't pass her
final exams. 她對自己沒能通
過期末考試感到惋惜。
相對上一句會顯得更加正
式，更書面語化。但在日常
表達中一般人都會加上
about 顯得自然。

22. to feel smug about 為 …感
到沾沾自喜
例：She used improper means
to acquire that small company
and felt smug about her
conspiracy. 她用不正當的手
段收購了那家小公司，並為
自己的陰謀而感到沾沾自
喜。

23. to set a precedent for　為 …
開先例
例：We can't set a precedent for
anyone who goes against the
regulations. 我們不能為任何
違反規定的人開先例。

24. lackadaisical 無精打采的
懶散的
例：This boy had been playing
the game for two days straight.

He slept less, and of course, he appeared lackadaisical while listening to the lectures in class. 這個男孩已經連續玩了兩天遊戲了。他睡得很少，當然，在課堂上聽講時，顯得無精打采。

25. to set goals for 為…制定目標
例：My habit is that I set goals for the consecutive years, at least 5 years personal plan to complete my study or buy a brand new car. 我習慣為連續的幾年制定目標，至少有一個為期五年的個人計畫，以完成我的學業或買一輛嶄新的車。

26. to brace for 為…做準備
例：Humanity is bracing for an impending alien attack and making preparations to defend itself. 人類正為即將來臨的外星人襲擊做足準備，誓要自我防衛。

27. meager 微薄的，不足的，少的
例：Ordinary people can only earn meager salaries just to make ends meet. 普通人只能靠微薄的薪水勉強維持生計。

28. puny 微薄的，微不足道的
例：As citizens of this country, each of us must contribute our puny efforts to make it better in the future. 作為這個國家的公民，我們每個人都必須貢獻自己 微薄的力量，讓未來變得更美好。

29. to browbeat sb into doing sth 威逼某人做某事
例：The board members browbeat the CEO into taking more effective steps to boost revenue; otherwise, they threatened to withdraw all their investments. 董事會成員威逼首席執行官採取更有效的措施來提升收入，否則他們將撤回所有投資。

30. derisory 微不足道的
例：Many people consider giving children $2000 as a derisory amount for a Lunar New Year gift. However, I ended up in the awkward position of having to borrow that money from my mom. 許多人認為給孩子 2000 美元作為壓歲錢是一個微不足道

的數目　。然而，我卻陷入了一個尷尬的境地，不得不向我媽媽借這筆錢。

31. to be unverified 未得到證實.

例：All details pertaining to this case remain unverified. 與本案有關的所有細節仍未得到證實。

32. to fall foul of 違反

例：You will be fired if you fall foul of the rules specified by the company. 如果你違反了公司規定，你就會被炒魷魚。

33. unassailable 無懈可擊的

例：Confronted with unreasonable questions, his answers remained unassailable. 面對無理質疑，他的回答依然無懈可擊。

34. to imperil 危及到 ...

例：Our economy is in a U-turn, which has imperiled its post-pandemic prosperity. 我們的經濟正在經歷一次大轉彎，這已危及了其疫情後的繁榮。

再比如：Russia grumbled about the EU deploying ballistic missiles in Ukraine, which imperiled the region's peaceful situation. 俄羅斯抱怨歐盟在烏克蘭部署彈道導彈，這危及了該地區的和平局勢。

35. in an attempt to 為了

例：The commercial banks raised mortgage interest rates in an attempt to cool down the surging property prices. 商業銀行為了給飛漲的房價降溫，提高了抵押貸款利率。

36. for the sake of 為了

例：For the sake of your convenience, they decided to reimburse you accordingly. 為了您的便利，他們決定相應地報銷您的費用

37. to ram one's point home 為了強調這一點

To ram his point home, he repeatedly emphasizes his idea about the bespoke procedures and measures tailored specifically for this project. 為了強調他的觀點，他反復強調關於為這個項目量身定制的獨特程式和措施的想法。

38. in pursuit of 為了追求

例：In pursuit of true love, she decided to quit her job and move to another city to live with her boyfriend 她為了追尋真愛，決定辭去工作，搬到另一個城市與男友同住。

39. nuanced 微妙的

例：John and Marry fell in love for a couple of months, unfortunately, their relationship has become a bit more nuanced than before given that they knew each other much better. 約翰和瑪麗相愛已有幾個月，然而，隨著彼此更加瞭解，他們的關係變得比以前更加微妙。

40. immaculately 惟妙惟肖地，完美地

例：This actress immaculately performed the figure in the novel. 這位女演員得惟妙惟肖地演繹了小說中的人物。

41. strangulation 畏縮

例：This policy caused the strangulation of civilian consumption, indicating the economy was dipping. 這一政策導致了民間消費的畏縮，顯示出經濟正在走下坡路。

42. to shrivel 萎縮

例：This year's revenue profits have shriveled due to the pandemic, and the company's board is devising a new plan to tackle this challenge. 由於疫情，今年的收入利潤大幅萎縮，公司董事會正在制定新計畫來應對這一挑戰。

43. umpteen 無數的

例：There are umpteen planets like Earth in the cosmos. 宇宙中存在著無數像地球一樣的行星。

44. tad 微小

例：She is very sensitive to every detail, especially to a tad of change. 她對每一個細節都非常敏感，尤其是對微小的變化。

45. unquenched 未得到滿足

例：We must pay close attention to seniors suffering from depression caused by unquenched sexual desires, as it may lead to serious consequences for society. 我們

必須特別關注因性欲未得到滿足而引發抑鬱的老年人，因為這可能會對我們的社會造成嚴重後果。

46. blandness 溫柔
例：I wanted to break up with my girlfriend; however, her blandness somehow softened my heart. 我原本想和女朋友分手，然而她的溫柔不知為何軟化了我的心。

47. meek 溫順的
例：In nature, some animals are meek, while others are ferocious. 在自然界中，有些動物性情溫順，有些則兇猛殘暴。

再例如：Many young women struggle to understand why men often prefer partners who are meek and empathetic. From a psychological perspective, men tend to feel uncomfortable with partners who are overly aggressive or dominant. 年輕的女士們不明白為什麼男人會選擇溫順和善解人意的女朋友。 心態上，男性不喜歡接受如此咄咄逼人和強勢的另一半。

48. with a clear conscience 問心無愧
例：She faced the allegation with a clear conscience. 她面對指控問心無愧。

49. gravitas 穩重
例：Gauging whether someone has truly grown up can be judged by the gravitas they carry. 衡量一個人是否真正成熟，可以通過他們所展現出的穩重來判斷。

50. to buzz 這個詞的意思太多，由於篇幅限制只能舉兩個常用的例子，比如：嗡嗡響、給某人打電話（非正式）
例：So many mosquitoes were buzzing around, it really got on my nerves — and I ended up covered in bites.
那麼多蚊子在我身邊嗡嗡叫，真的讓我煩透了——我被咬遍滿身。

再比如：Can I give you a buzz on Sunday morning?
我星期天早上給你打個電話好嗎？

51. ubiquitous 無處不在的
例：Taking all varieties of vitamins has become ubiquitous around the world. 服用各種各樣的維生素在世界各地已經變得無處不在。

52. omnipresent 無處不在的
例：In the digital age, social media has become omnipresent in our lives, shaping how we communicate and interact with others. 在數字時代，社交媒體已經變得無處不在，塑造了我們與他人交流和互動的方式。

53. impervious 無動於衷的
例：I am impervious to any blame from anybody. 我對來自任何人的指責無動於衷。

54. insuperable 無法克服的
例：In my eyes, there are no insuperable difficulties; I believe I can overcome any barriers on my path to success. 在我看來，沒有無法克服的困難；我相信我可以克服通往成功路上的任何障礙。

55. irretrievable 無法彌補的，無法挽回的
例：Teresa Teng's passing was an irretrievable loss. To my knowledge, no singer has been able to surpass her. 鄧麗君的去世是無法彌補的損失。根據我的瞭解，至今沒有哪位歌手能夠超越她。

56. innocuous 無關痛癢的
例：I was astonished by my boss's innocuous apology for his mistake, as it seemed almost too mild for the situation.
我對老闆因犯錯而做出無關痛癢的道歉感到震驚，因為這道歉對這件事來說似乎過於輕描淡寫。

57. to smudge 汙跡斑斑
After the accident, the entire car was deformed and smudged, with the people inside trapped. They urgently needed life-saving assistance. 事故發生後，整車變形、汙跡斑斑，車內的人被困。他們急需緊急救援。

58. Nor did it help that 無濟於事
例：Nor did it help that even a clever housewife couldn't cook a meal without ingredient and rice. 巧婦難為無米之炊。

59. insatiable 無盡的，無止境的
例：He couldn't contain his insatiable creativity about his novel, and in just one night, he wrote 10,000 words. 他無法抑制對小說的無盡創意，結果一夜之間寫下了 10,000 字。

60. to be tantamount to 無異于，完全等同於...
例：Inhaling second-hand cigarette smoke is tantamount to committing suicide. 吸入二手煙無異於自殺。

61. hiccup-free 無拘無束的
例:I prefer freelance photographers, freelance consultants, and similar roles because I find them hiccup-free, allowing me to control my schedule with ease. 我更喜歡自由攝影師、自由顧問等，因為我覺得這些工作無拘無束。 可以輕鬆掌控我的時間安排。

62. insipid 無聊的，乏味的
例：I dislike the insipid gossip about celebrities. 我不喜歡那些關於明星的無聊八卦新聞。

63. one way or another 無論如何；以某種方法
例：A mother, piteously pleading, beseeches the doctor in the emergency room to find one way or another to save her son's life. 一位母親在急診室裡苦苦哀求醫生無論如何挽救她兒子的生命。

64. indefinitely 無限期地
例：Due to the sagging economy, all employees at this company have been laid off indefinitely. 由於經濟不景氣，本公司所有員工必須無限期下崗。

65. ineptitude 無能
例：The failure to crack the murder case fully exposes the ineptitude of the local police and its government. 未能破解謀殺

案充分暴露當地員警及其政
府的無能。

X

1. apace 迅速地
例：The immigration application
is progressing apace. I truly hope
she receives approval soon. 移
民申請正在順利快速地推
進。我真心希望她能儘快獲
批。

2. to seek an outlet 尋求發洩的出口
例：Adrian sought an outlet to
relieve his mounting frustration.
艾德里安試圖尋找一個發洩
的出口，以緩解他日益增長
的挫敗感。

3. to pummel 襲擊，重創，打，連續揍某人
例：Torrential rain relentlessly
pummeled the eastern coast. 滂
沱大雨無情地襲擊了東海
岸。

再比如：The pandemics
continued to pummel the global
economy, which was already
sliding at an alarming rate. 疫情

持續重創本已以驚人速度下
滑的全球經濟。

4. nuts and bolts 細節
例：Your report on the current
marketing trend seems
incomplete. I'd prefer you to
include the nuts and bolts of each
step, so as to present a
comprehensive picture that
reflects its impact on
implementation. 你寫的這份關
於當前行銷趨勢的報告似乎
不夠完整。我更希望你能詳
盡說明每一個細節的關鍵要
素，以勾勒出一個全面的整
體圖景，從而體現其對實施
的影響。

5. to ransack 洗劫
例：A thief ransacked my house
and made off with all my
valuables. 一名小偷洗劫了我
的房子，所有值錢的東西都
被搶走了。

6. minutiae 細節

例：His new novel lays bare the minutiae of his life in the countryside. 他的新小說揭示了在農村生活的細節。

7. nitty-gritty 細節

例：After being hired by the company, I also received systematic training on the nitty-gritty of service delivery to clients. 被公司錄用後，我還接受了關於客戶服務細節的系統培訓。

8. mutatis mutandis 細節上做修改

例：Before publication, my book was revised mutatis mutandis—with the necessary changes made accordingly. 在出版之前，我的書做過細節上的修改。

9. of yore 昔日

例：He disliked mentioning the glories of yore. 他不喜歡提起昔日的輝煌。

再比如：You've changed tremendously; I can hardly recognize you. You're not the same one of yore. 你變化巨大，我幾乎認不出你了。你已經不是昔日的你了。

10. boondoggles 細小毫無意義之事

例：I found the relationships among colleagues in this company to be entangled in boondoggles. 我發現這家公司同事之間的關係糾纏在細小毫無意義之事上。

11. to dangle sb 吸引，誘惑某人

例：Her hot outlook dangled in front of many horny young men.. 她火辣的外表吸引了許多色迷迷的年輕男士。

12. to enwrap 吸引著 ...

例：The latest cartoon movie"Nezha 2" enwrapped children around the world in its charm. 最新的卡通電影深深吸引住了全世界的孩子們。

13. to overawe 嚇呆了

例：He suddenly collapsed and instantly lost consciousness. All the attendees at the scene were scarily overawed. 他突然倒下，立刻失去了意識。現場的所有人都被嚇呆了。

14. to freak out 嚇壞了

例：I lost hundreds of thousands of dollars in the stock market, and my wife is freaking out, but I'm not. 我在股市上損失了幾十萬美元，我妻子嚇壞了，但我沒有。

15. snotty 下賤的，傲慢的

例：Elijah's behavior has become so snotty that it can no longer be tolerated. 以利亞的行為太下賤了，不能再容忍了。

16. to show off 顯擺

例：That guy stupidly showed off a $100,000 watch, and as a result, he was robbed and nearly lost his life. 那個傢伙愚蠢地顯擺價值 10 萬美元的手錶，結果他被搶了，差點丟了命。

17. to mope around 閒逛

例：I moped through the sparsely populated mall, bought a cup of cold coffee, and sank into a seat to sip it slowly. A sense of solitude wrapped around me, leaving me adrift in my thoughts. 我在人不多的商場裡閒逛，買了杯冷咖啡，坐下來慢慢地啜飲。一種孤獨感包圍了我，讓我沉浸在自己的思緒中。

18. to traipse 閒逛

例：His parents traipsed through the mall while he was sleeping. 他睡覺的時候，他的父母在商場裡閒逛。

19. to reprimand 訓斥、指責，譴責。

例：The boss of the company reprimanded one of his employees for constantly being late. 這家公司的老闆因為一名員工總是遲到而對他進行了訓斥。

20. stark 鮮明的, 十足的, 明顯的

例：The colors in the painting are astonishingly stark，creating a bold and dramatic contrast. 這幅畫的色彩鮮明、對比驚人，呈現出大膽而誇張的視覺效果。

21. to descend into 陷入

例：the whole world descended into scare and turmoil due to the lethal virus spreading. 由於致命

病毒的傳播，整個世界陷入
了恐慌和混亂。

22. to dig into 陷入 …

例：Due to the sluggish economy, the company accumulated significant debt and has dug itself into an abysmal situation. 由於經濟低迷，公司債臺高築，已將自己陷入了深淵。

23. to beset 陷入 …困境

例：Her husband lost his job and was beset by a worsening financial situation. 她的丈夫失去了工作，陷入了日益惡化的財務困境之中。

24. to lapse into 陷入 …,

例:Constant inflation will cause the world economy to lapse into an abysmal state. 持續的通貨膨脹將使世界經濟陷入深淵。

再比如：The economy once again lapsed into turmoil due to the pandemic worsened.由於疫情惡化，經濟再次陷入了動盪。

25. in a funk 陷入沮喪

例：He had been trading in foreign exchange, and in the end, he made a mistake during a trade and lost everything in an instant, leaving him in a funk.他一直在進行外匯交易，最後在一次交易中犯了個錯誤，瞬間失去了所有，結果陷入了沮喪。

26. chastise 訓斥, 斥責,

例：Mateo made a critical mistake while preparing the quotation for his customer, and his boss sternly chastised him. 馬特奧在為客戶準備報價時犯了一個關鍵錯誤，他的老闆嚴厲地訓斥了他。

27. to batter 襲擊，連續打擊，嚴重破壞 …

例：A heavy snowstorm battered the city. 一場暴風雪襲擊了這個大城市。

28. to be compounded by 雪上加霜，使得…更加嚴重

例：His diabetes will be compounded by his over eating。過度飲食讓他的糖尿病狀況雪上加霜。

29. to keep a lid on 限制

例：Nowadays, it's quite outlandish to insist on hiring only those under 35. This unwise rule keeps a lid on recruiting more qualified candidates and reflects poor judgment on the part of any company or enterprise. 如今，堅持只招聘 35 歲以下的人員顯得非常離譜。這條不明智的規定限制了更有資歷人才的引進，體現出任何公司或企業在用人方面的判斷失誤。

30. to crimp 限制

例：Improper rules and regulations will undoubtedly crimp individuals' freedom to innovate; instead, they will encourage people to lie flat. 不當的規章制度無疑會限制個人的創新自由，反而會促使人們選擇躺平。

31. to impose curbs on 限制

例：Parents must impose curbs on their children playing games all day, as it can be harmful to their health.父母必須限制孩子整天玩遊戲的行為，因為這會損害他們的健康。

32. to stint someone from doing sth.限制某人做某事

例：Parents must stint their kids from using mobile phones in order to protect their eyes and brain development. 父母必須限制孩子使用手機，以保護他們的眼睛和大腦發育。

33. to opt out 選擇退出

例：If you disagree with the board's decision, you may opt out of the investment.如果您不同意董事會的決定，您可以選擇退出投資。

34. to twiddle one's thumbs 閑著

例：I understand you're busy, but I'm not just twiddling my thumbs. Nearly everyone went on vacation, and I had to take care of everything. Don't you think that's unfair to me? 我知道你很忙，但我可沒閑著。幾乎每個人都去度假了，而我卻得照看一切。你不覺得這樣對我不公平嗎？

35. to put out feelers to 向 ... 示好

例：He had secretly been in love with her for quite some time.

Now, he wanted to express his feelings, so he tried to put out feelers by inviting her to dinner. 他暗暗喜歡她已經很長時間了。現在，他想向她表達自己的感情，於是他邀請與她共進晚餐來示好她。

36. to catnip 向 ...示好

例：She tried to catnip to her boss to get more promotion opportunities. 她試圖向她的老闆示好，以獲得更多的晉升機會。

37. to beam to 向…傳送

例：Every year, the live World Cup soccer matches are almost beamed to countries around the world. 每年，世界盃足球賽的直播幾乎會通過衛星傳送到全世界各國。

38. bumpkin 鄉巴佬，土包子

例：For the first time, I visited the interior of a shuttle space. Sadly, I felt like a bumpkin. The various equipment made me dizzy, as if they weren't made by humans. 這是我第一次參觀航太艙內部，遺憾的是，我感到自己像個鄉巴佬。各種設備讓我頭暈，仿佛它們並非人類製造。

39. to be flanked by 相伴左右

例：He walked out dressed in black, flanked by numerous beauties at such a young age. 他穿著黑色衣服走出來，許多美女相伴左右，年紀輕輕就如此風光。

40. to be commensurate with 相匹配

例：Your experience and knowledge will be commensurate with the amount you can earn. 你的經驗和認知將與你能賺取的金額相匹配。

41. to want to have one's cake and eat it 想分一杯羹

例：Seeing the electric vehicle market flourish and become highly profitable, the company also wanted to have its cake and eat it, so it poured a huge amount of money into R&D. 看到電動汽車市場的繁榮並賺大錢，這家公司也想分一杯羹，所以他們在研發上投入了巨大的資金。

42. to relish 享受
例：I saw some people losing their jobs but they are still buying luxury cars or going to expensive restaurants to indulge in their lives. That's literally unbelievable. 我看到有些人丟了工作，但他們仍然買豪車或去昂貴的餐館享受生活，簡直 難以相信。

43. to envisage 想像，設想
例：He couldn't envisage how he could spend his life without gaming. It was very sad for him to be so deeply addicted that he couldn't break free from it. 他無法想像沒有遊戲的生活會是什麼樣子。對他來說，沉迷其中無法自拔是件非常悲哀的事。

44. pale 相形見絀
例：Humans pale in comparison to aliens in terms of intelligence. 人類和外星人的智力對比，人類顯得相形見絀。

45. sequinned 鑲著亮片的
例：She adorned herself with a stunning sequinned skirt, exuding beauty and captivating the attention of all who laid eyes upon her. The glimmering sequins on the skirt sparkled like stars, catching the light and adding a touch of glamour to her appearance. With each movement, she radiated confidence and allure, effortlessly attracting and captivating the audience around her. 她穿著一條閃閃發光的亮片裙子，美得吸引了所有觀眾的目光。裙子上閃耀的亮片猶如星星一般，在光線下閃爍，為她的造型增添了一抹魅力。每一次動作，她都散發出自信和誘惑力，毫不費力地吸引著周圍的觀眾。

46. gubbins 小部件
例：I rarely bought an old car because finding gubbins for the defective parts was quite challenging, causing prolonged delays and giving me a headache. 我很少購買舊車，因為很難找到替換損壞零件的小配件，這導致維修時間拖得很長，讓我感到很頭疼。

47. to whittle 削成
例：It is marvelous to see a turnip whittled to a vivid flower. 看

到蘿蔔被削成一朵鮮豔的花，真是太神奇了。

48. nosh 小吃
例：I want to share some extraordinary nosh with you. Can we go to a newly opened restaurant close to my house this Sunday? 我想和你分享一些特色小吃。這個星期天我們可以去我家附近新開的餐館嗎？

49. clown 小丑
例：Anyone who disrespects the fact can be dubbed a clown. 任何不尊重事實的人都可以被稱為小丑。

50. to promulgate 宣揚
例：Now the whole society adores promulgating positive energy instead of negative energy. 現在全社會都崇尚宣揚正能量，而不是負面能量。

51. gaggles of 喧鬧的、嘰嘰喳喳的
這個短語多用於形容小孩子或少年們的喧鬧。往往說這麼一群嬉笑的孩子們。

例：There are gaggles of teenagers on top of the mountain, playing around. 有一群嘰嘰喳喳的青少年在山頂上玩耍.

52. luridly 絢麗奪目地，色彩斑斕地
例：The colorful fireworks luridly ignited the sky. 五彩繽紛的煙花把天空照得絢麗奪目。

53. peccadillos 小過失
例：No one dares to claim they have never had any peccadillos in their entire life. 沒有人敢聲稱他們一輩子從未有過任何小過失。

54. embers 小火苗
例：Walking on a narrow path along the mountain at night, you will see embers flashing in succession, jumping intermittently. 在夜晚走在山間的小路上，你會看到小火苗接連閃爍，時而跳動。

55. to pare back 削減
例：A lot of factories have to pare back their budgets due to worsening financial situations. 由於財務狀況惡化，許多工廠不得不削減預算。

56. to whittle down 削減

例：During the pandemic, many companies whittled down employees' salaries. 疫情期間，許多公司削減了員工的工資。

57. to lop off 削減

例：In light of the economic downturn, the company has to lop off its costs and lay off some employees. 鑒於經濟衰退，公司不得不削減成本並裁減部分員工。

58. to be in stake 懸了

例：Given the sudden change in personnel, his position on the board is at stake. 由於人員的突然變動，他在董事會的位置懸了（處於風險之中）。

59. to stamp out 消除

例：Taking a specific medication can stamp out the H1N1 virus. 服用特定的藥物可以消除 H1N1 病毒。

60. a small fry 小人物，無足輕重的人

例：He felt frustrated and decided to resign because he believed he was treated like a small fry, despite being a director at the company. 他感到十分沮喪，決定辭職，因為他認為自己雖然是公司董事，卻被當作無足輕重的小人物看待。

61. to chip away at 削弱

例：As you continue to chip away at your advantage, you'll find it increasingly difficult to reach your target. It's essential to introspect and gain a clear understanding of yourself. 如果你持續削弱自己的優勢，達成目標將變得愈發困難。進行自我反思並清晰認識自己是至關重要的。

62. to dilute 削弱

例：With the increasing gun violence in the US, calling for gun control became spike, the division among the politicians and the dysfunction of law had diluted the gun-control legislation.隨著美國槍支暴力事件的不斷增加，要求控制槍支的呼聲越來越高，政客之間的分歧和法律的失靈削弱了控槍立法。

63. chest-thumping 虛張聲勢的

例：Whenever I was startled by the blaring sirens of fire trucks whizzing past me, I felt their actions were more of a chest-thumping display than a genuine emergency response.每當消防車鳴著刺耳的警笛從我身邊呼嘯而過時，我總覺得他們的行為更像是在虛張聲勢，而不是在應對真正的緊急情況。

64. swashbuckling 虛張聲勢的

例：Nowadays, our society is inundated with swashbuckling gestures that muddle public perception and insult people's intelligence. 如今，我們的社會充斥著各種虛張聲勢的、耀武揚威的舉動，混淆公眾認知，侮辱大眾智商。

65. to enfeeble 削弱

例：The war between Ukraine and Russia, Covid pandemics, inflation, and whatnot further enfeebled the world economy and global trade.烏克蘭和俄羅斯之間的戰爭、新冠病毒大流行、通貨膨脹等等，進一步削弱了世界經濟和全球貿易。

66. to debilitate 削弱

例：His tremendous loss in the stock market hasn't debilitated his ambition to achieve his goals. 他在股票市場上的巨大損失並不能削弱他實現目標的雄心。

67. to undercut 消弱 ...

例：The poor-quality products undercut their competitiveness against other manufacturers worldwide. 劣質產品削弱了他們在全球範圍內與其他製造商的競爭力。

68. to wane 消逝,消退,衰落

例：His severe pain waned after taking some special medications to alleviate the symptoms. 在服用了緩解症狀的特殊藥物後，他的劇烈疼痛逐漸消逝。

（要特別說明的是，在英語國家，人們在表達吃藥不會用 medicine,不說 take some medicines。大都用 medication,所以，護士到你病床前來讓你吃藥時，她們會說：It's time for you to take your medications。而 medicine 是對藥的總體表達，而非醫生給你開的治療具體疾病的處方藥物。

再比如：Time serves as the most potent remedy for healing your wounds, as they gradually wane over your pain .時間是治癒傷口最有效的良方，因為傷口會隨著時間的流逝逐漸消退，減輕你的痛苦。

69. bluff 虛張聲勢

例:He prefers to bluff rather than be pragmatic. He wouldn't devote himself to his studies and research, and as a result, he failed his final exam. 他更喜歡虛張聲勢，而不是腳踏實地。他沒有投入到學習和研究中，最終他的期末考試掛科了。

70. to trod 小心謹慎

例：He is brilliant because he trod very cautiously when dealing with his boss and colleagues. 他很聰明，因為在處理與老闆和同事的關係時，他非常小心謹慎。

71. circumspect 小心翼翼的、小心謹慎的

例：He used to splurge on luxury items without hesitation, but recently, I've noticed he has become quite circumspect about his spending. 他曾毫不猶豫地在奢侈品上揮霍錢財，但最近，我發現他變得相當謹慎，花錢變得小心翼翼。

72. to sabotage 蓄意破壞

例：In the US, the liberal party attempted to sabotage Trump's plans. .在美國，自由黨試圖蓄意破壞特朗普的計畫。

73. at large 逍遙法外

例：A man was murdered last night, and the police are actively searching for the suspect. Unfortunately, the killer remains at large. 昨晚一名男子被謀殺，警方正在追捕嫌疑人。不幸的是，兇手仍逍遙法外。

74. to desecrate 褻瀆，污辱

例：His behavior desecrated our sacred mission, undermining the values we hold dear. 他的行為褻瀆了我們的神聖使命，動搖了我們所珍視的價值觀。

75. satanic 邪惡的
例:This plan is downright satanic—so twisted and cruel that no one in their right mind could possibly accept it. 這個計畫妥妥的邪惡，扭曲而殘忍，任何一個頭腦正常的人都無法接受。

再比如：No matter which country initiates a war, such actions are undeniably satanic. 無論哪個國家先發動戰爭，這種行為都無疑是邪惡的。

76. nefarious 邪惡的
例：Their nefarious intent is to monopolize the entire market and plunder the local petroleum resources. 他們邪惡的圖謀是壟斷整個市場，並掠奪當地的石油資源。

77. to entail 需要
例：Carrying out this project will inevitably entail long-term commitment, but it holds great promise for benefiting future generations.實施這個專案勢必需要長期的投入與堅持，但它對後代將帶來巨大的益處。

78. disingenuous 虛偽的
例：No company would want to hire employees who are disingenuous; they all prefer those who are sincere and loyal. Of course, there is always an exception—perhaps the bosses themselves may be the ones who lack sincerity. 沒有公司願意雇傭虛偽的員工；他們更傾向于那些真誠忠誠的人。當然，也有例外——或許老闆們自己就是缺乏真誠的人。

79. to leak out of 洩露出
例：the newly designed iPhone has been leaked out of Apple.新設計的蘋果手機從蘋果公司洩露出去了。

80. pedigree 血統
例：Marriage with foreigners may dilute the pedigree of our offspring, which has raised widespread concerns.與外國人結婚可能會削弱我們後代的血統，這引起了廣泛關注。

81. gory 血腥的，血淋淋的
例：Some people fear gory autopsy scenes, so they are unable to become forensic doctors. 有些人害怕血腥的屍

檢場景，所以他們不能成為法醫生。

82. recumbent 斜倚在
例：When I entered the room, I saw him lying recumbent on the couch, fast asleep. 當我走進房間時，我看到他斜倚在沙發上，沉沉地睡著了。

83. distraught 心煩意亂的
例：I was distraught by this case, which was so complicated and intertwined. 這個案件讓我心煩意亂，因為它如此複雜且錯綜交織。

84. to harbor 心懷，隱藏
例:Young people must harbour their strong ambitions; decadence will lead to them being abandoned by society. 年輕人要心懷遠大志向； 頹廢會使他們被社會拋棄。

再比如：Given the complexity of our society, we must, to some extent, be adept at harboring our views to avoid being attacked. 考慮到我們社會的複雜性，在某種程度上我們必須善於隱藏自己的觀點，以避免遭受攻擊。

85. hypocritical 虛偽的
例：I think the so-called democracy in the Western world is hypocritical. 我認為西方世界所謂的民主是虛偽的。

86. to put one's faith in 信賴
例：As Western medical treatments continued to disappoint, people increasingly turned to traditional Chinese medicine, putting their faith in its methods instead. 隨著西方醫學的不斷失望，人們越來越多地轉向傳統中醫，將信任寄託在其方法上

87. tacit 心領神會的，心照不宣的
例：We are very good friends, so we can communicate with each other through tacit feelings, passions, and emotions. 我們是非常好的朋友，所以我們可以通過心領神會的感受、激情和情感來交流。

88. to embrace 欣然接受
例：After the pandemic, the entire world has changed tremendously. Each one of us must embrace this change. .在疫情之後，整個世界發生了

巨大的變化。我們每個人都必須欣然接受這種變化。

89. freshly-anointed 新上任的

例：Mr. Jackson became the freshly anointed CEO of our company. 傑克遜先生成為我們公司新上任的首席執行官。

90. nerve-racking 心神不寧的

例：She felt nerve-racking when she heard this news. 她聽到這個消息時感到心神不寧。

91. rapture 欣喜若狂，興高采烈

例：When he heard he had won 30 million dollars in the lottery, he suddenly went into rapture. 當他聽說自己中了 3000 萬美元的大獎時，他突然欣喜若狂。

92. whim 心血來潮

例：All the colleagues deeply suffered from their boss's whims, which often led to poor decisions. Furthermore, he frequently changed his mind. 所有同事都深受老闆心血來潮的影響，常常導致錯誤的決定。 此外，他還經常改變主意。

93. with a hard slog 辛辛苦苦地

例：It took me six years to finish this book with a great deal of hard slog. 我花了六年時間，經過辛辛苦苦地才完成了這本書。

94. newfangled 新穎的，新奇的

例：In 2022, Rolex rolled out a line of newfangled watches, which seems to mark a breakthrough and set a benchmark for all other watch manufacturers worldwide. 2022年，勞力士推出了一系列新穎的腕表，這似乎標誌著一次突破，並為全球其他手錶製造商設立了一個標杆。

95. temperamentally 性格上，喜怒無常地

例：I am temperamentally unsuited to work in this company because its politics seem to be quite complex. 我性格上不適合在這家公司工作，因為它的政治環境似乎非常複雜。

再比如：John is temperamentally unsuitable for this position due to his family background. 由於家庭背景，約翰在性格上不適合這個職位。

96. streak 性格特點
例：Different people have different streaks, so it's not easy to get along with everyone or make everyone satisfied with you. 每個人有不同的性格特點，因此與別人相處融洽或讓每個人都滿意並不容易。

97. firing squad 行刑隊
例：The drug smugglers were sentenced to death, and the criminals trembled as they faced the firing squad. 毒品走私犯被判處死刑，那些罪犯面對行刑隊時瑟瑟發抖。

98. to gloat over 幸災樂禍
例：He secretly gloated over others' misfortune, especially since they had hurt him when he was a child. sychologically speaking, he didn't do anything wrong. Whether he sought revenge or not, as an adult, he has the logical right to do whatever he wishes. 他偷偷地因他人不幸而幸災樂禍，畢竟他們曾在他小時候傷害過他。從心理學角度來看，他並沒有做錯什麼。無論他是否報復他人，作為一個成年人，他完全有權按自己的意願做任何事。

99. to crow over 幸災樂禍，得意洋洋
例：No one should crow over another person's pain. 沒有人應該因他人的痛苦而幸災樂禍。

100. to fritter away 消耗
例：Lorenzo became rich; unfortunately, he doesn't want to improve himself further. He is frittering away the rest of his life. 洛倫佐變得富有；不幸的是，他不想進一步提升自己，他正在消耗餘生。

101. go-getting 雄心勃勃的
例：This couple set up their go-getting plan to buy a bigger house next year; they are still steeped in their eagerness and happiness.這對夫婦制定了明年買大房子的雄心勃勃的計畫，他們仍然沉浸在他們的渴望和幸福中。

102. vanity 虛榮

例：I am deeply disappointed by his excessive vanity and overambitious attitude. 我對他那過於虛榮和野心勃勃的態度感到非常失望。

103. mendacious 虛假的

例：I found so many mendacious videos on the internet, bewildering people and spreading rumors, which make it difficult to discern the truth. 我在互聯網上發現了許多虛假的視頻，迷惑人們並傳播謠言，使得人們難以辨別事實。

104. to furlough 休假

例：This summer has been scorching, so everyone at the company has been furloughed; luckily, they are still getting paid. 今年夏天酷熱異常，因此公司裡的每個人都被暫時休假了；幸運的是，他們仍然會繼續領取工資。

105. fictitious 虛構的

例：All the characters in this novel are fictitious, and the true love between the young people doesn't exist; it is far removed from our real world. 這本小說中的所有人物都是虛構的，那些年輕人之間的真愛並不存在，這與我們的現實世界相去甚遠。

106. to sit on ones hands 袖手旁觀

例：During the war, the provisions seemed too lean, so he contacted the head office to request more food, but those people sat on their hands. 在戰爭期間，供應顯得過於緊張，於是他聯繫了總部要求提供更多食物，但那些人袖手旁觀。

107. fallow 休整的

例：After fallow 10 days, they decided to launch a new campaign against their hostiles. 休整的 10 天后，他們決定向敵人發動新的戰役。

108. to pin down 陷入被動

例：The pandemic pinned down governments, forcing them to take action by locking down entire cities or even whole countries to prevent the spread of infection. However, some medical professionals questioned the effectiveness of such measures.

疫情迫使各國政府陷入被動，封鎖整個城市，甚至全國，以防止人群感染。然而，一些醫學專家對這些措施的效果表示質疑。

Y

識，幫助中國成為全球領導者。

1. to squash 壓縮
例：Due to the economic downturn, companies around the world have decided to squash all kinds of expenditures 由於經濟衰退，全球各地的公司決定壓縮各類開支。

2. to belt out 引吭高歌
例：The soldier passionately belts out his love for his hometown and his mother, deeply moving many in the audience. 這位戰士引吭高歌激情表達了他對家鄉和母親的愛，感動了現場的許多觀眾。

3. visionary 遠見卓識的，有眼力的
例：The policy of opening up to the outside world is highly visionary, which helped China rise to become a global leader. 對外開放的政策具有遠見卓

4. to be averse to 厭惡
例：I am averse to their behavior of speaking loudly and snapping at someone who may accidentally irk them in public. 我厭惡他們在公共場合大聲說話並對那些可能無意激怒他們的人發火的行為。

5. revulsion 厭煩
例：I feel a strong revulsion toward advice that only benefits the person giving it, which seems selfish. 我厭煩那些只會給自己帶來好處的建議，這似乎很自私。

6. to paper over 掩蓋
例：The share issuers in the stock market colluded with the banks to paper over the fact that they were deceiving the shareholders. 股票市場上的股

票發行者們與銀行勾結，試圖掩蓋他們欺騙股民的事實。

7. to cloak 掩飾、掩蓋，隱藏

例：I was lucky to run into an experienced guy who kindly reminded me to cloak my talent or strong capabilities in front of colleagues and my boss, as it is likely to generate envy from them. 我幸運地遇到了一位經驗豐富的人，他友善地提醒我，在同事和老闆面前要掩飾自己的才能或強大能力，因為這容易引起他們的嫉妒。

8. to obscure 掩蓋，遮蓋

例：I felt deeply disappointed by their attempts to obscure the details of the investigation. 我對他們掩蓋調查細節感到非常失望。

9. draconian 嚴苛的

例：During the pandemic, the draconian citywide shutdown severely disrupted people's daily lives. 在疫情期間，嚴苛的城市封鎖嚴重影響了人們的日常生活。

10. to fulminate 嚴厲斥責

例：Many employees fulminated against their salaries being reduced year after year, which negatively impacted their lives. 許多員工嚴厲斥責對薪資逐年減少，這嚴重影響了他們的生活。

11. dressing-down 嚴厲批評

例：During the negotiation with the competitor, he made a significant mistake and was given a dressing-down by the board. 在與競爭對手的談判中，他犯了一個重大錯誤，受到了董事會的嚴厲批評。

12. to excoriate 嚴厲批評，苛責

例：Even though he tried to do everything well, his boss still excoriated him. 儘管他努力把每件事都做好，但他的老闆還是嚴厲批評他。

再比如：Regarding ideology, different countries have nuanced situations. We shouldn't excoriate one another; instead, we should be more inclusive and respectful to better adapt to various histories and cultures. 關於意

識形態，不同國家的情況各不相同。我們不應該互相苛責，反而應當更加包容和尊重，以適應不同的歷史和文化。

13. to brook 允許
例：As a clerk in this bank, she was not brooked to undertake any procedures beyond her authorization. 作為這家銀行的職員，她不允許進行任何超出授權的操作。

14. deferral payment 延期付款
例：He was just laid off and couldn't afford the monthly loan payments, so he decided to apply for a deferral. 他剛被裁員，負擔不起每月的貸款還款，於是決定申請延期付款。

15. to masquerade 掩飾
例：Someone who often shows kindness may be masquerading their underlying vicious instincts. 那些經常表現出善意的人，可能是在掩飾他們內心深處的惡劣本能。

16. acute 嚴重的，危險的，急性的
例：The water shortage will result in a severe drought this summer. 水資源短缺將導致今年夏天出現嚴重的乾旱。

17. toll 嚴重的不良影響
例：The abuse of children will take a profound, long-term psychological toll on their entire life. 對孩子的虐待將對他們的一生產生深遠的長期嚴重的不良影響。

18. to wreak havoc on 嚴重破壞，使陷入大混亂
例：COVID-19 wreaked havoc on global supply chains, causing commodity prices to surge tremendously. COVID-19 對全球供應鏈造成了嚴重破壞，導致商品價格暴漲。

19. gravity 嚴重性
例：Given the gravity of her illness, she had to quit her job and stay at home, unfortunately losing her source of income. Luckily, her friends lent a hand to help her through this difficult period in her life. 鑒於她病情的

嚴重性，她不得不辭掉工作，在家休養，不幸的是因此失去了收入來源。幸運的是，她的朋友們伸出援手，幫她度過了人生中這段艱難時光。

20. to simmer 醞釀
例：Rage against corruption has long simmered beneath the surface. 人們對腐敗的憤怒醞釀已久。

21. impotent 陽痿的
例：Because he was impotent, his wife eventually chose to divorce him. 因為他陽痿，他的妻子最終選擇了離婚。

22. supine 仰臥的
例：She was too exhausted to fall asleep and lay supine on the couch, staring at the ceiling, her mind completely blank. 她累得無法入睡，仰臥在沙發上，盯著天花板，腦子一片空白。

23. to wobble 搖擺不定
例：The market slowdown signals that the economy is wobbling. 市場放緩表明經濟正在搖擺不定。

24. saber-rattling 耀武揚威的
例：I'm not fond of his saber-rattling behavior, which stems from his privileged background. 我不太喜歡他那種炫耀武力的樣子，而這完全是因為他出身富裕。

25. rickety 搖搖晃晃的
例：Yesterday, I had the day off, so I hired a carpenter to fix my rickety stairs. 昨天我休息，所以我雇了個木匠把搖搖晃晃的樓梯修好。

26. to grit their teeth 要咬緊牙關
例：We must grit our teeth and put in great effort to combat the rapid spread of Omicron, as the saying goes, 'Seize the moment, save a life. 我們必須咬緊牙關，付出巨大努力來抗擊奧密克戎的快速傳播，正如那句俗話所說："抓住時機，拯救生命"。

27. tottering 搖搖欲墜的
例：Amidst its tottering economy, the devaluation of the currency only served to exacerbate the situation further. 在其搖搖欲墜的經濟背景

下，貨幣貶值進一步加劇了這一局勢。

28. to plod 一步步地、辛勤勞作

例：He began to plod through his application for enrollment at Harvard University, and in the end, he succeeded in gaining admission. 他開始一步步地申請哈佛大學的入學，最後終於如願以償。

29. to be duty-bound to 義不容辭

例：Kindergartens are duty-bound to protect all the children, including their health, safety, education and more. 幼稚園義不容辭保護所有孩子，包括他們的健康、安全、教育等方面。

30. one-off 一錘子的，一次性的

例：We dislike one-off deals; instead, we prefer long-term sustainability 我們不喜歡一錘子的買賣；相反，我們更傾向於長期的可持續性。

31. a smidgen of 一點點

例：She is sensitive to alcohol and can't tolerate even a smidgen of champagne. 她對酒精非常敏感，甚至一點點香檳都不能忍受。

32. to outbid 以高價勝出

例：In the final round of bidding, a mysterious bidder outbid the others by 60%, securing the win. 在競標的最後一輪，一位神秘的競標者以高出 60%的價格超過其他競標者，贏得了競標。

33. Alas for，哎！遺憾的是

例：Alas for my sister, she couldn't stop him from divorce. 哎!遺憾的是我姐姐沒能阻止他提出離婚。

34. gobs of 一行行，一串串，一滴滴，一捆捆等

例：She was so emotional while watching the blockbuster that globs of tears rolled down her cheeks. 她在觀看那部大片時情緒太激動了，淚水一行行順著臉頰滾落下來。

35. to be predisposed to 易患 ...病, 傾向傾向於...的狀態

例：Smokers are predisposed to developing lung cancer. 吸煙者易患肺癌。

36. stamina 毅力

例：The youngest diver, Hongchan Quan, demonstrated tremendous stamina and endured arduous effort to clinch the world championship in shining glory. 最年輕的跳水運動員全紅嬋展現了驚人的耐力，並付出了艱苦的努力，最終以輝煌的成績贏得了世界冠軍。

37. a cluster of 一連串 ...

例：A cluster of issues reveals a major flaw in our management system. 一連串問題暴露了我們管理體系中存在的一個重大缺陷 。

它的另一種說法： a barrage of

38. a spate of 一連串的

例：To crack this case, you must gather a spate of clues from which the truth can be unearthed. 要破這個案子，你必須收集一連串的線索，從中挖掘出真相。

39. stellar 一流的

例：Her stellar talent deeply impressed the interviewer, and naturally, she landed the offer. 她一流的才華給面試官留下了深刻的印象，當然，她順利地拿到了那份錄用通知。

40. to portend 預示

例：From my perspective, heavier summer rainfall may portend a snowier winter, and vice versa. 在我看來，夏季降雨越多，可能預示著冬季會有更多降雪，反之亦然。

再比如：Too many aftershocks may portend a major earthquake in the future. 太多的餘震可能預示著未來會發生大地震。

41. ilk 一路人，類型

例：We can't be friends because we're not of the same ilk. 我們不能做朋友，因為我們不是一路人。

42. to be abuzz 引發關注、議論紛紛、沸沸揚揚

例：The approval allowing every American to carry guns has been abuzz worldwide after the Supreme Court voted 6-3 in favor of it. 允許每個美國人攜帶槍支的批准在美國最高法院以六比三的投票結果通過後，已在全球引發了廣泛關注。

43. lest 以免

例：Young people must seriously listen to the advice of seniors lest they make big mistakes and waste more time and energy in their lives. 年輕人一定要認真聽取前輩的建議，以免犯大錯，浪費更多的時間和精力。

44. in one go 一條龍

例：This company can apply for a visa, a passport, or an air ticket in one go. 本公司可一條龍辦理簽證、護照、機票。

45. to limp 一瘸一拐的走路

例：I guess Kai got injured, which is why he's limping. 我猜凱可能受傷了，所以他在一瘸一拐地走。

46. to remain elusive 依然遙不可及、依然渺茫

例：His hope of starting a new company remains elusive due to financial issues and other internal disruptions. 由於財務問題和其他內部干擾，他希望成立新公司的願望依然遙不可及。

47. to scoop up 一掃而光（搶購商品）

例：Thanks to their superior quality, almost all the toilet cushions in Japan were scooped up by Chinese tourists. 由於其優越的品質，日本幾乎所有的馬桶墊都被中國遊客一掃而光。

48. threadbare 衣衫襤褸的

例：I gave some money to a threadbare older man, and I can't imagine how he has managed to get through his life. 我給了一個衣衫襤褸的老人一些錢，真不敢想像他是如何度過自己的一生的。

49. on a whim 一時興起、一拍腦袋

例：George, on a whim, suddenly flew to Hawaii for a

vacation without notifying anyone. 喬治一時興起，突然飛往夏威夷度假，連任何人都沒有通知。

再比如：My mom is a knowledgeable woman, but my dad often acts on a whim, never considering the consequences. 我媽媽是個知識淵博的女人，而我爸爸總是一拍腦袋做事，從不考慮後果。

50. scrupulous 一絲不苟的，嚴謹認真的

例：My mom pays scrupulous attention to her work, which earned her high praise from her company. 我媽媽對工作一絲不苟，因此得到了公司高度的評價。

再比如：The quality of German-made machinery is renowned worldwide, thanks to its scrupulous quality control, superior raw materials, and, in particular, its exquisite craftsmanship. 德國製造的機械因其嚴格的品質控制、更優質的原材料，尤其是精湛的工藝，而在全世界享有盛譽。

51. to opine 以為

例：He opines that he is right. Unfortunately, he made the wrong decision, which led to irreversible consequences. 他自以為是對的。不幸的是，他做出了錯誤的決定，導致了無法挽回的後果。

52. one silver lining 一線希望

例：Even though I flunked this exam, fortunately, I heard there's another one next month, so there's still a silver lining for me. 雖然我這次考試掛了，但幸運的是，我聽說下個月還有一次同樣的考試，對我來說也算是不幸中的一線希望。

53. It is a fantasy to think 簡直就是異想天開，癡人說夢

例：It's a fantasy to think you can drain the ocean in a day. 在一天之內把海洋抽幹是異想天開。

54. a vignette of 一小段插曲

例：She selected a vignette from the poem and began to elocute it. Her voice was so touching that it brought tears to my eyes. .她選了一小段插

曲，開始富有激情般地朗誦，聽起來很感人，讓我熱淚盈眶。

55. to nibble 一小口一小口的吃
例：He enjoys nibbling on ice cream while lounging on the sofa and watching TV. 他喜歡一邊躺在沙發上看電視，一邊一小口一小口吃著霜淇淋。

56. a tiny pellet of 一小粒
Given the potency of this medicine, the patient is allowed only a tiny pellet each day, carefully stored in a special jar. 鑒於這種藥物的效力，患者每天只能服用一小粒藥丸，這顆藥被小心地儲存在一個特殊的藥瓶中。

57. tit-for-tat 以牙還牙的，針鋒相對
例：Anyone who dares to invade our country will face a tit-for-tat retaliation 任何膽敢侵犯我們國家的人，我們都將以牙還牙、進行針鋒相對的反擊。

58. in a sleek 以圓滑的方式，以時髦的方式
例：Maverick prefers to talk in a sleek. 馬弗裡克喜歡以圓滑的方式說話。

59. in a trice 一眨眼，一轉眼
例：He ran away in a trice. I am wondering when he left. 他一眨眼就跑掉了。我不知道他什麼時候走的。

60. not so much...as 與其說…還不如…
例：He wants to go to university not so much to gain knowledge as to earn a diploma. 他想上大學，與其說是為了獲得知識，不如說是為了拿到文憑。

61. to tame 抑制
例：As inflation worsened, the government stepped in to tame the surging prices. 通貨膨脹變得嚴重，因此政府採取了措施來抑制飛漲的物價。

62. to roll back 抑制，減少
例：The government is taking an effective measure to roll back the surging gas price. 政府正在

採取有效措施，以抑制高漲
的油價。

63. to smother 壓制
例：Owen tried to smother his ire toward his colleague so he could focus on finding a better solution. 歐文努力壓抑對同事的怒火，以便能專注於尋找更好的解決辦法。

64. to quash 抑制，鎮壓
例：The local government attempted to quash the soaring prices in the real estate market. 當地政府試圖抑制房地產市場日益上漲的價格。

65. dilettante 門外漢、一知半解者、業餘愛好者
例：In my childhood, I set a personal goal to become a professional in a field rather than a mere dilettante. 在我小時候，我就為自己設定了一個目標：要成為某個領域的專業人士，而不是一個淺嘗輒止的門外漢。

66. iron-willed 意志堅強的
例：All boys should be encouraged to become strong-willed individuals; otherwise, they may not have good prospects. 所有男孩都應該被鼓勵成為意志堅定的人，否則他們可能沒有好的前景。

67. at the fastest clip 以最快的速度
例：This movie is seasonal, so the team is trying to put it on screen at the fastest clip. 這部電影的季節性很強，所以團隊正在努力以最快的速度將它搬上銀幕。

68. to be undone by 因 ...付諸東流，被 ...抵消
例：Our revenue was undone by overspending due to investment losses. 我們的收益因投資損失的過度支出而付諸東流。

69. to take flak for 因 ...受到嚴厲批評
例:This expert took a lot of flak for advocating an increase in hydro fees. 這位專家因主張提高水電費而受到嚴厲批評。

70. to be overly chummy with someone 與某人過度親密

例：We must remember to avoid being overly chummy with anyone in the real world. 我們必須記住，在現實生活中避免與任何人過於親密。

71. to resonate with 引發 ...的共鳴

例：This dynamic movie resonates with young people. 這部充滿活力的電影在年輕人群體中引發共鳴。

72. to trigger rows about 引發對…的爭吵

例：This incident triggered a row about whether we should permanently adopt daylight saving time. 這一事件引發了關於我們是否應該永久實行夏令時的爭論。

73. to coil 引發騷動

例：The unexpected downturn in Nasdaq stock trading has sharply captured the attention of global investors, coiling heir minds and stirring up a swift, intense impact on their decisions. 納斯達克股票交易的突如其來的下跌迅速吸引了全球投資者的注意，引發了騷動並迅速、強烈地影響著他們的決策。

74. to spark a debate about 引發有關…的爭論

例：Recently, many media outlets have sparked a debate over whether high school students should engage in romantic relationships. 最近，許多媒體引發了一場關於高中生是否應該談戀愛的討論。

75. prurient 淫穢的，好色的

例：Public perception of the esteemed novel The Plum in the Golden Vase is riddled with bias and inaccuracies. Despite its literary significance and popularity, it has controversially been dismissed as merely a prurient book. 公眾對名著《金瓶梅》的認知中存在著大量偏見與誤解。儘管它具有重要的文學價值並廣受關注，卻仍飽受爭議地被貼上了淫穢小說的標籤。

76. promiscuous 淫亂的

例：So far, some critics argue that sex education in North American countries has led to a promiscuous mindset among children, potentially causing distorted perceptions. 迄今為止，一些批評者認為，北美國家的性教育導致了兒童的縱欲思想，可能會造成扭曲的認知。

再比如：Some believe that avoiding promiscuous women after the age of 60 contributes to longevity. 有人認為，60歲之後遠離淫亂的女性有助於延年益壽。

77. to strain relations with sb 與某人關係緊張

例：I have a friend whose relationship with his mother became strained after he moved abroad. 我有一個朋友，自從他出國後，和母親的關係就變得緊張起來。

78. to give the limelight to 引起關注

例：Environmental improvement has taken the limelight in public discourse. 環境改善已引發公眾的關注。

79. blithe 愉悅的、愉快的，樂觀的

例：Even after enduring years of endless suffering, she remains optimistic and carries herself with a blithe spirit. 儘管多年來經歷了無盡的苦難，她依然樂觀，帶著愉悅的神采。

80. to be striking 引人矚目，令人震驚

例：The speech he delivered was truly striking. 他發表的演講引人矚目。

再比如：The divergence between East and West is striking. 東西方之間的差異令人震驚。

81. insidious 陰險的

例：Many people speak highly of him because they don't truly know him but his behavior is very insidious. 許多人對他讚譽有加，只是因為不瞭解他，但他的行為很陰險。

82. implicit 隱形的

例：In some countries, implicit discrimination persists, which has deeply frustrated many people. 在一些國家，隱形歧視依然

存在，這讓許多人感到極為
憤慨。

83. to pander to sb 迎合某人
例：Parents should not pander to their children's whims, as this could negatively impact their future lives. 父母不迎合孩子的任性，這將對他們未來的生活產生負面影響。

84. mirthful 愉快的
例：Many people are drawn to the Apple Store not only for its bright, expansive ambiance that exudes joy, but also for the comprehensive and mirthful shopping experience it offers. 許多人被蘋果店吸引，不僅因為它明亮寬敞的氛圍充滿喜悅，還因為它提供的全面而愉快的購物體驗。

85. to parrot 鸚鵡學舌
例：Our teachers must guide our children to avoid merely parroting others' rhetoric. Instead, they should provide opportunities for them to think critically and express themselves independently. 我們的老師必須引導孩子們避免僅僅鸚鵡學舌他人的言辭。相反，他們應該提供更多機會，讓孩子們獨立思考並表達自己的想法。

86. sway 影響、左右
例：Many companies prefer to make use of celebrities' sway to sell their products. 許多公司更傾向于利用名人的影響來銷售他們的產品。

再比如：I have a mind of my own; I won't be swayed by anyone else. 我有自己的主見，不會被任何人左右。

87. daft 愚蠢的
例：The way he handled this issue seems rather daft. Unfortunately, he didn't realize it. 他處理這個問題的方式顯得有些愚蠢。不幸的是，他沒有意識到這一點。

88. to impinge on 影響(多指負面的)
例：During the pandemic, wearing a mask, especially an N95, can impinge on people's breathing while exercising. 在疫情期間，佩戴口罩，尤其是N95口罩，會對運動時人們的呼吸造成影響。

89. to mingle with 與...混入
例：Mila prepared her salad mingled with barbecue sauce, which gave it a uniquely special taste. 米拉在她的沙拉中混入了燒烤醬，使其味道格外獨特。

90. perpetual 永久的，永無休止的
例：He lost his son in a car accident, which left him in perpetual suffering for the rest of his life. 他在一場車禍中失去了兒子，這讓他在餘生中承受著永久的痛苦。

91. to pile into 蜂擁而入
例：The promise of high profits has led many young people to pile into art schools to study performance, hosting, and broadcasting. 高利潤的前景促使許多年輕人蜂擁進入藝術院校，學習表演、主持和播音。

92. bloated 臃腫的
例：He gained a significant amount of weight, and sadly, being overweight has made him look bloated. 他的體重大幅增加，令人遺憾的是，超重使他看起來臃腫。

93. toperverse 有駁常理的，不通情理的
It would be perverse for sb to do sth。做 ...事是有駁常理的。

例：It would be perverse for a frog to survive sealed inside a stone, cut off from air and without any food, for nearly 40 million years. 一隻青蛙被封在石頭中，既無空氣，又無食物，竟能存活將近四千萬年，這簡直太有駁常理。

94. to cajole the public into 誘導 ...養成 ...
例：The gaming companies cajoled children into developing impulsive spending habits 那些遊戲公司誘導孩子們養成了衝動消費的習慣。

95. glum 鬱悶
例：His salary was unreasonably cut by the board, which left him feeling rather glum. 他的工資被董事會無理削減，這讓他感到有些鬱悶。

96. to decoy 誘餌

例：While hunting on the suburban outskirts of the city, Mateo decoyed wild boars by placing a slice of meat. 在城市郊區狩獵時，馬特奧通過放置一片肉來誘捕野豬。

97. malign 有害的

例：Eating food with more poisonous chemicals will malign the health of people of all ages. 食用含有更多有害的化學物質的食物會對所有年齡段的人身健康造成惡劣影響。

98. pernicious 有害的

例：Pornography is pernicious to both children and adults, as a survey showed that persistent exposure to such content can lead to long-term sexual apathy, particularly after marriage. 色情對孩子和成人都有害，調查顯示，持續接觸此類內容會導致長期的性冷淡，尤其是在婚後。

99. to pan out 有結果，成功

例：Despite their love lasting for several years, their marriage unfortunately didn't pan out in the end. 儘管他們相愛多年，但遺憾的是，他們的婚姻最終無果。

100. punchy 有力度的

例：His approach to revitalizing the sluggish economy appears punchier and more effective. 他振興疲軟經濟的做法看起來更有力，也更有效。

101. to be a whizz(whiz) at 在 ...方面有兩下子，有奇才

例：This buddy is a whizz at cooking fish. 這哥們兒做魚有兩下子。

102. stodgy 油膩的，不易消化的

例：Cutting down on stodgy food will benefit your health. 減少油膩難消化的食物有益於你的健康。

103. cogent 有說服力的，令人信服的

例: During the board meeting, the CEO presented a cogent marketing plan aimed at further exploring and expanding the Asia-Pacific market, with the goal of securing more funding and workforce to bring it to fruition. 在董事會上，首席執行官提出

了一項有說服力的行銷計畫，旨在進一步開拓和擴展亞太市場，並爭取更多的資金和人力來實現這一目標。

104. sludge 下水道油污，淤泥

例：The sewage was blocked, so there may be some sludge that needs to be cleaned out. 下水道被堵塞了，可能有一些油污需要清理。

105. to make a serious dent 有效遏制 ...（後面一般表述的是負面內容）

例：To make a serious dent in reducing inflation, the government rolled out a series of practical measures to raise interest rates. 為了有效遏制通貨膨脹，政府推出了一系列切實可行的加息措施。

106. salutary 有益的

例：He accumulated a wealth of salutary experience in business negotiation, and decided to document and publish it to benefit younger generations. 他在商務談判中積累了大量有益的經驗，決定將其記錄下來並出版，以造福年輕一代。

107. wholesome 有益身心健康的

例：We should avoid junk food and instead eat more wholesome options, such as organic, hormone-free, and non-genetically modified foods. 我們應當避免垃圾食品，轉而多攝取更有益身心健康的食物，比如有機的、無激素的、非轉基因的食品。

108. to grapple with 與 ...作鬥爭，應對

例：We must grapple with all kinds of difficulties and challenges in the new era to achieve our goals.在新時代，實現我們的奮鬥目標，必須同各種困難和挑戰作鬥爭。

再比如：She is very independent and self-motivated. She has grappled with challenging situations and has done her best to change her future. 她非常獨立且自我驅動。她積極應對挑戰，盡力改變自己的未來。

109. owing to 由於…多指負面的原因

例：The local travel industry has seriously been affected owing to the inclement weather. 由於天氣惡劣，當地旅遊行業受到了嚴重影響。

110. waffling 猶豫不決的，優柔寡斷的

例：I love John's personality, but his waffling expressions sometimes leave me confused. 我喜歡約翰的個性，但他優柔寡斷的表達有時讓我感到困惑。

111. melancholy 憂鬱的

例：I felt a sense of melancholy from his behavior and expression. 他的行為和表情讓我感到一陣憂鬱。

112. contentious 有爭議的

例：His performance is quite contentious. Some people preferred it, while others didn't. 他的表演頗具爭議，有些人喜歡，而另一些人則不喜歡。

113. to have the feel of shakedown of 有種被敲詐的感覺

例：Charging additional fees suddenly has the feel of a shakedown by tourist agents, a practice that has gradually become rampant. 突然收取額外費用讓人有種旅遊代理商敲詐的感覺，這種做法逐漸變得猖獗。

114. glib 油嘴滑舌的

例：Anyone who is glib cannot earn the trust of others. .任何油嘴滑舌的人都無法贏得他人的信任。

115. to reconcile with 與…和解

例：After years of quarreling with his colleagues, he decided to reconcile with them in order to form a better team. 經過多年和同事們的爭吵，他決定與他們和解，以便組建一個更強的團隊。

116. to put on a par with 與…並駕齊驅

例：Achieving precision technology in OLED screen production has put South Korea on a par with Japan. 在 OLED 螢幕精密製造技術方面取得突破，使韓國與日本並駕齊驅。

117. to be at odds with 與…不和、與…發生爭執

例：Rowan was at odds with his executive, so he reluctantly had to resign, even though he loved the job. 羅文與上司意見不和，因此即使他非常熱愛這份工作，也不得不勉強辭職。

118. to row with 與…吵架，發生爭執

例：He's always rowing with his colleagues, so no one wants to cooperate with him. 他總是與同事們吵架，所以沒有人願意和他合作。

119. to scuffle with 與…動手，扭打

例：A common phenomenon in the Western world is that while you can shout or argue with someone, you must never scuffle with them — or you'll land yourself in serious trouble. 在西方社會，一個普遍現像是你可以和別人爭吵甚至怒吼，但絕不能與他人動手，否則你會給自己惹來大麻煩。

120. to contrast sth with sth 與…對比

例：If he contrasts pink with purple and he prefers pink, it may indicate that he has experienced depression. Psychologically speaking, those who prefer pink are, to some extent, more vulnerable to depression. 如果他在粉色和紫色之間對比，而他偏愛粉色，這可能表明他曾經歷過抑鬱。從心理學角度來說，偏愛粉色的人或多或少更容易受到抑鬱情緒的影響。

121. to pit against 與…對抗

例: The Sino–US trade war, in fact, pits two nations against each other in a clash rooted in ideological differences. 中美貿易戰實際上是兩種意識形態之間的對抗。

122. to skirmish with 與…發生爭執、衝突

例：Samsung has skirmished with Apple over a patent concern. 三星(Samsung)與蘋果(Apple)

在一項專利問題上發生了衝突。

123. to be alien to 與…格格不入

例：Nowadays, the lifestyle of young people is alien to the older generation. 如今，年輕人的生活方式對老一輩人來說格格不入。

124. to be incongruous with 與…格格不入

例：The values he pursues seem to be incongruous with the development of the world. 他追求的價值觀似乎與這個世界的發展格格不入。

125. to converse with 與…溝通

例：As parents, we must make an effort to converse with our kids, especially during their teenage years when they may exhibit strong reverse psychology tendencies. This will ultimately help mitigate the extension of their rebellious phase. 作為父母，我們必須努力與孩子溝通，特別是在他們的青少年時期，當他們可能表現出強烈的反向心理傾向時。這樣

做最終有助於減少他們叛逆期的延長。

126. to vie against 與…角逐、競爭

例：Even though car designs have become uglier than ever, automakers continue to vie against one another with no sign of letting up. 儘管汽車設計變得比以往任何時候都醜，但各大車企之間的競爭絲毫沒有減弱的跡象，仍在激烈角逐。

127. to bear scant relation to 與…沒關係

例：Some of the approaches drivers demonstrated during their road tests bear little relation to real-world driving. 司機在路試中展示的一些方法與現實世界中的駕駛方法幾乎沒有關係。

128. to flirt with 與…眉來眼去

例：From my point of view, any woman flirting with young men suggests she is neither serious nor decent. 在我看來，任何與年輕男人眉來眼去的女人都表明她不正經也不正派。

129. to gallivant with someone 與…某人閒逛

例：Living alone abroad led to nothing, so sometimes, I had to gallivant with a few friends at nightclubs. 獨自在國外生活使我無事可做，所以有時,我不得不和幾個朋友去夜總會閒逛。

130. to confer with 與…商量

例: I have to confer with my wife to decide whether we should place the order with you. 我必須與我的妻子商量，以決定我們是否可以向您下訂單。

131. to be haggled with 與…討價還價

例：It is pretty common to be haggling with each other during the negotiation, especially for business, project, and payment transactions.在談判中，尤其是商業、專案和支付交易中，彼此討價還價是很常見的。

132. to fall short 與…匹配

例：Young people's imagination often falls short of reality. 年輕人的想像力往往難以與現實相匹配。

133. to dovetail with 與…吻合

例：The plots of many TV series don't dovetail with historical facts, which may mislead audiences and lead them to misjudge or misunderstand historical figures. 許多電視劇的情節與歷史事實不吻合，這可能會誤導觀眾，使他們對歷史人物產生誤判或誤解。

134. to draw parallel with 與…相提並論

例：You can't draw a parallel between his capability and talent. 你無法與他的能力和才華相提並論。

135. to be correlated with 與…密切相關

例：His failure in the final exam is correlated with his study habits. 他期末考試的失敗與他的學習方式密切相關。

136. to consummate 與…圓房

例：Everyone knew this man deeply loved the woman, but he never consummated their marriage. Still, no one could believe it. 所有人都知道這個男人非常愛這個女人，但婚

後他從未與妻子圓房，這讓人難以置信。

137. to hamstring 因…受阻
例：The project designed by this company was hamstrung by a shortage of funds and poor policy. 這家公司設計的專案因資金短缺和政策不利而受阻。

138. to spook 使驚嚇
例：The surging inflation spooked everyone, especially those who could barely afford food and other necessities 通貨膨脹的飆升嚇壞了所有人，尤其是那些連基本食物和生活必需品都快負擔不起的人。

Z

1. to be vulnerable to 在…方面有風險，脆弱
例：All of Europe is vulnerable to shortages of energy resources. 整個歐洲都面臨能源短缺的風險。

2. to be in flux 在…變化莫測
例：Young people's emotions—especially those of teenagers—are often unpredictable and in constant flux. They are easily swayed by new and exciting things. So if they tell you they love you, don't take their words too seriously—they might change their mind at any moment. 年輕人的情緒——尤其是青少年——常常變化莫測，難以捉摸。他們很容易被新鮮事物牽著走。如果他們對你說"我愛你"，千萬別太當真——他們可能隨時改變主意。

3. there is little sb can do about sth without unnecessarily doing sth 在不造成 …的情況下， 某人或某機構對 … 幾乎無能為力。
例：There is little our institute can do to address the manpower shortage without unduly affecting this year's overall financial budget. 在不對今年整體財政預算造成不必要影響的情況下，我們研究所對人力短缺問題幾乎無能為力。

4. the scourge 災禍

例：Food shortages will become the scourge of the 21st century. 糧食短缺將成為 21 世紀的災禍。

5. onus is on someone to do something 做某事是某人的責任

例：The onus is on all teachers to educate children to abide by the law. 所有教師都有責任教育孩子遵紀守法。

6. to be afoot 在進行中

例：We're too late — the performance is already afoot. 我們來晚了，演出在進行中了。

7. to come a cropper 栽了，失敗了

例：This expert made many predictions, but none of them came true — he came a cropper. 這位專家預言了許多事情會發生，但但沒一個成真 ，他顯然是栽了。

8. to tear 左右為難

例：As her son, he was torn between honoring his filial duty and following through on his decision to study abroad. 作為她的兒子，他在孝道與出國深造的決定之間左右為難。

9. squalid 髒的，污穢的

例：I found a room and called the owner to say I'd like to take a look. But when I arrived, it was squalid and had a nasty smell, so I ended up giving it up. 我找到了一個房間，於是打電話給房東說我想去看看。但到了那兒才發現房間又髒又臭，最後只能放棄了 。

10. to exact a grim toll on 造成了嚴重影響

例：Drought has exacted a grim toll on the harvest, and as a result, we are likely to suffer a food shortage. 乾旱給收成造成了嚴重影響，因此我們將面臨糧食短缺。

11. crummy 糟糕透頂的、劣質的、微不足道的、不愉快的

例：The broadband at my home is crummy and painfully slow, even though the internet service provider claims it's running at their highest speed ever. 我家的寬頻糟透頂，速度慢得要

命，儘管網路服務提供商聲稱這是他們有史以來的最高速度。

12. to fiddle 造假 （暗中）
例：They tried to fiddle with the quality of their line of products. 他們試圖暗中對自己產品線的品質造假。

再比如：Many historical TV serials fiddle with fabricated contents, deviating from the truth. 許多歷史題材的電視連續劇內容造假，偏離了事實。

13. to falsify 造假，偽造，扭曲，篡改
例：Recently, we discovered that some scholars had falsified their theses. It's both disgraceful and unacceptable. 最近，我們發現有些學者在造假他們的論文。這種行為既醜陋又不可接受。

14. to reel from 遭受災難，受 ...的不良影響
例：Omicron spreads rampantly around the world. any country without exception was reeling from the catastrophe. 奧米克戎在全球範圍內廣泛傳播。 任何國家都無一例外地遭受著這場災難。

15. precocious 早熟的
例：We need to pay close attention to precocious teenagers to prevent them from being misled by misguided beliefs. 我們必須關注那些早熟的青少年，以防他們被錯誤的認知誤導。

16. opprobrium 責罵
例：Every day, we must be mentally prepared to bear any opprobrium from others. Are you ready to face this challenge? 每天，我們都必須在心理上準備好承受來自他人的任何責罵。你準備好迎接這個挑戰了嗎？

17. to resent 憎惡，討厭
例：I resent his constant rattling on about his talent and genius. 我憎惡他喋喋不休地吹噓自己的才能和天賦。

Resent 基本就等於 hate. 不同的是 resent 語氣比較委婉，表示一種不公待遇，通常壓抑在內心，帶有長期性。 而

hate 表達更直接，有強烈的厭惡或敵意。

18. to bequeath sth to 贈給
例："According to his will, the famous scientist decided to bequeath all his patents to the university where he had studied. 根據他的遺囑，這位著名科學家決定將所有專利贈給他曾經就讀的大學。

19. to prop up 支撐、支持
例：African countries need sufficient funds from the IMF to prop up their failing economies. 非洲國家需要國際貨幣基金組織提供足夠的資金來支撐其衰退的經濟。

20. untenable 站不住腳
例：Since you failed to prove it correct, your argument is untenable. .既然你未能證明它是正確的，你的論點就站不住腳。

21. to hold less water 站不住腳的
例：His analysis on winning the bid holds little water due to its lack of persuasiveness and realistic expectations. 他關於中目標分析由於缺乏說服力和現實預期，站不住腳。

22. lame 站不住腳的，無說服力的；差勁的，拙劣的
例:Your statement on this issue is seriously lame. 你在這個問題上的說法實在是站不住腳。

這個詞的意思非常多，還有殘疾的，差勁的，拙劣的等。所以，在具體使用時，還要根據上下文來決定。

23. to gain the upper hand over 占上風
例：In my memory, the female students had the upper hand over the males in primary school, especially in terms of grades — girls always ranked in the top three. 在我的記憶中，小學時女生在成績上總是占上風，勝過男生，女生幾乎總是排在前三名。

24. to envisage a bright future of...展望一個光明的未來
例：China's rapid development has been widely acknowledged around the world. We can envision a bright future in which it

becomes the leading economic power. 中國的快速發展在全球範圍內廣受認可，我們可以展望一個光明的未來成為世界第一大經濟體。

25. to unspool through 展現 (緩緩）

例：His life unspools through his latest novel, revealing his deepest instincts and passions along the way. 他的一生通過他最新的小說緩緩展現，字裡行間流露出他那最深層的本能與激情。

26. to encroach 佔用

例：I wouldn't want to encroach on your valuable time and energy. 我不想佔用你寶貴的時間和精力。

27. to gain an edge over 佔優勢

例：This manufacturer invented a new product, gaining an edge over its competitors. 這家製造商發明了一款新產品，因而在競爭對手中占了優勢。

28. to toss and turn 輾轉反側

例:Failure to find a job left people tossing and turning; they suffered greatly. 找不到工作使人們輾轉反側，吃盡了苦頭。

29. to squat on the toilet without taking a shit 占著茅坑不拉屎

例：The government must fire those carders squatting on the toilet without taking a shit and hire more young talents to serve the people. 政府必須開除那些占著茅坑不拉屎的幹部，多招青年人才為人民服務。

30. snag 障礙

例：The critical snag in English learning for Chinese learners is that they don't know which words and expressions are commonly used by native speakers. Instead, they are often misled into memorizing the entire dictionary or the textbook by rote. 對於中國學習者來說，學習英語的關鍵障礙在於他們不知道哪些詞彙和表達方式是母語人士常用的。相反，他們常常被誤導，死記硬背整本詞典或課本。

再比如：Leilani was driving her car so fast that she suddenly lost control and hit a snag on the roadside. 萊拉尼開車太快，

突然失去控制，撞上了路邊的障礙物。

31. hurdle 障礙，跨欄（體育）

例：This case may face many hurdles before it can be verified. 這個案件在被驗證之前可能會面臨許多障礙。

再比如：Ryan won the 400-meter hurdles event in the Olympic Games. 裡安在奧運會上贏得了 400 米跨欄比賽。

32. to buff up 彰顯

例：Her gesture clearly aims to buff up her authority. 她的舉動顯然是為了彰顯自己的權威形象。

33. hush up 張揚出去

例：There is an old saying in China that a family's scandal must never be hushed up. 中國有句老話，家醜不可外揚。

34. to regurgitate the text book 照本宣科

例：Professors should avoid merely regurgitating the textbook and instead highlight key content, integrating their expertise and theories to enhance and fully unlock the students' potential. 教授應避免單純照本宣科，而應強調關鍵知識點，將他們的專業知識和理論相結合，以促進並充分發揮學生的潛力。

35. to retrieve 找回

例：Since their divorce, it's been difficult for them to retrieve the love they once had. 自從離婚後，他們很難找回曾經的那份愛情。

36. corral 召集在一起

例：The Ministry of Education corrals top talents from various schools and universities to discuss the renovation and reform of the current education model. 教育部把來自各類學校和大學的精英召集在一起討論當前教育模式的革新與改革。

37. to find a pretext for 找藉口

例：I've found that many people often try to find a pretext for rejecting others. I really don't like that it feels so hypocritical. 我發現很多人經常設法找藉口

來拒絕別人。我真的很反感這種行為感覺太虛偽了

38. ostentatious 招搖的，引人注目的

例：These days, many "stars" flaunt an ostentatious image, completely oblivious to the value of staying low-key. 現在不少"明星"一副招搖的樣子，完全不懂得低調才是真正的修養。

39. to incur 招致

例：Illegal random parking will incur a penalty. 亂停亂放將會被處罰。

40. to spell 除了"拼寫"的意思外，還有招致，替換等含義。

例：His ignorance spells a great deal of trouble for him. 他的無知給自己招致很多煩惱。

再比如：She had been working for almost 10 hours, so her colleague came to spell her. 她已經工作了將近 10 個小時，所以她的同事來替換她。

41. excruciating 折磨人的

例：The side effects from the covid excruciating 新冠病毒的副作用很折磨人。

42. unfeigned 真誠的，不虛偽的

例：Nowadays, everything can be fake, but the care and love your parents show you should be unfeigned. 如今，一切都可以是假的，但只有父母對你的關心和愛應該是真誠的。

43. to target 針對

例：All our teachers should lay out a better education program that targets the character of each student. 我們所有的老師都應該針對每個學生的特點制定更好的教育方案。

44. uplifting 振奮人心的，令人振奮的

例：He posted an uplifting article on the website and attracted hundreds of millions of fans to follow him. 他在網站上發佈了一篇振奮人心的 文章，吸引了數億粉絲跟隨他。

45. to butt heads 針鋒相對

例：A couple doesn't need to butt heads over daily trifles to prevent their stressed relationship from escalating, which could ultimately lead to divorce. 一對夫婦不需要在日常瑣事上針鋒相對，以防止緊張的關係升級，最終可能導致離婚。

46. to pep up 振作起

例：Failure is not scary; the end of the world is that you lose confidence in pepping up your spirit to rekindle your future.失敗並不可怕；最可怕的是你失去了振作起來重新點燃未來的信心。

47. to wrangle with 與 ...爭吵

例：例：She often wrangles with her colleagues, which has led many people in the company to isolate her. 她經常與同事爭吵，這導致公司裡許多人把她孤立起來。

再比如：You must keep in mind that you try to avoid wrangling with your colleagues, otherwise, it will affect your long-term relationship.儘量避免與同事爭吵，這會影響你們的長期關係.

48. to perpetrate 做（惡）

例：Everyone hopes the state can issue a new law to maximize curbing the crimes that can be perpetrated through the smuggling of children 大家希望國家能夠出臺一項新法律，最大程度地遏制那些可能通過兒童走私實施的犯罪。

49. to spar with 與 ...爭吵

例：He spars with his team members on some trivial issues, so nobody would like to work with him.他在一些瑣碎的問題上與他的團隊成員爭吵，所以沒有人願意和他一起工作。

50. to end up doing sth 最終做了

例：With his great exertion and dedication, he ended up accomplishing a task that once seemed impossible.憑藉巨大的努力和奉獻精神，他最終完成了一個曾被認為不可能完成的任務。

51. to subdue 征服

例：Her super fast mental calculations subdue the audience, astonishingly even faster than a computer can perform. 她的心算能力令人震驚、征服了觀眾，甚至比電腦還快。

52. to neaten 整理，修整

例 I'm neatening up all the items on my shelf to make them look more orderly. 我正在把架子上的所有物品整理整齊，讓它們看起來更有條理。

53. to squabble over 爭吵、爭論

例：Supporters of gas-powered cars squabbled with those in favor of electric vehicles. 燃油車的支持者和電動車的支持者發生了爭吵。

54. to vindicate 證明…的清白、證明…的無辜

例：I hope the result of your investigation can vindicate me. 我希望你的調查結果能證明我的清白。

55. overriding 最重要的

例：The current overriding issue is how we can figure out a better way to stop the virus variant from spreading across the country. 當前最重要的問題是，我們如何想出一個更好的方法來防止病毒變種在全國範圍內進一步傳播。

56. to face squarely 正視

例：You must face the challenge ahead squarely. 你必須有足夠的勇氣正視擺在你面前的挑戰。

57. to levy tax on 徵稅

例：Western governments levy heavy taxes on everything, which significantly impacts the daily lives of ordinary people. 西方政府對所有事物征重稅，這嚴重影響了普通民眾的日常生活。

58. to tell a lie with one's eyes wide open 睜眼說瞎話

例：Clearly, this foolish decision was made by her boss. Unfortunately, he continues to tell a lie with his eyes wide open, which is utterly absurd and ridiculous. 顯然，這個愚蠢的

決定是她的老闆做出的。不幸的是，他依然睜著眼睛說瞎話，這簡直荒謬可笑。

59. to vault 蒸蒸日上，蓬勃發展

例：His career is vaulting to new heights thanks to his ability and talent. 由於他的能力和天賦，他的事業蒸蒸日上。

60. altercation 爭執

例：The altercation between the two countries could potentially lead to a catastrophe in economic, political, and cultural spheres. 兩國之間的爭執可能會導致經濟、政治和文化領域的災難。　。

61.　the hardest-borne 最艱難的

例：You might encounter the hardest-borne moments on your life journey, but you shouldn't get discouraged. Overcoming them is key to realizing your true value. 在人生的旅程中，你可能會遇到最最艱難的時刻，但你不應灰心喪氣。克服這些困難是實現自我價值的關鍵。

62. to espouse 支持

例：Almost all the employees, but a few espouse the policy the board conjured up, so the boss undoubtedly decided to implement it. 除了少數員工外，幾乎所有的員工都支持董事會制定的政策，因此老闆無疑決定實施它。

63. fidgeting 坐立不安

例：A police officer noticed via the monitor that a middle-aged man was fidgeting around near the entrance of the mall. 一名員警通過監視器注意到一名中年男子在商場入口附近坐立不安。

64. to root for 支持，力挺

例：Stella encountered many difficulties during the implementation of this critical project. Luckily, her boss roots for her. 斯特拉在這個重點項目的實施過程中遇到了很多困難，幸運的是她的老闆很支持她。

65. to conjure up 制定

例：From my point of view, a government, whether in rich or developing countries, must conjure up a realistic policy to help people under the poverty line improve the quality of their living standards. 在我看來，無論是富國還是窮國的政府都必須制定一個現實的政策來幫助那些在貧困線下掙扎的人們提高他們的生活水準。

66. to gawp at 直盯盯地看著

例：He was sitting in a coffee shop on the corner of the street when he looked up and saw a beautiful girl walking by. He couldn't help but gawp at her, so stunned by her presence that he dropped his cup, spilling coffee all over the floor. 他正坐在街角的咖啡店裡，抬頭看到一位美麗的女孩走過。他忍不住目瞪口呆直盯盯地看著她，不小心把杯子掉了，咖啡灑了一地。

67. to draw up one's own plan 制定某人自己的計畫

例：To achieve your goal of entering top universities, you should consider drawing up your own study plan in advance. 為了實現進入頂尖大學的目標，你應該考慮提前制定自己的學習計畫。

68. to defray 支付

例：Her family members will visit the USA next month. As one of her sons and a guarantor, I will defray all the expenses during their visit. 她的家人將在下個月訪問美國。作為她的兒子和擔保人，我將支付他們訪問期間的所有費用。

69. swaggering 趾高氣揚的

例：I came across numerous videos online showcasing single ladies exuding swaggering self-confidence, one of whom unrealistically demanded her boyfriend earn 2 million dollars while she only made $1000 a month. I wonder where she got that confidence from. 我在網上看到很多視頻，展示一些單身女士擺出一副趾高氣揚、自信滿滿的姿態，其中一位不切實際地要求她的男朋友賺兩百萬美元，而她每月僅賺 1000 美元。我不禁想知道是誰賦予了她這樣的自信。

70. to counterweight 制衡

例：Some scholars conducted years of research on Chinese history and discovered an interesting phenomenon: emperors tended to hire both loyal and treacherous ministers, deliberately using one group to counterweight the other in order to consolidate their power. 一些學者經過多年研究中國歷史，發現一個有趣的現象：皇帝往往任用忠臣和奸臣，故意讓一方去制衡另一方，以鞏固自己的權力。

71. brainchild 智慧結晶
例：The invention of vehicles is a remarkable brainchild of humankind. 車輛的發明是人類非凡智慧結晶。

72. forthright 直截了當的
例：You may consider taking a tactful rather than a forthright approach when dealing with issues during times of trouble. 在遇到困難時，你可以考慮採取一種更圓滑而非直截了當的方式來處理問題。

73. reputed 知名的
例：It's bizarre that so many reputed experts have suddenly put forward a slew of absurdities that not only bewilder and mislead the public but also overturn people's understanding, moral standards, and worldviews. 令人匪夷所思的是，許多知名的專家突然提出了一連串荒謬的言論，不僅讓大眾感到困惑和誤導，甚至顛覆了人們的認知、道德標準和世界觀。

74. an unvarnished depiction of 質樸無華
varnished 本意為給…塗漆，裝飾，前面加了一個 un 變成了否定，故此譯為質樸無華，不加修飾的意思。

比如：It fully reveals an unvarnished depiction of his way of life. 它充分展示了他生活方式的質樸無華。

75. finger-wagging 指手畫腳
例："Stop the finger-wagging during our discussion," he raged. He also warned that anyone who tried to sag our efforts and energy in researching and developing a new product would be fired. "別在我們討論的時候指手畫腳了"。他怒吼道。他還指出，任何想要削弱我們在研發新產品上的努力和精力的人都會被解雇。

76. red-hot 炙手可得的
例：Being a civil servant has suddenly become red-hot, even though nobody was interested in it in the past. 曾無人問津的公務員工作，如今卻突然變得炙手可得。

77. exponentially 呈指數增長地
例：During the pandemic, the number of people infected by the virus increased exponentially. 在疫情期間，感染病毒的人數呈指數級增長。

78. to be outspoken 直言不諱
例：I am outspoken, but that doesn't mean I'm malicious. 我可能說話直言不諱，但這並不代表我有惡意。

79. to be blunt about 直言不諱地談論
例：Her grandpa was blunt about his granddaughter's unrealistic expectations for her future husband, warning that such expectations might leave her single forever. 她爺爺直言不諱地指出她對未來丈夫的不切實際的期待，並警告說這可能會讓她永遠單身。

80. only by doing sth...can sb do sth...只有…才能 …
例：Only by relentlessly exerting our efforts toward a single goal and never giving up can we ultimately achieve success.只有堅持不懈地朝著一個目標努力，絕不放棄，我們最終才能取得成功。

81. to purport 旨在，意圖
例：This manual purports to make writers' articles more readable.本手冊旨在提升作者文章的可讀性。

82. to fumble 支支吾吾
例：The big loss this year triggered panic within the company. However, the president fumbled during his talk with the board, and almost nobody believed in him, which ultimately led to his resignation. 今年的大損失引發了公司內部的恐慌。然而，總裁在與董事會的談話中表現得支支吾吾，幾乎沒有人相信他，最終導致他辭職。

83. to stanch 止住
例：Day traders must sell all their stocks to stanch any losses

before the market closes, in case their stocks sharply drop, especially when the market opens the next day. 日間交易者必須在股市收盤前賣掉所有股票，以止損，防止股票在次日開盤時急劇下跌。

84. fealty 忠誠

例：Under most circumstances, companies prioritize their employees' fealty, while employees are more inclined to pursue financial gain. 在大多數情況下，公司更看重員工的忠誠，而員工則更傾向於追求經濟利益。

85. to take a hammering 重創、打擊

例：Owing to his failure to accurately anticipate the future, his company's further development took a hammering. 由於他未能準確預估未來，他公司的後續發展受到了重創。

86. to hit the jacket 中頭獎，中大獎

例：Samantha hit the $70 million jackpot this week, and she was so excited that she couldn't sleep for three days. 薩曼莎本周中了七千萬美元的彩票大獎，激動得三天都沒能睡著覺。

87. to roll around 周而復始，沒完沒了的

例：The argument over whether to issue a $2,000 basic income to each Canadian keeps rolling around in Parliament. 關於是否應該向每位加拿大人發放2000加元基本收入的爭論在議會裡周而復始地上演，遲遲沒有定論。

88. to phase it out 逐步淘汰

例：The facilities in this country have become worn out and should be phased out and replaced with new ones. 這個國家的設施已經破舊不堪，應當逐步淘汰，並用新的設施替代。

89. to be doomed to 註定

例：The marketing strategy implemented by the company is doomed to lead to bankruptcy. 該公司實施的行銷策略註定會失敗，並最終導致破產。

90. to ratchet up 逐漸升溫、逐年飆升

例：The Sino-US trade war was ratcheting up as both countries continued to escalate import tariffs. 隨著中美兩國不斷加征進口關稅，中美貿易戰正在不斷升級。

再比如：Everyone's expenditures have ratcheted up year by year due to unchecked inflation 由於通脹失控，每個人的開支都在逐年飆升。

91. staple food 主食

例：Chinese people take rice as their staple food, while Westerners tend to prefer bread. Although flour-based food is also common in China, rice still accounts for about 70% of their daily diet 中國人以大米為主食，而西方人則更傾向於麵包。雖然中國也常吃麵食，但大米在他們的日常飲食中仍占大約 70%。

92. to nab 抓起來，逮捕

例：Anyone who produces poisonous food should be nabbed and sentenced to life imprisonment. 任何製造有毒食物的人都應該被抓起來判無期徒刑。

93. high-handed 專橫跋扈的

例：His boss offended many employees because of his high-handed manner. 他的老闆因為專橫跋扈的性格得罪了很多員工

94. to be bent on 專心致力於

例：All the 12th-grade students are bent on improving their scores in order to gain smooth admission to top universities. 所有十二年級的學生都專心致力於提高成績，以順利進入頂尖大學。

95. to ram 撞擊

例：This morning, two drivers rammed into each other on the highway. One of them died on the spot, and the other sustained serious injuries and later died in the hospital. 今天早上，兩名司機在高速公路上互相猛烈撞擊，一人當場死亡，另一人重傷，隨後在醫院去世。

96. pageantry 壯觀，華麗

例：The ancient buildings exuded pageantry through their

unique architectural traditions and cultural heritage. 這些古老的建築通過其獨特的建築傳統和文化傳承展現出一種壯觀而華麗的氣派。

97. to hold one's accountable 追究某人責任

例：It's rather peculiar that almost all online taxi companies establish a so-called "safety team" to handle rider complaints, yet drivers have no direct way to contact them — let alone engage in face-to-face discussions. I question what they're hiding and what exactly they fear. This mechanism leads to numerous wrongful convictions and the unjust dismissal of many outstanding drivers. I firmly believe that governments worldwide must hold these companies accountable to ensure the basic rights of both drivers and riders are equally protected. 令人費解的是，幾乎所有網約車公司都設立了所謂的"安全團隊"來處理乘客的投訴，但司機卻無法直接聯繫他們，更別提面對面溝通了。我不禁質疑他們到底在隱藏什麼，又究竟在害怕什麼。這種機制導致了大量冤假錯案，許多優秀司機被不公正地辭退。我堅信，各國政府應當追究這些公司的責任，以確保司機和乘客的基本權利都能得到平等保障。

98. to plump for 支持、選出

例：I plump for pursuing true love. Unfortunately, it seems to have vanished from the real world — existing only in novels or the virtual realm.我支持追求真愛。不幸的是，它似乎早已從現實世界中消失，只存在於小說或虛擬世界裡。

再比如：When visiting a new restaurant for the first time, diners often find it challenging to plump for a specific dish—especially when the menu is filled with a variety of tempting options. 第一次光顧一家新餐廳時，顧客往往很難挑選出一道具體的菜品，尤其是在功能表上滿是各種誘人選擇的情況下。

99. searing 灼熱的

例：She walked alone through the searing desert, with no one to accompany her. Everyone showed genuine concern for her safety. 她獨自穿越灼熱的沙

漠，無人陪伴。每個人都真切地關心她的安危。

100. to set one's sights on 著眼於
例：The company is ambitiously setting its sights on launching a bold marketing strategy across Europe. 這家公司正著眼於計畫在整個歐洲推出一項大膽的行銷策略。

101. insolvent 資不抵債的
例：He acquired numerous properties and faced significant financial challenges that ultimately rendered him insolvent. 他購買了許多房產，遇到了嚴重的財務問題，最終導致了他資不抵債

102. uppity 自大的，傲慢的
例：He was born with uppity traits, so he wasn't interested in participating in this program; instead, he was busy designing his own. 他天生帶有高傲的特質，因此他不願參加這個項目；相反，他忙於設計自己的專案。

103. unprompted 自發的
例：So many people came to the impoverished villages to help the local children unprompted. 所以許多人自發地來到貧窮的村莊幫助當地的孩子。

104. wannabe 自封的
例：She is a wannabe beauty, but nobody acknowledges it. 她自封為美女，但沒人認同。

105. to plug naturally into 自然融入到
例：Tens of thousands of new immigrants arrive in Canada each year, eager to plug themselves naturally into the new environment by adapting their customs to blend in with the locals and pursue a better life. 每年，成千上萬的新移民來到加拿大，他們渴望通過自然地融入新環境，適應當地的風俗習慣，與當地人融合，追求更好的生活。

106. to bludgeon 自衛反擊，打擊
例：A road rage incident escalated into the drivers bludgeoning each other. In the end, they were all arrested and

sent to prison. My question is—was it really worth it? 一場路怒事件最終升級為司機們互相毆打，結果他們全都被逮捕並送進了監獄。我的問題是：這真的值得嗎？

107. to mull over 仔細考慮

例：One of my friends once told me that life is all about mulling over how to pull money out of others' pockets into your own. It struck me as both enlightening and profoundly far-reaching. 我有個朋友曾告訴我，人生的意義就在於仔細考慮如何把別人口袋裡的錢掏進自己的口袋。這句話讓我覺得既啟發人心，又深遠得令人驚歎。

108. to pore over 仔細研究

例：He pores over car models and is planning to build one based on his own design.他仔細研究各種汽車模型，並計畫打造一款屬於自己設計的車型。

再比如：As a supervisor, he must pore over every line of code to ensure quality control and guarantee that the program runs smoothly. 作為一名主管，他必須逐行仔細檢查程式設計代碼，以確保品質控制，從而保證程式順利運行。

109. totakestock仔細斟酌

例：This will be vital for the rest of my life , please allow me a moment to take stock of it. 這對我的餘生至關重要，請讓我來仔細斟酌一下。

110. tobeself-absorbed自以為是，固執己見

例：Carter is so self-absorbed that he refuses to heed anyone's advice , his failure was inevitable. 卡特自己為是，聽不進任何人的勸告。所以，他的失敗是註定的。

111. self-inflicted自作的

例：Your current situation was self-inflicted due to your carelessness and negligence. 由於你的粗心大意和疏忽，目前的處境是你自作的。

112. criss-crossed縱橫交錯的

例：In China, the dazzling network of crisscrossing highways has left many Western visitors in awe, marveling at the tremendous transformation over the past 30 years. 在中國，那些縱橫交錯、令人眼花繚亂的高速公路令許多西方遊客驚歎不已，他們為過去三十年來的巨大變化感到震撼。

113. to connive 睜一隻眼閉一隻眼、縱容

例：Unfair and encroaching laws will end up conniving at crimes. 不公且侵權的法律最終會對犯罪行為睜一隻眼閉一隻眼。

114. to snarl 阻礙

例：A survey revealed that an aggressive personality may snarl a person's career development in the future. 一項調查顯示，一個人的好鬥性格可能會阻礙其未來的職業發展。

115. to enmesh 阻礙

例：Your timidity will enmesh you in self-doubt, preventing you from realizing your dreams and fully exploiting your potential. 你的膽怯會讓你陷入自我懷疑，阻礙你實現夢想、充分發揮潛能。

116. to shield sb from doing sth 阻擋某人做某事

例：No one can shield others' rights from knowing the truth. 任何人都不能阻擋他人瞭解真相的權力。

117. to suffice 足夠

例：A phone discussion with the clients will suffice; why do you need to be there in person?" his boss questioned him. 與客戶通過電話討論就足夠了；為什麼一定要親自去呢?"他的老闆質問他。

118. to preclude from 阻止（非常正式的用法）

例：With the development of AI, companies could have better ways to preclude their staff from playing games during working hours. 隨著人工智慧的發展，公司可以通過更好的方式來阻止員工在工作時間玩遊戲。

119. to forestall 阻止，防止

例：He frequently appeared in public to forestall the spread of rumors about his death. 他經常公開露面，以阻止關於他死亡的謠言傳播。

120. to dissuade...from 阻止⋯做⋯

例：Even though this young man was paralyzed, it never dissuaded him from learning to drive. 儘管這個年輕人已經癱瘓，但並...沒有阻止他學習駕駛汽車。

121. to delve into 鑽研，深入研究

例:She was a famous journalist, but now she delves into Buddhism. 她曾是一位元著名的記者，現在她深入鑽研佛教。

122. incipient 最初的

例：The incipient idea may lead to the realization of a dream, so I advocate for people to have ideas, regardless of whether they are realistic or not, at least they dare to think about it. 最初的想法可能會引領夢想的實現，所以我提倡人們要有想法，不管它是否現實，至少你敢去想。

123. doggedly 執著地

例：Sawyer doggedly loved a girl who, by all appearances, might not have felt the same way about him. 索耶執著地愛著一個女孩，而這個女孩顯然可能並沒有同樣地愛他。

Index 索引

A

alight on 突然想到... T-67

alimony 贍養費 S-20

altercation 爭執 Z-60

ameliorate 改善 G-02

amble 慢吞吞移動 M-08

among other things 除此之外 C-100

anthropogenic 人為的 R-31

angst 焦慮，擔憂 J-82

anodyne 平和的 P-34

apace 迅速地 X-01

ape 模仿 M-52

apogee 巔峰，最高點 D-66

appall 使...大為震驚 S-50

apply a broad brush to 大刀闊斧地做...D-10

arcane 晦澀難懂的，神秘的 H-60

arduous slog 艱巨的任務 J-54

ardour 熱情 R-27

archetypal 典型的 D-73

aspire to 渴望得到 K-20

at every turn 處處，到處 C-99

at large 逍遙法外 X-73

at one's mercy 受...擺佈 S-103

at the fastest clip 以最快的速度 Y-67

atone for 贖罪 S-129

B

babble at 對...喋喋不休 D-112

back down 放棄，讓步 D-31, F-23

backfire 事與願違 S-100

backlog 積壓的貨物，積壓的工作 J-31

badger 煩擾 J-128

badger sb 死纏著某人...S-86

baffle 把...難住 B-10

balk at 回避 H-48

bane 禍根 H-73

bandish 討好，奉承 S-09

bandy words with sb 和某人頂嘴 H-16

barely...when 剛...就... G-13

batter 肆虐，連續打擊，嚴重破壞... X-27

be about to go up in smoke 化為烏有，白費了，付諸東流 H-40

be abuzz 議論紛紛，沸沸揚揚 Y-42

be adept at 擅長...S-17

be aggrieved 受委屈 S-121

be agog for 渴望 D-138

be akin to 就像個...相當於 J-130

be duty-bound to 義不容辭做... Y-29

be embroiled in 捲入 J-18

be etched into 銘刻在... M-49

be extremely reticent about 諱莫如深 H-56

be fraught with 充滿了... C-106

be fiercely critical of 強烈批評 Q-32

be flanked by 相伴左右 X-39

be given no heads-up about 沒有事先通知 M-26

be gleeful at 對...幸災樂禍 D-139

be haggled with 與...討價還價 Y-131

be hamstrung by 受到阻礙 S-112

be iffy about 對...不滿意 D-101

be immersed in 沉浸在... C-72

be incongruous with 與...格格不入 Y-124

be inflated by 被誇大 B-72

be in flux 在變化 Z-02

be in stake 懸了 X-58

be inimical to 損害，有害 S-53

be in jeopardy 處在風險中，岌岌可危 C-109

be in sore need of 急需 J-30

be inundated with 充斥著 C-91

be in cahoots 勾結在一起 G-32

be less susceptible to sth, 不易受...影響 B-168

be less vulnerable to 受影響的程度不大，不那麼脆弱 S-124

be loth to 不願意... B-172

be lavish in 對...大加讚賞 D-111

be littered with 佈滿，充滿 B-153

be loaded with 充滿了... C-94

be lukewarm about 並不熱衷 B-113

be morphed into 變成...B-93

be no match for sb at 在某方面某人不是某人的對手 B-12

be nostalgia for 懷念 H-41

be not inferior to 不比...差 B-125

be not up to snuff 不合格 B-140

be not much more than 不超過，僅僅 B-127

be not much use for 對...用處不大 D-143

be not without 並非沒有 B-114

be oblivious to 對...毫不在意 M-27

be obsessed with 對...著迷 D-149

be off to a good start 開了一個好頭 K-02

be vulnerable to 在...方面都很脆弱 Z-01

be yoked to 跟...扯上關係 G-25

be wary of ...警惕，留神 J-119

be a whizz(whiz) at 在...方面有兩下子，有奇才 Y-101

be widely scattered 分散各處 F-52

be never wonky about 不存僥倖 B-167

beam to 向...傳送 X-37

bear scant relation to 與...沒關係 Y-127

bear weight 承受，負重 C-85

become a stain on someone 成為某人的污點 C-84

become so entrenched 變得如此根深蒂固的 B-96

bed-hopping 反復無常的 F-11

bedevil 困擾 K-54

beef up 加強 J-42

beget 產生 C-49

beguile 使著迷 S-101

begrudge 吝嗇 L-38

beholden to sb 欠某人人情 Q-17

bemoan 抱怨，惋惜 B-55

belch out 噴發 P-19

bellow 大聲吼叫 D-27

belt out 引吭高歌 Y-02

bend 屈從 Q-56

bend someone to one's will 使別人屈從自己的意志 S-70

beset 陷入...困境 X-23

besmirch 敗壞，玷污，誹謗 B-28

bespectacled 戴眼鏡的 D-39

bespoke 定制的 D-78

bequeath sth to 贈給 Z-18

bewail 痛哭 T-40

bicker 吵嘴 C-65

bilk 欺騙 Q-07

bill oneself as 把自己標榜為 B-24

bingeing 暴飲暴食 B-53

blatant 公然的，喧囂的，華麗的 G-30

blanch 焯菜 C-64

bland 平淡無味的 P-32

blandness 溫柔 W-46

blandish 討好，奉承 T-09

blandishment 奉承 F-57

blast off 發射升空 F-06

blisteringly 極熱、極冷等 J-06

blithe 愉快的，樂觀的 Y-79

bluff 虛張聲勢 X-69

bludgeon 自衛反擊，打擊 Z-106

blunder 錯誤 C-41

blur 變得模糊，不清楚 B-95

blurt out 不加思考脫口而出 B-145

blustering 氣勢洶洶的 Q-80

C

conundrum 難題 N-06

convoluted 錯綜複雜的，曲折的 C-42

convulsion 抽搐 C-95

cooling-off period 冷靜期 L-24

copious 大量的 D-20

corner someone 逼某人 B-90

cosy up to 討好 T-08

counter-productive 適得其反的 S-72

counterweight 制衡 Z-70

court 導致，招致 D-47

courtesy of 多虧... D-159

coveted 夢魅以求的 M-30

converse with 與...溝通 Y-125

covertly 偷偷摸摸地 T-49

corral 召集人們在一起 Z-36

cow 恐嚇，威脅 K-27

be coy about 對...閃爍其詞 D-128

crank out 胡亂做... H-30

crank up 把聲音調大 B-23

crank up one's power 使足了勁兒 S-102

crimp 限制 X-30

cringe 感到難為情，感到難堪，畏縮 G-06

cringeworthy 令人感到尷尬的 L-44

criss-crossed 縱橫交錯的 Z-112

crony 裙帶的，親密的 Q-47

crop up 突發 T-59

crow about 吹噓 C-116

crow over 幸災樂禍，得意洋洋 X-99

crumbling 破破爛爛的,搖搖欲墜的 、破滅，粉碎 P-33

crummy 糟糕透頂的，劣質的，微不足道的，不愉快的 Z-11

cudgel 棍棒 G-59

cull 撲殺 P-53

cultish 狂熱的 K-46

cumbersome 繁瑣的，麻煩的 F-13

cupidity 貪婪 T-04

curtail 減少，限制 J-67

curry favour with 拍馬屁,巴結 P-08

cut a mustard 達到標準，符合條件 D-80

cut euphemism 不要繞彎子 B-180

cut loose 解雇 J-90

D

dabble 涉足 S-26

daft 愚蠢的 Y-87

dangle sb 吸引，誘惑某人 X-11

discernment 洞察力，眼力　D-81

discredit 抹黑　M-55

discretionary 可自由支配的　K-24

disengage 掰了（多指關係上）B-29

disgorge 吐出來　T-58

dishearten 讓人心灰意冷，讓人心寒　R-20

disingenuous 虛偽的　X-78

disorientate 迷失方向　M-37

disown 脫離關係　T-16

disparage 貶低　B-98

dissect 剖析　P-51

dissipate 浪費，揮霍　L-09

dissonant 不和諧的　B-142

dissuade...from 阻止...做...　Z-120

distraught 心煩意亂的　X-83

ditch 丟棄，拋棄（非正式用法）　B-115

dither 發抖，顫抖　F-01

divergent 分歧的　F-51

divest oneself of 擺脫　B-32

divulge 透露，洩露，洩露　T-45

divvy up 分攤，分配　F-53

do soul-searching about 對...反省　D-113

dodgy 狡猾的，不可靠的　J-78

doff 脫帽，脫衣　T-37

dogged 頑強的　W-12

dog someone 困擾某人　K-48

doggedly 頑強的　Z-123

dole out 發放　F-02

dovetail with 與...吻合　Y-133

doughty 彪悍的　B-106

double-whammy 雙重打擊　S-136

dowdy 邋遢　L-03

downplay 小看，低估　B-97

downright 徹頭徹尾的　C-67

drab 單調的，乏味的　C-74

draconian 嚴苛的　Y-09

drag on 拖延　T-81

drawback 缺點，不足之處　Q-78

drawn-out 長期的　C-51

draw parallel with 與...相提並論　Y-134

draw up one's own plan 制定某人自己的計畫　Z-67

dredge up 挖出　W-01

dressing-down 嚴厲批評　Y-11

dribble 帶球，運球　D-37

drift into 紛紛湧入　F-56

drivel 胡言亂語　H-34

drum up 鼓起　G-36

dry 慘澹的，冷清的　C-09

dud 白費了，無用的，爛的　B-27

duff 蹩腳的，錯誤的　B-109

dwindle 減少　J-66

E

exact a toll 釀成代價 N-20

exact one's own toll 付出某人代價 F-66

exact a grim toll on 造成了嚴重 Z-10

excise 切除 Q-41

excoriate 嚴厲批評 Y-12

excruciating 折磨人的 Z-41

exercise restraint 保持克制 B-40

exponentially 呈指數增長地 Z-77

expedient 權宜之計的 Q-77

extort 勒索，敲詐 L-20

eyebrow-raising 驚人之舉的 J-116

F

face squarely 正視 Z-56

fab 絕妙的，難以置信的 J-40

face a stern test 面臨著嚴峻的考驗 M-40

fallback 備用的，應急的 B-81

fall foul of 違反 W-32

fall on deaf ears 沒人理睬，對...置若罔聞 M-19

fall out with 鬧掰了 N-12

fall short 與...脫節 Y-132

fallow 不活躍的 X-107

fallow 休整的 B-144

fanfare 熱鬧非凡，大張旗鼓 R-24

fanatical 狂熱的 K-45

far-fetched 牽強的，離譜的 Q-18

far-flung 偏遠的 P-26

fare 表現 B-108

farcical 鬧劇的 N-14

fart 放屁 F-19

fawn over 奉承 F-58

fealty 忠誠 Z-84

fecund 肥沃的，生育能力強 F-44

feel aggrieved 感到倒楣，感到委屈 D-45

feel chill to the bone 後背發涼 H-27

feel daunted 望而卻步 W-16

feel disillusioned with 對...絕望 D-120

feel no shame in 對...不感到羞恥 D-97

feel queasy 感到噁心 G-04

feel smugger about 為...感到沾沾自喜 W-22

fete 盛宴 S-47

fervid 慷慨激昂的 K-07

fester 使...惡化 S-52

fickle 多變的，變幻莫測的 D-157

fictitious 虛構的 X-105

froth 泡沫 P-14

frown upon 看不慣，不滿，不贊成 K-05

frumpy 土氣，傻裡傻氣的 T-62

fudge 捏造，敷衍 N-22

fuel panic 加劇恐慌 J-38

fulminate 嚴厲斥責 Y-10

full-blown 全面的 Q-71

full-fledge 全面的 Q-72

fumble 支支吾吾 Z-82

fume about 憤怒，生氣 F-04

fungible 可替換的 K-18

furlough 休假 X-104

furore 公憤 G-20

furtive 偷偷摸摸的 T-48

fussy 愛挑剔的 A-04

fuzzy 模糊不清的, 毛茸茸的 M-56

G

gaggles of 喧鬧的 X-51

gain an edge over 佔優勢 Z-27

gain the upper hand over 占上風 Z-23

gallivant with someone 與...某人閒逛 Y-129

garble 篡改 C-35

garrulous 喋喋不休的 D-75

gasp at 對...驚歎 D-119

gauge 估計，判斷 G-39

gawp at 直盯盯地看著 Z-66

geek 高手(在某領域） G-16

gee up 促使 C-33

get a square dinner 一頓豐盛的晚餐 C-124

get around to doing 抽時間做... C-98

get by on 靠...勉強度日 C-28

get cold feet about 對...冷淡 B-94

get hitched 結婚 J-92

get in the way 擋路，妨礙 D-43

get lumbered with 迫使扛起 P-48

get riled by 被...激怒 B-60

get burned 被炒魷魚 B-66

giddy 頭暈眼花，眼花繚亂的 T-54

gin up the economy 振興經濟 J-71

give the limelight to 引起關注 Y-78

give sb a leg up 給某人幫助和支持 G-72

glib 油嘴滑舌的 Y-114

gloat over 幸災樂禍 X-98

glum 鬱悶 Y-95

gobs of 一行行，一串串，一滴滴，一捆捆等 Y-34

H

hark back to 回想起，回憶起 H-62

hash out 討論來討論去，沒完沒了的討論 T-11

haunting 難以忘懷的，縈繞心頭的 N-08

have a bearing on 對...有影響 D-145

have/has hogged the limelight 搶盡了風頭，備受矚目 Q-28

have/has little incentive to 對...沒什麼積極性 D-123

have no inkling of 對...一無所知 D-142

have one's hands full 忙得不可開交 M-10

have plenty going for 對...大有好處。 D-160

have scruples about 對......有顧慮 D-152

have the feel of shakedown of 有種被敲詐的感覺 Y-113

heady 得意忘形的，濃郁醇厚的 D-50

heap the derision on D-105

heart-rending 令人心碎的 L-52

heartthrob 萬人迷 W-14

heckle 起哄 Q-03

hectic 忙碌的，繁忙的，忙亂的 M-11

heft 實力 S-77

hefty 高大健壯的 G-14

heinous 滔天的，極其罪惡的 T-14

hiatus 脫節 T-79

hiccup-free 無拘無束的 W-61

hide its strengths and bide its time 韜光養晦等待時機 T-07

high-grossing 叫座率高，高票房率 J-89

high-handed 專橫跋扈的 Z-93

hinge on 取決於 Q-63

hip 時髦的 S-78

hit the jacket 中頭獎，中大獎 Z-86

hoax 惡作劇 E-10

hobble 蹣跚 P-11

hobnob 交談 J-85

hold less water 站不住腳的 Z-21

hold one's accountable 追究某人責任 Z-97

hold someone in thrall 將某人陶醉其中 J-75

hold troubling implications for 對...產生不安的影響 D-103

hold vigils for 守夜 S-123

hollow sth out 把...挖空 B-16

home in on 鎖定 S-117

hone sth. 磨練 M-25

hoover up 獲得（錢） H-83

hound 糾纏 J-126

howl 嚎叫，憤怒 H-11

hubbub 大聲喧嘩 D-28

in the doldrums 低迷 D-57

in the offing 即將發生 J-12

incense 憤怒，激怒 F-50

incipient 最初的 Z-122

inconceivable 難以想像的，不可思議的 N-09

inconstancy 變幻莫測 B-101

incontinent 大小便失禁 D-32

incur 招致 Z-39

indefinitely 無限期的 W-64

indolent 懶惰的 L-07

in droves 群體 Q-66

ineptitude 無能 W-65

incessant 不停的 B-159

inexorably 無情地，無法阻擋地 W-04

inextricably 密切地,不可分開地 M-36

infallible 絕對正確的 J-110

inferno 地獄 D-62

infiltrate 滲透 S-38

infringed someone's right to sth 侵犯了某人的...權利 Q-46

infringe upon 給...帶來痛苦 G-22

infuriate sb 使...發怒，激怒 S-55

innocuous 無關痛癢的 W-56

insatiable 無盡的，無止境的 W-59

inscrutable 神秘莫測的，難以理解的 S-36

insidious 陰險的 Y-81

insipid 枯燥的 W-62

insolvent 資不抵債的 Z-101

insouciance 漠不關心 M-03

insouciant 漠不關心的,漫不經心的 M-50

instigate 挑撥 T-29

instill 逐漸灌輸 G-53

insular 孤立的；與世隔絕的 G-42

insulate 含沙射影的，旁敲側擊 H-03

insuperable 無法克服的 W-54

interminable 沒完沒了的，冗長的 M-22

internment 拘留 J-139

intersperse 點綴 D-74

intransigent 強硬的 Q-34

intractable 棘手的 J-23

intrigue 讓...著迷 R-08

intrinsic 內在的 N-17

introspection 反思 F-12

ipso facto （來自拉丁語）事實 S-91

irascible 暴躁的，易怒的 B-59

irk 惹惱 R-23

iron out 解決，消除 J-94

iron-willed 意志堅強的 Y-66

irrational 非理性的，不合邏輯的，荒謬的 F-41

irretrievable 無法彌補的，無法挽回的 W-55

L

M

matter less to 對...不當回事,沒拿它當回事 D-96

maul 撕咬 S-01

mayhem 混亂 H-65

maverik 特立獨行 T-17

mawkish 令人作嘔的 L-54

meager 微薄的，不足的，少的 W-27

mean 平均的 P-36

meddle 干涉 G-10

mediate 促成 C-76

meek 溫順的 W-47

melancholy 憂鬱的 Y-111

mellow 柔和的 R-19

mendacious 虛假的 X-103

mesmerize 讓...著迷 R-09

meticulous 非常細緻入微的 F-35

mimic 模仿 M-51

mind-boggling 令人難以置信的 L-46

mirthful 愉快的 Y-84

mirror 反映 F-15

miscreant 惡劣的 E-01

misfire 不發揮效力的 B-126

mingle with 與...混合 Y-89

minutiae 細節 X-06

moat 壕溝 H-08

momentum 慣性 C-92

monolithic 鐵板一塊，整體的 T-34

mope around 閒逛 X-17

moribund 垂死的；停滯不前的 C-114

mouldering 破碎的，崩塌的 P-50

muggy 悶熱的 M-28

mull over 仔細考慮 Z-107

murky 不光彩的，不可告人的等 B-137

muse on 認真思考 R-38

muster 聚集 J-136

mutatis mutandis 細節上做修改 X-08

mutilate 毀壞 H-53

myriad 大量的 D_03

N

nab 抓起來，逮捕 Z-92

nadir 低谷 D-51

nag 嘮叨 L-15

nagging 嘮叨的 L-16

nannyish 婆婆媽媽的，過於謹慎的 P-46

namesake 同名同姓 T-42

neaten 整理，修整 Z-52

nebulous 含糊其辭的／模糊的 H-02

neck and neck 不分上下，並駕齊驅 B-131

nefarious 邪惡的 X-76

O

P

pin the blame for 把...歸咎於... B-6

pin high hopes on 對...寄予厚望 D-117

pinpoint 確定 Q-79

pious 虔誠的，盡責的 Q-15

round up 四捨五入 S-58

pit against 與...對抗 Y-121

pitch in 投入 T-47

pithy 精煉的，簡潔的 J-112

pivot 關鍵點，支點 G-52

place a bet on 將賭注押在...上 J-73

plagiarize 剽竊 P-28

plastic 可塑性 K-16

plateau 飽和 B-46

plausible 似乎有道理的 S-81

play havoc with 嚴重破壞，使陷入大混亂 Y-18

pliant 順從的 S-105

plod 一步步地，辛勤勞作 Y-28

plop 撲通一聲扔到...落下 P-22

pluck up the courage to 鼓起勇氣... G-43

plug naturally into 自然融入到 Z-105

plummet 暴跌 B-42

plump for 追求，選擇 Z-98

plunge sb into 使...陷入... S-61

ply 從事... C-26

poach 竊取，挖走(人才) Q-45

poignant 慘痛的，悲傷的 C-11

point of no return 停不下來了，無法挽回了 T-35

poke 嘲笑，奚落 C-61

poke around 窺探 K-51

poke into 打聽 K-52

poke fun at 取消，嘲弄 Q-68

polish 改進，潤色 G-01

polish off 快速完成 K-41

pomp 排場，盛況 P-01

ponderous 冗長的，死板的 R-43

Ponzi scheme 龐氏騙局 P-12

pooh-pooh 對...不屑一顧 D-108

pooling purchase 團購 T-68

pore over 仔細研究 Z-108

pose a danger to 對...構成威脅 D-115

pose an unprecedented challenge to 對...提出挑戰 D-135

posh 豪華的，時髦的 H-09

potent 強大的 Q-25

pour into 投入 T-46

pout 撅嘴 J-120

precarious 不穩定的 B-162

precipitate 加速（一般指不好的事）J-43

precipitous 陡峭的，險峻的 T-65

Q

quackery – 騙子的行為 P-27
quash – 抑制，鎮壓 Y-64
quench – 壓抑，壓制 W-66
querulous - 愛抱怨的 A-01

quiescent - 沉默的，不動聲色的 C-4quip - 打趣，譏諷，嘲弄 D-25
quirk - 怪癖 G-49
quixotic – 不切實際的，堂吉歌德式的 T-01

R

rack up 積攢，積累 J-33 rags to riches 白手起家 B-31 rail against 譴責 Q-21
rake in , 大賺了一把，迅速大量取得 D-34
ram 撞擊 Z-95
ram one's point home 為了強調這一點 W-37
ramification 後果 H-78
rancid 變質的，不新鮮的 B-105
rancorous 惡意的 E-06
rankle 惹怒，激怒 R-25
ransack 洗劫 X-05
誇誇其談，慷慨陳詞 D-29
rapacious 貪婪的 T-05
rapture 欣喜若狂，興高采烈 X-91
ratchet up 逐漸升溫，逐漸增加 Z-90
rational 合理的 H-15

rattle 驚慌失措，神經緊張 J-111
raucous 沙啞的，喧鬧的，刺耳的，粗聲的 S-14
ravage 破壞 P-39
rave about 對...讚不絕口 D-146
reap 獲得 H-71
rebuff 斷然拒絕 D-93
recalcitrant 不聽話的 B-160
reconcile with 與...和解 Y-115
recondite 深奧的 S-29
recoup 收回，償還 S-114
recumbent 斜倚在 X-82
red-hot 炙手可得的 Z-76
reek 臭氣熏天，散發著臭氣 C-97
reel 顛簸，跟蹌 D-65
reel from 遭受災難，受...的不良影響 Z-14
reel from competition 內卷 N-15
reel off 流利背出 L-58

row with 與...吵架，發生爭執 Y-118

ruffle feathers 冒犯某些人 M-13

rumble on 沒完沒了的 M-21

ruminate 反芻 S-37

ruminative 沉思默想的 C-77

rummage 亂翻 L-53

run-of-the-mill 普通的 P-47

ruse 詭計 G-57

S

saber-rattling 耀武揚威 Y-24

sabotage 蓄意破壞 X-72 sack 解雇 J-91

saddle sb with 背負 B-67 B-68

salient 突出的，顯著的 T-57

saliva, drool, slobber 口水 K-33

sally out 出發，出擊 C-101

salubrious 天氣清爽 T-26

salutary 有益的 Y-106

sanity 神智 S-39

sap 使削弱 S-98

satanic 邪惡的 X-75

sardonic 嘲諷的 C-56 scarcely day, month, year without sb doing sth 幾乎...都做... J-08 savage 蠻橫 M-06

savvy 這個詞是一個非正式用法表示聰慧的，精明的 C-01

scamper about 蹦蹦跳跳 B-83

scant 缺乏的，不足的 Q-30

scarcely day month year without sb doing sth 幾乎...都做... J-08

scathing 尖銳的，嚴厲的 J-65

scoop out 挖掉 W-02

scupper 毀掉 H-52

schizophrenia. 精神分裂症 J-117

scintillating with wit 才思敏捷，妙語連珠 C-07

scoop up 一掃而光（搶購商品） Y-47

scoot about 跑來跑去 P-12

scourge 災禍 Z-04

scotch 遏制 E-08

scowl at sb 怒視某人 N-03

scramble 倉促完成 C-13

scramble to 慌亂，手忙腳亂做。。 H-81

scrap 放棄，廢棄，報廢 F-28

scrape 勉強做 M-42

scrape together 東拼西湊 D-84

screed 冗長的文章 R-02

scrub 刪除 S-18

scruffy 邋遢，骯髒的 L-04

scrupulous 一絲不苟的，嚴謹認真的 Y-50

scuffle with 與...動手，扭打 Y-119

skimp 對...不夠用心；捨不得給 D-08

skimpy 低廉的，不足的，吝嗇的 D-55

skimp on 克扣，節省 K-30

skirmish with 與...發生爭執，衝突 Y-122

skittish 不安的 小心翼翼的，不安的（多用於動物和人）B-124

skulduggery 欺騙，造假 Q-09

slack off 偷懶 T-44

slacken 放緩 F-20

slam on 給 ...帶來猛烈衝擊 G-69

slap with sth to sb 甩...給某人 S-132

slather on 塗抹 T-61

sleaze 卑鄙，不道德的人 B-62

sleazy 爛的，低級庸俗的 L-06

sleight 手法，技巧 S-113

slick 花裡胡哨的 H-38

slight 輕視 Q-51

slither 跟蹌走 L-36

slop 灑在... S-03

sloppy 草率的 C-15

slosh around 四處遊蕩 S-82

slot 插入 C-46

sludge 下水道油污，淤泥 Y-104

sluggish 緩慢的 H-84

slurp 大聲吃喝 D-26

smother 抑制，壓制 Y-63

smug 舒適的，整潔的 S-128

smudge 汙跡斑斑 W-57

snaffle 竊取 Q-44

snag 障礙 Z-30

snarl 阻礙 Z-114

snap 突然情緒崩潰 T-66

snappier 活潑的 H-75

snap up 搶購 Q-26

snappy 時髦的 S-79

snarky 刻薄的，尖刻的 K-12

snarl 阻礙

snazzy 時髦的，時尚的 S-80

sneak 頭偷偷摸摸地做 T-52

snigger 嘲笑 C-60

snog 接吻擁抱 J-100

sniff at 對...嗤之以鼻 D-106

snotty 下賤的，傲慢的 X-15

snub 瞧不起 Q-37

snuff out 遏制，扼殺 E-09

sober 冷靜的，清醒的 Q-54

sobering 發人深省的，耐人尋味的 F-05

soggy 濕透的 S-94

solace 安慰之物 A-07

solidify 使變可靠 G-28

someone could scarcely believe 簡直不敢相信... J-70

sour 關係變差 G-54

sought-after 很吃香的，最受青睞的 H-17

T

take wing 日益凸顯，成為現實 R-41

tally 統計，計算，合計 T-39

tame 抑制 Y-61

tramp... spread 遏制...的傳播 E-12

tamper with 篡改，損害 C-34

tantalize 逗某人 D-89

tantalizing 令人矚目的，垂涎三尺 C-115

tangle 糾纏，混亂 J-25

tap 利用 L-30

tap into 挖掘，充分利用 W-03

target 針對 Z-43

tarnish 玷污，損壞...的形象，或聲譽 D-71

tear 左右為難 Z-08

tease out 梳理 S-127

tee up 安排 A-06

tell of 談到，講述 T-03

tell a lie with one's eyes wide open 睜眼說瞎話 Z-58

temperamentally 性格上，喜怒無常地 X-95

taint 玷污 D-70

tease out 梳理 S-127 tenacious 堅韌不拔的，頑強的 J-64

terse 簡潔的 J-52

tether one's hope to 把某人的希望寄託在... B-21

testy 暴跳如雷 B-51 tetchily 惱火地 N-13

tetchy 暴躁的，易怒的 B-58

tether one's hope to 把某人的希望寄託在... B-21

that's not much use for 對...沒有多大用 D-124

there comes one flood too many 洪水氾濫 H-24

there is little sb can do about sth without unnecessarily doing sth 在不造成 ...的情況下，某人或某機構對...幾乎無能為力 Z-03

thorny issue 棘手的問題 J-26

thrash out 絞盡腦汁去做 J-81

threadbare 衣衫襤褸的 Y-48

throttle 扼殺，壓制，卡頓，減速，遏制 E-05

throw off 戒掉，擺脫 B-176

throw sth to the winds 把...拋到九霄雲外，拋到腦後 B-13

thuggishly 殘忍地 C-10

thump to the ground 撲通摔倒在地上 P-44

tick up 起色，上升 Q-10

ticklish 棘手的 J-24

tide over 度過 D-92

tighten one's belt 勒緊褲腰帶 L-19

time-worn rhetoric 陳詞濫調 C-69

tinged with 帶有...氣息、色彩 D-40

tinker with 改裝，修補 G-71

U

ulterior motives 別有用心 B-110

umpteen 無數的 W-43

unassailable 無懈可擊的 W-33

uncannily 驚人地，異乎尋常地 J-115

unencumbered 不受阻礙的 / 無拘無束的 B-158

underbelly 薄弱部分 B-50

undercut 削弱... X-67

underlie 成為...的基礎 / 是...的根源 C-83

underlying 潛在的，表面下的，根本的 Q-20

undermine the reputation of 損害...的名譽或聲譽 S-115

underpin 提供（證據） T-22

underwhelm 令...失望 L-40

underwhelming 平淡無奇，有點平庸，未留下深刻印象 P-31

undulate 起伏蕩漾 Q-01

unfashionable 不是新鮮事了，不時髦了 B-157

unfeigned 真誠的，不虛偽的 Z-42

unpalatable 難吃的 N-04

unravel 分崩離析 F-47

unscathed 毫髮無損的 H-07

unspool through 展現 Z-25

unyielding 不服 B-133

upbeat 樂觀的，積極向上的 L-17

upend 顛覆 D-67

ubiquitous 無處不在的 W-51

uppity 自大的，傲慢的 Z-102

upstart 暴發戶 B-45

undying 不朽的 B-166

unencumbered 不受阻礙的 B-158

unpalatable 難吃的 M-04

unprompted 自發的 Z-103

unquench 未能得到滿足 W-66

unremitting effort 不懈的努力 B-164

unreservedly 毫無保留地 H-13

unrivaled 無與倫比的

unspoken 不言而喻的 B-167

unspool through 展現 Z-25

untenable 站不住腳的 Z-20

unviable 不可行的 / 不成功的 B-148

行不懂的（特指財政方面） B-128

unwind 放鬆，展開 F-31

unwittingly 不知不覺的 B-174

unwavering 堅定不移的，不動搖的 J-49

uphill 艱巨的，艱難的 J-53

uplifting 振奮人心的，令人振奮的 Z-44

waver 動搖，猶豫 D-122
wayward 任性的 R-35
wean sb off 使某人擺脫對...的依賴 B-177
weed out 清除 Q-49
well-heeled 富有的 F-73
wherewithal 必備的資金 B-86
wheeling and dealing 不擇手段，爾虞我詐 B-173
whims 心血來潮 X-92
whip up 打雞蛋 D-17
whiplash 沉重的打擊 C-78
whisk 攪拌 J-77
whittle 削成 X-47
whittle down 削減 X-56
whizzy 飛速發展的，出色的 F-43
wholesome 有益身心健康的 Y-107
whoop 歡呼，大聲呼叫 H-43
whopping 巨大的 J-132
wield 揮舞（棍棒或手中的權力） H-61
wilful 故意的 G-46
willy-nilly 不得不，不情願地 B-130
wince 退縮 T-74
wind down 放鬆，結束 F-30

wind up 結束 J-98
windfalls 橫財，意外之財 H-19
winnow 挑選，篩選 T-31
wink at 對...使眼色，對...視而不見 D-133
without blushing 毫不臉紅 H-05
with a clear conscience 問心無愧 W-48
with a hard slog 辛辛苦苦地 X-93
wobble 搖擺，脆弱 Y-23
woolgather 胡思亂想，心不在焉 H-32
wow 博得...追捧 B-117
wrangle with 與...爭吵 Z-47
wreak havoc on 對...造成嚴重破壞 D-147
wrenching 極為痛苦的 J-28
writ 令狀（一般指法院發佈的） L-56
wringer 令人心煩意亂 L-51
write off 抵消，一筆勾銷 D-59
wretched 惡劣的，討厭的，極壞的，可憐的 E-02

yammer about 對...嘮叨 D-121
yawning income 收入可觀 S-120

Y

yoke together 生拼硬湊在一起 S-43

www.ingramcontent.com/pod-product-compliance
Lightning Source LLC
Chambersburg PA
CBHW070904120626
46546CB00001B/126